Celebrating 50
years of the
Doctor Who
family

Celebrating 50
years of the
Doctor Who
family

Paula Hammond

First published in the UK in 2013 by
Telos Publishing Ltd
www.telos.co.uk

Telos Publishing Ltd values feedback. Please e-mail us with any
comments you may have about this book to: feedback@telos.co.uk

ISBN: 978-1-84583-092-2 (paperback)

50 for 50 © 2013 Paula Hammond

The moral right of the author has been asserted.

Internal design, typesetting and layout by Arnold T Blumberg
www.atbpublishing.com

Printed in the UK by Berforts Group Ltd

British Library Cataloguing in Publication Data.
A catalogue record for this book is available from the British Library.

To all those who are wise enough to appreciate that a straight line may be the shortest distance between two points, but it is by no means the most interesting.

Introduction

You know you're a *Doctor Who* fan if …

- You regularly use phrases such as 'Oh! My Giddy Aunt'; 'Jumping Jehosaphat' or 'Allons-y!'
- You know how to play the spoons.
- You once saw a man in green bubble wrap crawl down a corridor and couldn't sleep for a week.
- You spent a whole summer begging your mum to knit you a long, multi-coloured scarf.
- You can't walk past a churchyard without expecting the statues to move when you're not looking at them.
- Every time you walk into a pub you have the urge to order five rounds rapid.
- You think bow ties are cool.
- You've actually tried fish fingers and custard.
- You can't travel past Earl's Court tube station in London without stopping for a photo opportunity.
- Even as an adult you can't say '*Om mani padme hum*' without half-expecting a giant spider to materialise on your back.

If you grew up watching *Doctor Who* then you'll know that there's simply something about the show that grabs your imagination and refuses to let go. Exactly why this TV series – rather than any other – should have captivated so many people, is hard to pin down. Part of it is the fun, the mystery and the adventure. Part of it is the ethos of the show that even 50 years on is still infused with that '60s sense of optimism. But mostly it's the Doctor himself. He is, after all, a rationalist, a liberal, a pacifist, an intellectual, an explorer and perhaps … just perhaps … a little bit of a trickster. He's all of the world's great literary heroes rolled into one. He's Sherlock Holmes, Peter Pan and the Wizard of Oz. But there's more to it than that. The Doctor may be 900-and-a-bit years old, but he still views the universe with a child's eyes. He doesn't care if you're black, white, gay, straight, android or human. He's only interested in what's right. And he sees that with the clarity and the certainty of a six-year-old. Who wouldn't want to be as wise, as witty, as giving and as forgiving as the Doctor?

But then you already know all this because you're a fan. And hopefully because you're a fan, you've just bought – or are contemplating buying –

50 for 50 … So what's it all about?

This book tells the story of 50 years of *Doctor Who* as experienced by 50 people who've contributed to the show's success. You won't find interviews with Tom Baker or Matt Smith, Peter Davison or David Tennant in these pages. Not because they weren't 'worth' interviewing but because they've already been interviewed so many times before. The focus here is on the wider *Doctor Who* family. Those actors, directors, writers, designers, model-makers, illustrators and stunt-coordinators who have all made a contribution to the *Doctor Who* story but are rarely – if ever – interviewed. People like Bernard Lodge, who was tasked with creating the iconic *Doctor Who* title sequence. People like screenwriter Bob Baker, who turned up at the BBC to pitch a story about an old army chum and ended up creating K-9, the Axons and Omega. People like Jeremy Young, who had the distinction of playing the first ever *Doctor Who* villain. And people like Yee Jee Tso, whose many good experiences filming the *Doctor Who* television movie were almost overshadowed by one very bad one. There are some exceptions to this rule … but then Frazer Hines, Debbie Watling, Richard Franklin, Louise Jameson, Colin Baker, and Sylvester McCoy were just far too interesting to leave out …

This book is designed to be a 'magazine style' publication, with interviews written in different styles to give variety and colour. The approach taken for each piece depends very much on the circumstances of the interview. Some were conducted by phone or e-mail. Some were face-to-face. Some interviews were short and sweet – 15 minutes grabbed in a green room, at a convention or theatre. Others were leisurely affairs over a cup of tea and a slice of cake. However, everything you read in quotes are the interviewees' own words, and where they've asked me to keep something strictly 'off the record' then I have.

Like you, I'm a *Who* fan, but the experience of writing this book has made me even more enamoured of the show and the incredible people involved in it. People who have opened their doors to me and shared their stories. I've laughed – a lot. I've been surprised. I've been shocked. And during one interview, I cried like a baby … It's been a real labour of love. Thanks everyone. To paraphrase the Brigadier: You're wonderful chaps. All of you.

Paula Hammond
London
September 2013

Contents

Chapter One: The '60s..12

1. The Title Sequence: Bernard Lodge
Co-creator of the Doctor Who *title sequences: first to fourth Doctor*....14

2. The First Director: Waris Hussein
Director of '100,000 BC' and 'Marco Polo'...20

3. The First Baddie: Jeremy Young
Kal, '100,000 BC'..25

4. The War Lord: Derren Nesbitt
Tegana, 'Marco Polo'...30

5. The Rocket Man: Peter Purves
Companion Steven Taylor..35

6. The Gunslinger: Shane Rimmer
Seth Harper, 'The Gunfighters'..39

7. The Man of a Million Voices: David Graham
Dalek voices, 'The Gunfighters' and 'City of Death'..............................43

8. The Doctor's Most Faithful Companion: Bernard Cribbins
'Daleks – Invasion Earth: 2150 AD' and Wilfred Mott.........................46

9. The Highlander: Frazer Hines
Companion Jamie McCrimmon...49

10. The Storyteller: Victor Pemberton
Script editor and writer, 'Fury From The Deep'....................................54

11. The Victorian Miss: Deborah Watling
Companion Victoria Waterfield..59

12. The Triple Jumper: Peter Craze
'The Space Museum', 'The War Games' and 'The Nightmare of Eden'...63

Chapter Two: The '70s...68

13. The Captain: Richard Franklin
Captain Mike Yates 70

14. The Director: Michael E Briant
Director 'Colony in Space', 'The Sea Devils', 'The Green Death', 'Death to the Daleks', 'Revenge of the Cybermen' and 'The Robots of Death' 76

15. The Golden One: Bernard Holley
'The Tomb of the Cybermen' and 'The Claws of Axos 79

16. The Cyber Controller: Michael Kilgarriff
Cyber Controller, Ogron and Giant Robot 84

17. The Thal: Jane How
Rebec, 'Planet of the Daleks' 91

18. The Bristol Boy: Bob Baker
Writer and co-creator of K-9, Omega and the Axons 93

19. The Archer: Jeremy Bulloch
'The Space Museum' and 'The Time Warrior' 97

20. The Savage: Louise Jameson
Companion Leela 102

21. The Shaman: David Garfield
'The War Games' and 'The Face of Evil' 106

22. The Faithful Pooch: John Leeson
Companion K-9 109

23. The Grifter: Nigel Plaskett
Unstoffe, 'The Ribos Operation' 116

24. The Mentiad: David Warwick
'The Pirate Planet' and 'Army of Ghosts' 120

25. The Ones We Left Behind: Mary Tamm
Remembering Mary Tamm 124

26. The Meglos Survivor: Crawford Logan
Deedrix, Meglos 127

Chapter Three: The '80s 131

27. The Megalomaniac: Terry Molloy
Davros 133

28. The Aristocrat: Sarah Sutton
Companion Nyssa 139

29. The Space Pirate: Liza Goddard
Kari, 'Terminus' 143

30. The Sixth Doctor: Colin Baker 147

31. The Other Side of the Table
Sylvester McCoy, Lalla Ward, Peter Purves and Mary Tamm talk fandom 150

32. The Movellan & the Evil Henchman: Tony Osoba
'Destiny of the Daleks' and 'Dragonfire' 153

33. The Werewolf: Jessica Martin
'The Greatest Show in the Galaxy' and 'Voyage of the Damned' 159

34. The Other Brigadier: Angela Bruce
Brigadier Winifred Bambera, 'Battlefield' 164

35. The Cheetah Woman: Lisa Bowerman
Karra, 'Survival' 168

Chapter Four: The '90s 172

36. The Appreciation Society: Antony Wainer
Press and Publicity Officer, The Doctor Who *Appreciation Society* 174

37. The Target Man: Nigel Robinson
Editor of Target Books and New Adventures author 177

38. The Illustrator: Andrew Skilleter
"… the man who draws Doctor Who *…"* 181

39. The Producers: Nick Briggs and Gary Russell
Big Finish..185

40. The Filmmaker: Keith Barnfather
Reeltime Pictures 192

41: The Fanzine: Stephen James Walker
Co-founder and joint editor of The Frame, *1987-1993* 195

42. The Kid: Yee Jee Tso
Chang Lee, 'Doctor Who' 1996 203

43. The Doctor's Doctor: Daphne Ashbrook
Companion Dr Grace Holloway, 'Doctor Who' 1996................206

Chapter Five: The '00s 210

44. The Animator: Steve Meyer
'Scream of the Shalka', 'The Invasion' and 'The Infinite Quest'............212

45. The Gaffer: Mark Hutchings
Lighting Gaffer...215

46. The Model Maker: Mike Tucker
Model maker on classic and new Who, Virgin New Adventures *& Big Finish author*...217

47. The Fight Coordinator: Kevin McCurdy
2005 Doctor Who *Christmas Special: 'The Christmas Invasion'* 222

48. The Companion's Companion: Noel Clarke
Companion Mickey Smith..227

49. The Costume Designer: Ray Holman
Designer on Torchwood, *2006-2008 &* Doctor Who *2007-2010, including Matt Smith's costume*...232

50. The BFI: Dick Fiddy and Justin Johnson
The British Film Institute on the cultural importance of Doctor Who..236

Chapter One: The '60s

'Have you ever thought what it's like to be wanderers in the fourth dimension? Have you? To be exiles? Susan and I are cut off from our own planet – without friends or protection. But one day we shall get back. Yes, one day …'
(The Doctor, '100,000 BC')

There's no word that better sums up the 1960s than 'change'. This was the era that saw post-War 'make-do-and-mend' give way to fast food and disposable fashion. It was a time when teenagers were no longer simply adults in waiting. Suddenly, it was cool to be young. Big bands and easy listening were out. Teen pop and psychedelia were in. This was the decade of sex, drugs and rock and roll. Of mini skirts, Doc Martens, Paisley and love beads. While children thrilled to the Supermarionation adventures of John, Scott, Virgil, Gordon and Alan, their Project Mercury counterparts – Glenn, Carpenter, Grissom, Cooper and Shepherd – were boldly going for real. This was the decade when a spotty teenager became a web-slinging superhero. It was the decade when your favourite UNCLE was either Kuryakin or Solo. And it was the decade when a battered old police box was transformed into a time machine.

However, when the first episode of *Doctor Who* aired on 23 November 1963, the set-up of a schoolgirl travelling with her teachers and grandfather probably owed more to the fusty '50s than to the era of peace and love. Although that first episode, 'An Unearthly Child', makes many references to pop culture, the tone is still very much one of Mother – or at least Grandfather – knows best.

The Doctor's companion, Susan, had been conceived as an all-action girl, but that idea was quickly dropped. Writer Anthony Coburn added the grandfather-granddaughter relationship because he felt there was something 'not quite proper' about an old man travelling with a young girl for a companion.

All that quickly changed as the show caught up with the libertarian spirit of the age. Susan's teachers, Barbara and Ian, become confidants and friends. 'Grandfather' evolved from the stern paterfamilias into a strange and other-worldly alien. The stories may still have had an educational remit, but the Daleks, Sensorites and Zarbi were pure, futuristic fantasy. Just a year after the show was launched, the 16-year-old Susan left the TARDIS behind for the love of a freedom fighter. How '60s is that?

When, on 29 October 1966, the familiar features of William Hartnell as the Doctor regenerated into those of Patrick Troughton (although the term regeneration wasn't used at the time) the show's own transformation was complete. The second Doctor – complete with Beatle haircut and anti-authoritarian stance – is '60s incarnate. The first Doctor was often content to let history take its course, but the second was an anarchist and an agitator. He not only gets involved, he berates those who don't – including his own people, the Time Lords.

Bringing in a new Doctor was *Doctor Who*'s biggest gamble. Could the show really survive without the actor who created and came to embody its hero? Perhaps only Patrick Troughton could have made the transition from grandfather to cosmic hobo believable. Perhaps the show was just too good to fail. Or perhaps, somehow, that battered old police box and its strangely compelling owner had simply sunk into the British psyche. Whatever the truth, with Troughton at the helm, the '60s were safe.

The Title Sequence:
Bernard Lodge

'… there weren't many creative expectations of us at the BBC. We all wanted to do super-duper things but you didn't get much chance.'

Friday 13 September: probably not the day you'd choose to try to reproduce a notoriously elaborate camera trick. However, regardless of the vagaries of Lady Luck, at BBC Television Centre, Crew 1 are setting up their equipment. The studio has been booked from 9:30 through to 17:45 and, although no-one knows it, they're about to make television history.

Studio 2 still uses the old CPS-Emitron Cameras, which had their first outing during the 1948 London Olympics. These big beasts suffer from an effect known as 'vision peel-off' during outside broadcasts, which is why they've been moved indoors. Luckily Bernard Lodge and a technical team, headed by Ben Palmer, are hoping to create some visual distortions of their own. By pointing the black and white Emitron at a monitor playing the camera's own output, an effect known as howl-around is created.

It's an effect the origins of which are buried deep in the mists of time. Peter Jarrett, writing in *Prospero* magazine (August 2011), recalls working as a vision control operator with either Crew 4 or 9 in Riverside Studio 1 when the technical operations manager, Norman Taylor, asked them to set up Camera 3 facing a monitor. Although the Image Orthicon cameras used at Riverside didn't 'peel-off', the howl-around was similar, but tricky to reproduce, as the distance between the monitor and the camera had to be 'just so'. However John Billett, who was then a studio engineer, claims that the howl-around came as the result of a conversation between him and Ben Palmer and was first reproduced at Riverside 2. Whatever the truth, this startling effect is about to become synonymous with one of the most loved and iconic TV shows of all time: *Doctor Who*.

Making History

Bernard Lodge began working for the BBC early in the 1960s after leaving London's prestigious Royal College of Art. At the time, he didn't have much of an idea what he wanted to do for a living but, having tried teaching, he was looking for something to stretch his artistic muscles. 'To be honest though', he says, 'there weren't many creative expectations of us at the BBC. We all wanted to do super-duper things but you didn't get much chance'.

That chance finally came when a young producer called Verity Lambert gave Bernard the script for a new family television show to read. 'She said that she wanted to use this electronic technique of howl-around and I ought to look at it in order to do the lettering over it. So I went and spent about an hour looking at this 35mm film that had been shot for a children's programme called *Tobias and the Angel*.[1] I thought that it was absolutely amazing.

'In the Graphic Design Department, we were doing all sorts of experiments with flexible mirrors and projected lettering. It was really quite hot – creatively – but nothing compared with what just I'd seen. We didn't deal with electronic gear, we worked on film all the time, so I asked Verity if she could set up a session.'

Despite the BBC's famously tight budgets, Lambert was able to persuade the Head of Drama to let her use a studio for what was listed on the crew's roster as the 'Dr Who Experiment'.

Bernard is keen to emphasise that, at this point, he was just 'one of a whole team of people' and very much the 'alien' in the group. He'd never even met the technical guys before. 'However, Ben Palmer,' he says, 'was a real wizard, doing some amazing stuff.' When they put Bernard's logo and lettering into the howl-around, and added light spots using a pen torch, the effect 'absolutely blew my mind'. Bernard then took the resulting film and edited it. But it was when the eerily otherworldly theme music, created by Ron Grainer, Delia Derbyshire and Dick Mills, was added to the finished titles that the magic happened.

Bernard: 'I met Ron in the producer's office and he asked "When's my moment of drama?" I said that 20 seconds from the beginning, the lettering would be formed and it would go backwards, and he said "Fine" and went away. Then the day came when I got the music, put it on and it absolutely looked like he'd designed it for every frame. But he didn't. He didn't have my film and I didn't have his music! It just came together. It was terrific!'

Back to the Drawing Board

If the first *Doctor Who* titles were terrific then Bernard's titles for the

---

1 *Tobias and the Angel* was transmitted on 19 May 1960. In previous interviews, Lodge has stated that the programme in question was *Amahl and the Night Visitors*, transmitted on 24 December 1959; but it seems that it was in fact *Tobias and the Angel*, as he states here.

Doctor's second incarnation were award-winning. Bernard won the 1968 British Design & Art Direction Award for his Troughton sequence. The Awards, known as Yellow Pencils, are highly coveted and Lodge was up against the best of the best.

During the original experiment, a member of the crew had stood in front of the camera to show how the effect would work with William Hartnell's face incorporated into the sequence. The unnerving sight of his features disintegrating into a vortex of chaos was ultimately vetoed by Verity Lambert. It was considered way 'too horrific' for what was, after all, a family show! This time round, though, Bernard decided he'd like to include the new Doctor's face.

A photography session was arranged and the painstaking process of producing the *Doctor Who* Mark 2 titles began. 'It was', Lodge remembers, 'very, very difficult. We could spend the whole evening talking about it!'

The secret to his success was to film the howl-around with Troughton's face in the foreground. Working with an outside film company, Lodge set up a board of polystyrene. When facing the camera, it looked pure white, but as it turned, the shadows created by its rough texture increased until the screen went black. The finished effect meant that instead of the Doctor's face seeming to disintegrate, it actually appears to form out of the shadows.

Colour came in with Jon Pertwee's Doctor, and once again Lodge was asked to redesign the titles. 'I thought wow! With a colour camera this howl-around technique is going to be amazing – but it wasn't, because the colour cameras don't do it. So … we shot it in black and white and added colour as a film optical. I also added some geometric shapes to control the whole thing. On the first *Who* titles, all those howl-around clouds looked very exciting, but I was getting a bit bored with it. So, besides the new lettering and the face, I used concentric diamond shapes. You don't really see them, but they are there – controlling the way the waves work – holding it all together.' It's a beautifully subtle piece of design and still a firm fan favourite.

Expensive Experiments

If the BBC had baulked at the cost of a day's studio work to produce the initial howl-around, then it's fortunate they never actually saw the bill for Lodge's next take on the titles, commissioned by *Doctor Who* producer Barry Letts in 1973. 'I used an outside company for the shoot and they never caught up with the cost!' Bernard laughs. 'I overspent horribly, but the way costs were controlled at the BBC at the time was very, very sloppy. Sometimes you'd get away with it. Thank goodness nobody seemed to ask!'

What was so expensive was a technique called slit-scan, which was used in a very famous film of the era. Bernard explains: 'This time round ... the producer wanted to do something completely different. I'd been influenced by a technique used in the film *2001: A Space Odyssey*. At the end of the film, there's an amazing sequence where they're travelling towards Jupiter and they go through a spectacular corridor of light. It's a sensational effect, but the director Stanley Kubrick had a huge studio out in Elstree and money was no object. A few of us in the Design Department kept reading this magazine article about how it was done, and a couple of us had a go, but it didn't work. Then it suddenly dawned on me how they did it.'

A rostrum camera is basically a camera mounted on a frame, pointing downwards. The camera can move up or down the frame. What Bernard realised was that, if you moved the camera all the way down the frame, keeping the aperture open so that one frame is exposed, then the effect produced would be something like a motion blur. It's the same effect you get with a stills camera if the shutter is left open on a street at night, so that it records passing traffic as a series of blurs. Add a single light source (the slit) and interesting things start to happen. A circular slit creates a tunnel of light. If you put torn strips of polystyrene between the slit and the light, then patterns begin to emerge. And if you stop and restart the camera at different points on the frame, then these patterns gradually build into something fabulous. 'So,' Bernard continues, 'I found a company that had a fairly sophisticated rostrum camera and could do it, but it was absolutely terrifying!'

The excellent result was well worth the stress. Consequently the fifth and last set of *Doctor Who* titles that Bernard produced, for Tom Baker's debut season, used the same effect. These two sets of titles are, he says, his 'favourites'.

So, looking back, is there anything he would have done differently? 'Well you find faults in all of them. I find with the third *Doctor Who* titles, that the Doctor's face is too clear. He's only really on screen for about two or three frames but, for me, that's too long. Thinking about it now, I'd have liked to have got some sort of space motif, where things are turning over and inside out, but I did what I could, and I was quite pleased with it at the time. Other people have since had a go and brought in stars – which was an obvious thing to do – but I wanted to keep the magic. With the howl-around, you put the viewer in a really strange space. I don't think that the present title sequence is particularly adventurous. It's very ordinary. They could have done something mind-blowing with the techniques available now. Mind you, I would have hated to have done the sequence that came just after mine. Those poor chaps didn't have much to work with – they came in just a bit too early for computers to help them out.'

A New Life
Bernard left the BBC in 1977, having become, as he comments, 'rather fed up with it … We had about 80 people in the Department but Alan Jeapes, Charles McKee and I in particular were really very, very keen to do good work. In my case, not for the BBC, but because I needed to make up a showreel of interesting stuff!'

Bernard had left the BBC once before, in the late 1960s, but after a stint with a production company, had returned when the Beeb went over to colour. 'So,' he says, 'I did two stints. In for seven years, out for two and in for another seven. But I thought: why have I come back? I did some good stuff, but then I wanted to go freelance, and my wife was very understanding considering I had no real prospects! So I persuaded Colin Cheesman, who was Head of Department at that time, to come out and join me, and it started to work out quite well.'

After a dodgy first year, the workload began to increase. In fact Lodge-Cheesman enjoyed seven fruitful years together. 'Not everything was fun,' Bernard admits, 'but the work was so varied outside the BBC and I did some good things.'

Those good things included more classic sci-fi in the form of work on the feature films *Alien* and *Blade Runner*. 'In *Blade Runner* I did the little bits where [the lead character, Deckard] talks to the computer and messages come up … They had to be rather special and showy, which was a tricky job. I also did the explosion in outer space at the climax of *Alien*. They probably wouldn't use me now because I wouldn't be able to do it with a computer. But at that time there were no computers and the people who did all the physical effects tried and tried, but Ridley Scott didn't like any of it. So he asked me, and we looked at some library film of actual atomic explosions – the post-war ones they did in the Pacific – and they seemed to spread out in an organic way. So I took bits of black card diffused through tracing paper. We had the card opening up on a couple of film bobbins, under glass. It's very, very crude but it looked okay. Then I went out to Elstree and they ran it at Cinemascope, which stretched it out, and I thought 'My God! That's better. That looks good!' In its way, in its time, it worked. But it was nothing but two bits of black card moving out symmetrically, with bits of coloured gel underneath and the whole thing diffused by tracing paper. That's it!'

These days, Bernard has given up the world of television and film to follow another passion: print-making. Lino-cutting and wood-cutting are techniques that he's always loved, and he's clearly happy to have escaped the rat-race once and for all. 'My wife and I moved down near Brighton and I have this huge printing press that I brought with me. And now I just do printmaking. I don't earn a lot, but I sell my art at local fairs and it pays for the paper and ink.'

What about *Doctor Who*? Is he ever tempted to go to conventions or write about his experiences? 'Really, it's a real drag, the *Doctor Who* thing. Really, I'm fed up with it!' he says, not altogether seriously. 'I don't do conventions. I'm enjoying having a really quiet life. I've got a nice house, the printing press, and I spend every moment I can making these prints. The other things belong to another life. I was 30 then and he was a different chap. Today, I don't have any deadlines!' And that seems fair enough. After all, if the Doctor can regenerate, who could begrudge the man who played such a pivotal role in the show's evolution a new life too?

The First Director:
Waris Hussein

On 23 November 1963, *Doctor Who* made its television debut. It was a modestly-budgeted family show, but somehow those 25-minutes of monochrome – along with the Doctor and his TARDIS – managed to lodge themselves in the British psyche. For Waris Hussein, watching that show at home, '100,000 BC' represented two months of blood, sweat and tears. Little did he know that he'd still be talking about it 50 years later …

Tell us a little about yourself.
I was born in India and brought up in England from the age of nine. I went to school here, then university. So basically India is my background, but where I'm from is Britain. I was always passionate about theatre as a child. I used to play act – as kids do – but it was at university that I came into my own. I joined the various theatre societies, and as a result of something I did, I was asked to an interview at the BBC Drama Department. I applied for their television course and after a quite a struggle, because it was a competitive thing to get into, I got to the final five and was selected. They trained me for six months then put me under contract. So I ended up at the BBC for nearly six years.

What directing job have you been most proud of and why?
It's very difficult to say because I've done different colours throughout my career. I've won awards and, obviously, something that you win an award for, you feel proud of. There was the abdication drama, *Edward and Mrs Simpson* with Edward Fox, for which I won an Emmy and a BAFTA[2] . I also did a musical for American television based on Barry Manilow's *Copacabana* and I won an Emmy for that. So you can see my spectrum is quite wide!

How did you come to be offered the job directing '100,000 BC'?
No-one else wanted to do it! I was the most junior director at the BBC under contract at the time and *Doctor Who* was my first proper assignment. The show's originator, Sydney Newman, was a newly-hired executive, originally from Canada. And Newman brought in a young production assistant, Verity Lambert, to be the show's first producer.

---

2 British Academy of Film and Television Arts.

When you think about the storyline, that first storyline … there was a spaceship and an eccentric man called Doctor Who … I think that the whole concept scared people and they didn't know what to do with it! So they just threw it at me. We started off with no plot, they relegated us to the oldest, smallest studio space they had, with the oldest cameras. Everything had to be shot continuously on four cameras and one of the cameramen literally cricked his back moving these big old cameras around. The facilities were that bad!

It sounds like they didn't have much faith in the show?
Verity and I were both very young and trying very, very hard to prove ourselves, you know? But we didn't have the facilities to be able to make it any better within the budget. They'd handicapped us quite severely, although nobody appeared to notice that! But when you think about that first episode and what we got out of it – it was a miracle. We had to create all of these amazing things from nothing. I guess I should be proud of it now but, at the time, I was very much frustrated by it.

It was quite unusual for British television to do a pilot episode. How did the pilot episode for *Doctor Who* come about?
We recorded the first episode and Sydney Newman, who was Head of Drama, and actually behind the concept of *Doctor Who* (though he has never been given enough credit for it), saw it and it was really not good. So he took Verity and me out to dinner and he said 'By rights I should be firing both of you but I'm going to give you a chance to do it again.' I really felt that the pilot was pretty erratic and very embarrassing at the time.

Is it true that William Hartnell was initially reluctant to be involved?
William Hartnell was the first person to be cast and actually nobody really thought he would want to do it. We didn't think he'd want to do it either, so we took him out to two very expensive lunches and he got quite pissed – we all got a bit drunk! Anyway … after the second lunch he said, 'Now do you really think you can get through this thing?' And I said, 'I wouldn't be here if I didn't.' He said he wanted time to think about it, and a week later his agent called and said he'd agreed to do it. I think he thought it would last a few weeks and that would be the end of it.

Did you get on?
I think he thought I was a bit of a curiosity. There was this Indian bloke,

speaking with an English accent, saying weird things … And when we started working together, he was very crotchety on the first day. He was testing me like mad, you know? It was like a tennis match. He was watching the ball always but, after two or three days, he trusted me. So we got on well. He was a very interesting man, William Hartnell.

How did you come to cast William Russell, Jacqueline Hill and Carole Ann Ford?

We were fortunate. Let's face it, William Russell already had a good reputation … Jacqueline was a friend of Verity's and she came in on it on the basis of knowing her. So we were left looking for a girl to play Susan. We're talking about the early '60s when girls all had a specific look. They all had blonde hair, black make-up round their eyes and mini dresses and they all looked like each other. We wanted someone different … I was at the BBC one day and there was a viewing room where you could actually see the monitors of the shows running on the studio floor. I saw this very unusual young girl. She was standing there, waiting for a shot. She had very short hair and these extraordinary eyes. She just looked so interesting that I immediately called Verity in her office and she came down and we both looked at the monitor. We asked Carole Ann to come in and see us and that was that.

You were young and Indian … Back then the BBC was primarily an organisation of middle-aged white men. Did that present any problems?

The key thing was to be in total control. I have to say that I used to get stage fright every time I walked onto the studio floor! You've got 30 people all watching you like hawks and me desperately trying to be terrific, you know? I always thought I had to be better than everyone else and that's a hard thing to do at that level.

Tell us a little about that first story.

The concept of going back into the Stone Age was daunting to say the least. We had to somehow make sense of a story where people are dressed in furs, and I was determined not to make it look silly. The story itself has certain danger points in it, thrills and tension, especially in 'The Cave of Skulls' episode. But honestly it was not the best start. However I think it spawned enough interest to generate a buzz. Once the Daleks came along, of course, that was a huge leap forwards for the show.

'Marco Polo' was the fourth *Doctor Who* serial – and the second one you worked on. Thanks to the success of the Daleks, *Doctor Who* was suddenly big news. Did that mean more money or better equipment for you?

Unfortunately, as you are aware, those episodes are lost, which is a great shame, because by then the sets and stories were a huge improvement. In those days the budget was £2,000 an episode but, by the time we got to 'Marco Polo', we were getting much more, because the BBC suddenly realised they had a cash cow on their hands.[3]

Can you share one memory of working on 'Marco Polo'?

Well, I wanted this character, Kuiju the mercenary bandit, to have a strange quality, and I thought that some sort of companion would work well. So I wondered if I could get a small actor – in those days, being un-PC, I'd probably have asked for a dwarf. Verity Lambert said very definitely 'No – we will not have a dwarf!' So I suggested a little monkey. We found this spider monkey somewhere and he was supposed to sit on this guy's shoulder all the way through the recording, but then he escaped and the poor thing was pooping everywhere. The studio was very hot, and everyone had to perform with this terrible smell!

You didn't direct the fourth episode of 'Marco Polo'. Why did you feel the need to hand over the reins for one episode?

It was a very complicated show. The story moved from A-Z, going across the whole Gobi Desert, and there was a point at which there was absolutely no way I could have done all seven episodes. The fight sequence, for instance, was being filmed while we were rehearsing, so there was no way I could have done two things at the same time.

Although we don't have 'Marco Polo' to watch anymore, it's thanks to you that we have telesnap images of the serial. Can you tell us how they came about?

We used to pay this guy called John Cura to do frame by frame photographs of shows because, in those days, we didn't have any videos or other ways of recording images. He'd literally photograph the whole shoot and then would produce long strips of narrative photographs. So that's how I came

---

3 Surviving documentation shows that the standard budget actually remained at £2,500 per episode. However, for '100,000 BC' a large chunk of the available money had been eaten up by the construction of the TARDIS interior set, so on 'Marco Polo' there would have been more money available for other aspects of the production.

to have the *Doctor Who* telesnaps. I found them in a cupboard. I'd had them for 40 years and when I found them it was like 'Oh my!'

Why didn't you carry on working on *Doctor Who* after 'Marco Polo'?
I did four episodes, then seven. That was almost a year's work, and at the end I thought, 'No, that's it.'

Do you ever go back and watch those first episodes again?
To be honest with you, I don't. It's interesting but I don't like doing it because it brings you face to face with the past and things you've forgotten about.

Would you like to be involved with the new series?
The new series is totally different now and has millions of pounds spent on every episode. I envy them all that. On the one hand, I'd love to be involved. On the other, I have been involved and I don't want to go back!

Does the continuing interest in the show surprise you?
I had no idea what was going to happen – none of us did. Yet this extraordinary thing has now become a phenomenon, which all of us have benefited by. It was my first ever proper drama show. It launched me into my career. I feel I've come a full circle now and I'm very glad to be around to witness it.

The First Baddie:
Jeremy Young

**'Fans tell me I was the first *Doctor Who* baddie …
He who finds fire will control the tribe! First the tribe,
then the world! I felt like a Bond villain!'**

Jeremy Young isn't the sort of man you'd peg as the archetypal baddie. Yet for much of the '60s, he was the guy casting directors went to when they were looking for someone thoroughly despicable. 'There were series like *The Saint* and *The Avengers* and I used to do the rounds playing the villain,' he laughs. 'Peter Bowles was the same. We used to follow each other round being the villain for the week!'

So how did such a nice guy end up playing bad guys? Jeremy explains: 'My mother taught me to read before I went to school and because of that, if we were going to do a little playlet, the teachers would always give me a part. I enjoyed it, but what I didn't enjoy was swimming. I found out that those kids who didn't go swimming stayed behind and did playlets. So, I don't know how, but my mother managed to get me out of swimming. That's really how it began.'

However, in grammar school, Jeremy's stage career hit an unexpected glitch. 'I was told that I couldn't be in the school plays because I didn't talk right,' Jeremy says, dropping into broad Scouse. 'So I decided there and then, at about 13, to iron out my Liverpool accent so I could carry on acting.'

After school and National Service, Jeremy determined to make a go of it as a professional actor. He'd met a guy in the army who mentioned that there was a good repertory company in Peterborough. Jeremy duly went along and presented himself at the stage door. 'Of course,' he says, 'I was terribly naïve, and quite rightly they told me to go away and get some experience! I eventually got to know one of the young actresses. She was all of 18 and told me, in a rather superior way, that I could find adverts for acting jobs in *The Stage* newspaper. So I bought it, wrote after an ad, and they said yes. Sheer luck!'

Luck & Lunches
After several years working his way through the 'repertory system', Jeremy was spotted by a casting director for Associated Television (ATV) called

Montague Lyon. 'He told me later that he'd seen me over a period of three years in different companies. I must have made an impression, because when ATV were casting a new series, called *Deadline Midnight*, he asked me to audition. So I was lucky he already knew my work.'

Jeremy got the part of thrusting young reporter Neville Crane, and actually worked at the *Daily Mirror* for two weeks in preparation. While there, Jeremy accompanied one of their leading reporters, Desmond Wilcox, whom he partly based his character on. The prep clearly paid off because, by the time *Doctor Who* came along, he was a familiar enough face on TV to be offered the role of Kal – the first bone fide *Who* villain.

'I got a call from the young director, Waris Hussein. I think this was one of his first television jobs, because he asked me if I would come to lunch with him to discuss a part. Maybe it was because of his slight inexperience that he thought this was the way to do it. But I thought it was great, because I had a free lunch at the BBC! He went through the idea and the script with me and asked if I was interested. It seemed all right to me, so I said to count me in.'

'100,000 BC' is now considered a television classic but, back then, it seemed that few people at the BBC had any faith in the show. Resources were tight, nerves were frayed, and the hard-pressed cast and crew were relegated to Lime Grove's Studio D – the Beeb's smallest, oldest recording space. Was Jeremy aware of any tension on set? 'No more than on any other show,' he says. 'It's always a bit tense on studio days, because the directors are under pressure to get it done. The main difficulty of shooting at Lime Grove was that the studios were tiny and the cameras themselves took up quite a lot of space. That's why they used to film inserts separately and drop them into the show. But you just had to concentrate and be on your game … because there was no time for retakes. You treated it like live theatre and, as in theatre, people used to forget their lines at times.' In fact, if a show was going out live, there used to be somebody standing by with a cut-out button that would cut the sound so that a prompt could be given. 'It didn't happen a helluva lot though,' Jeremy adds, 'because, as actors, you don't forget your lines, or else!'

Strangely, these difficult conditions actually seemed to help the actors bond. 'We were like a little family, because we were all in the same boat together,' Jeremy recalls. 'It sounds dreadful but it was actually fun! Beats working for a living!'

Fun, Fur & Fists
When I ask Jeremy if he has any specific memories of the production, he

laughs. 'Have you got three hours to spare?

'Well, first of all, we all had dirt and filth and God-knows-what daubed on us and were put into these awful old fur skins. They imported a huge amount of sand into the studio as part of the set. They added a few boulders and a bit of scrubland and that looked fine.' Unfortunately Studio D had old-style tungsten lights, which got incredibly hot. 'As the lights started to warm the sand, suddenly these sand fleas started to bite!' Jeremy says. 'As an actor you're used to being thrown into a river for a scene so you just put up with it. But there was one girl who'd been a bit iffy about having mud daubed all over her and she got more and more upset until, in the end, she stormed out – animal skins and all! Apparently she was a model and her agent had told her to get down to Lime Grove Studios because they were modelling furs!'

Jeremy played Kal, who is trying to learn the secret of fire so that he can take over from the leader of the tribe, Za. 'Fans tell me that I was the first *Doctor Who* baddie ... He who finds fire will control the tribe! First the tribe, then the world! I felt like a Bond villain!' Jeremy says with evident glee.

Za was played by Derek Newark – 'a bloody good actor' – who Jeremy had suggested would be good in the fight to the death that the rivals have. Because they were dressed in furs, Jeremy suggested they make the fight as animalistic as possible. The resulting rumble was one of the highlights of the story but, as Jeremy explains, there was one problem: 'So there we were, pretending to tear each other to shreds, rolling and scratching in all that mud, loving every minute. But at the time there was a programme called *Junior Points of View* where kids used to write in and request things. They asked for the fight sequence to be shown again and then for the action to be stopped because, at one point, the furs flip up and you see what the best dressed cavemen are wearing underneath for modesty!' For those who are curious: Marks and Spencer knickers!

No Bug-Eyed Monsters

The BBC were reportedly very nervous about the whole concept of 'sci-fi'. *Doctor Who* was given the green light only on the understanding that it would be semi-educational with absolutely no bug-eyed monsters! It was a remit that the scriptwriters took very seriously. 'The speeches we had as cavemen were quite involved and long and I thought it was all a bit erudite. So I asked Waris if I could change some of it to grunts and be more guttural and he said, "Yes but you mustn't frighten the children." So there was quite a lot of control over the whole thing, and the producer, Verity Lambert, was very tough at times. In fact when I was finally killed off, I let out a blood curdling scream, and they said, "No, no please don't do that, it's too frightening." Then, when Za picked up a big polystyrene rock and bashed my head in, they had somebody standing by with a sledgehammer and a watermelon for this grisly sound effect. But they cut that out too as they were so wary about frightening the kids.'

Almost a year later, Jeremy returned to the world of *Who* with an appearance in 'Mission to the Unknown'. This stand-alone episode was a prequel to the 12-part 'The Daleks' Master Plan' adventure. None of the regular cast appeared.

'I was up at the Edinburgh Festival doing the Scottish Play,' Jeremy recalls, 'and I got a phone call from Verity saying that there was this part of Gordon Lowery, who is the space commander of a crashed spaceship. I explained that I was busy, but she said if I could get time off from rehearsals, they could shoot it in about four days. So I shot down from Edinburgh for the recording.'

Full Circle

As with so many episodes of '60s *Doctor Who*, all that exists of 'Mission to the Unknown' are audio recordings made off-air by fans at the time. So what memories can Jeremy share for those of us who weren't lucky enough to see this one-off oddity when it was originally broadcast in October 1965?

'Well, we're marooned and the scene opens with the bottom eighth of the spaceship, because they hadn't got the money to build the whole ship! Nor the room in the studio, because it was very cramped. So it opens with the three of us. Edward De Souza plays a space investigator [Marc Cory]. Barry Jackson [Jeff Garvey] was a member of the crew and I was supposed to be the "space commander". I'm complaining about having to get the spaceship fixed. Incidentally, during rehearsals, I asked if there were any instruments that I needed to learn to use to actually fix this spaceship, and they asked the workmen who were putting up the set if they had any tools. They picked out a hammer and chisel! So there's me, bashing away at this spaceship, with not even a sonic screwdriver. Then the Varga plants start to appear and, if you get pricked by one, you change into a Varga plant. Of course, the inevitable happens. Barry and I get pricked and start changing, which leaves the space investigator alone and, as we are lying there dying, the Daleks suddenly arrive and that's the end of the episode.'

'Mission to the Unknown' marked the fourth appearance of the Daleks, who had very quickly become the show's iconic baddie. Kids both loved them and loved to be frightened by them. However, as Jeremy discovered, Daleks had the power to chill and thrill adults too. 'When we were in rehearsals, the actors inside would take the top of the Dalek props off. So all we could see were these bodies and heads sticking out of the pepper pot bottom half, which trundled along on casters. I couldn't see what all the fuss was about. They looked fairly harmless. I even knew one of the actors inside – a charming fellow called John Scott Martin – so there was no menace there. But when we were actually recording and I was lying there doing my best to die as a Varga plant, the lights suddenly changed, the music started up and, as they advanced across the studio floor with their tops now in place, I thought "Mmm, yes, I see what they mean now!"'

Fifty years separate the Jeremy Young who tried to bash the Doctor's brains in with a rock from the man I'm speaking to today. That man is warm, funny and incredibly modest. As we chat he often uses the word 'luck', when other actors might talk about 'success' or 'ability'. When I ask him to sum up 'an actor's life' he uses that word again. 'I've been lucky', he says. 'I've always worked – in theatre, seaside shows, radio, telly … and one thing led to another. Back then, ATV was booming, so there was work there all the time. I've seen all sides of the business too. Not just as an actor but as a director – that's the bossy Leo in me coming out. But it's a strange profession. There's the insecurity. Not actually knowing what the next job will be, unless you're in a run. When you're starting out, you're always waiting for something to happen, but you need to enjoy the moments. Now, I work in drama colleges. I enjoy teaching young actors about Shakespeare and the 18th Century playwrights. I enjoy giving back. We are just the storytellers of the tribe after all.' As he talks, it suddenly seems that things have gone full circle and Jeremy is back in furs and those all-important M&S knickers, helping tell great tales.

The War Lord: Derren Nesbitt

Derren Nesbitt is outrageous, outspoken, opinionated, and not altogether serious about anything except, perhaps, acting. If you've been lucky enough to have seen him on stage, you'll surely agree that his recent decision to 'never again do a play' is a crying shame. Even today, fans still talk in glowing terms about his turn as the Mongol War Lord Tegana in the first Doctor's serial 'Marco Polo'. The story was last shown in Ethiopia in 1971 and remains one of only three with not a single frame of broadcast footage currently known to survive. Fortunately Derren was happy to chat about it – and pretty much everything else …

You had a pretty high-profile career in the '60s and '70s but went off radar for a while in the '80s. Where were you?
I was in Australia. I got married to this Australian beauty queen, went over to meet her family and ended up staying there. It's a wonderful country. I was Head of Drama at an amazing university. I really enjoyed it but I found the very great disadvantage in marrying a beauty queen was her boyfriends! I found that situation rather upsetting, so I decided that we had to leave and go to Sydney. Unfortunately the lady made that totally impossible. I thought 'I've been here before. No more,' so I went home and married another lady whom I've known for 20 years. Should have married her 20 years ago, but what can you do?

It sounds like you're collecting wives. How many have you had?
Ha! Yes. I'm on my fourth.

That's really quite modest for showbusiness … are you going to go for the full Henry VIII-style six?
No, no, no! But … if I could have killed a few …

Do you have any children?
God knows how many! [Laughs.] Six, from various wives.

Are any planning to follow in your footsteps?
No way! They know it's a crazy life. I've discouraged them. You've got to be very lucky or very different to do it. And luck is 90 percent of it.

So what drew you to this crazy life? Is in it your blood?
Absolutely. I was actually was born in Finsbury Park Empire! My father and uncle [Max and Harry Nesbitt] were extremely famous music hall stars. My mother was a chorus girl. So I've never known anything else. I'm stuck with it.

Sounds like quite a family …?
It is. In fact my mother frightens the living daylights out of me. Once I said to her, 'Mother, the thing I'd like to ask you is, was I born on the 19th or the 20th?' and she said imperiously, 'I don't remember!' Every year she goes on a world cruise and I get cards addressed to 'Durran and Miranda' and I say, 'Mother you're sending me cards, but it's to Durran and Miranda. My name's Derren.' And she says, 'No it's not. Where did you get the name Derren from?' I said 'Well, Mother, you!' And she goes, 'No, no, no. I named you after a loaf of bread.' So thank God it wasn't Hovis! In fact, I found out there was a bread back in the day called something like Durran bread, so there you go …!

You started out as a Shakespearian actor. In fact, you won the Shakespeare Award at RADA[4]. How come we rarely see you in classical roles?
I've always believed in having a great deal of fun. Maybe I've been on too many holidays, but I've never been compulsive. After *Where Eagles Dare*, I was in the South of France for three years. My mother has a house there and things were bad with my first wife. So I decided to sit things out and listen to cow bells. It was either that or commit suicide.

In *The Victim* you play a rather nasty blackmailer. In *Where Eagles Dare*, you're an ice-cold SS Officer … You've played some nasty guys. Do you worry about typecasting?
No. You just do it.

So, what does it take to be a convincing bad guy?
Never playing 'a *bad* guy'. One plays oneself in differing situations. You can't be somebody else. You make up the reasons for why he is how he is, and you make it yours – and you just hope it works.

---

4 Royal Academy of Dramatic Art.

You've worked on classic television shows like *The Persuaders, The Protectors* and *The Prisoner*, as well as high budget films such as *The Blue Max*. Of all the things you've done, what was the most fun?
None of them was fun because it's a serious game. You can enjoy filming – it's so different from any other thing – but plays are very hard work to do. You can look back and say 'I enjoyed that' – and you do meet interesting people – but at the time it's hard work.

You've also worked on *Comic Strip Presents* and with comedians Hale and Pace on *Eat the Rich* … Is comedy really harder than playing it straight?
Not in the least. In comedy you – usually – hear the laughter. So, in that way, it's easier. But one should *never* think of anything as either comedy or drama. You are just the character in certain situations. Comedy actors are rarely able to play realistic characters in dramatic renderings – one has to be real! I watch with dismay certain UK soaps in which actors, unburdened by talent, appear unable to present the truth in a truthful situation. They act their impression of reality and that's not true reality.

You had a reoccurring role in *The Prisoner* as Number 2. Do you have any memories of that?
The one thing I recall is I was in my dressing room, and there's a knock on the door, and in comes the director to tell me my scene is next. Then he pauses and says, 'Can I ask you a question?' And I say, 'Sure. Fire away.' And he says, 'Do you know what it's all about?' I mean, he's the director; I was going to ask him! Anyway he went away and watched the first episode and came back and I said, 'You saw it?' 'Yes … and I still have no idea …' So while we were filming, Patrick McGoohan comes up to me and says, 'Derren, why so glum? You look like you don't know what's going on …!'

Were you asked to be in *Doctor Who* or did you audition?
I was asked.

Did you know about the show before you worked on it, and did you have any preconceptions about it being science fiction?
No. I believe no-one did. It was just another job and it appeared fairly low-key. A bit of a quickie.

Do you have any specific memories about 'Marco Polo'?
I remember it distinctly because after we did the shooting – night-time

shooting – my wife made me Italian meatballs. I remember because it's the only time she ever cooked anything! We'd just got married, which should have told me something!

Anything else ...?
The monkey [carried by Kuiju, the mercenary bandit]. The poor thing escaped into the gantries and it was so terrified that it couldn't stop going to the toilet. So you'd be standing there, doing a scene and suddenly phhhhop – monkey poop. And all I could think was: 'Everywhere I go there are critics!' Who would have known that such a small monkey would have had such a massive output? But there I was, this very sedate mandarin, covered in shit. The worst thing was that I got hit and no-one gave a damn. I had to go for coffee covered in poo!

Do you have any specific memories of working with William Hartnell that you'd like to share?
Hartnell was a gentleman. I was a big West End actor who appeared rather embarrassed to be working on something as low-key as a children's show ... such an unimportant TV series that did not match his fame, nor talent! Ha ha!

You have a much-talked-about swordfight with Mark Eden, playing Marco Polo, at the end of 'Marco Polo'. How much preparation did that take?
I had done many, many swordfights through working on *William Tell* and *The Adventures of Sir Lancelot*. In fact all the stuntmen – and I became one (by mistake) – were extremely good at fighting. So it didn't take long at all and I was very careful with Mark!

Your character commits suicide at the end. That's pretty hardcore for a family show. Were you given any specific direction on how to play that?
The most important thing for an actor is to keep away from directors! No-one took any notice whatsoever about what was either right or proper for a show watched by children. Certainly the director left it entirely to me – thankfully.

If the story were rediscovered today, how would you feel about seeing it for the first time in 50 years?
Slight curiosity.

What's been your strangest fan experience?

Oh! This is a classic. I did a play in the West End called *The Business of Murder*, and a man wrote a letter to me saying he enjoyed the show, he'd seen it twice, and was coming on Saturday week with his colleagues from an insurance company. There was a big trunk on stage where everybody thinks the body is and he actually wanted to get into the trunk. Then, when we all did our curtain calls, he wanted to come of the box and say: 'You can't keep a man from the Nationwide Insurance Company down.' I showed the letter to the company manager and he said, 'No, he'll never do it.' But … the next Saturday, we had to stop him. He was going to come out of the box!

Is there any role you'd still like to play?

My best friend in life is an actor called Bill Kenwright. I've known him for 40 years and he keeps on asking me to do tours. I really don't want to do any more. But I adore Shakespeare and – when I say adore Shakespeare – I love the tragedies. So I suppose in the back of my mind I would like to play King Lear. Maybe my swansong could be Lear. But I don't imagine it will happen.

Is that because you're not interested in actively pursuing roles?

I'm just very lazy!

Can you tell us a little about what you've been doing recently?

I've just done a film with Michael Caine and Debbie Moore called *Flawless*. Then *The Hot Potato* with my old friend Ray Winstone. I am also Chief Executive of the New Era Academy of Drama, which has now become one of the leading Drama Examination Awarding bodies in the UK. We have recently opened a branch in Sri Lanka, so I am extremely busy.

The Rocket Man: Peter Purves

**'I saw all of Billy's faults – and he had a lot –
but he cared about the work and the people he worked with.'**

Peter Purves played companion Steven Taylor to William Hartnell's Doctor, filling the gap left when William Russell (Ian) and Jacqueline Hill (Barbara) suddenly announced their departure. However, Peter has a rather unusual claim to fame: he played two different characters in the same *Doctor Who* story ... as he explains:

'In 1965 I got the lead in a television play called *The Girl in the Picture*, which was about a Blackpool beach photographer, and that was really the reason I got *Doctor Who*.' Peter was invited to see Richard Martin, who was directing the *Doctor Who* story 'The Web Planet' and looking for actors who could move well in giant insect costumes. As Peter had been in the chorus of the London Palladium, they assumed he could dance. He was actually in the singing chorus, but no-one checked! 'I saw Richard Martin the day after they transmitted the play', Peter says, 'but he told me, "No you're far better than these parts, these are rubbish parts. You'd have nothing to say or do. I wouldn't cast you, but if I'm casting people, I'll think of you." I took that with a pinch of salt, but he was as good as his word and he cast me in a cameo role in a story called "The Chase" about six months later.'

Peter played hillbilly hick Morton Dill, complete with 'cod accent and Stetson'. The director encouraged him to 'go over the top' and the result was a wonderfully comic turn. Not only did Peter enjoy it, but so did William Hartnell.

Getting to Know Who
At the end of the recording, producer Verity Lambert and story editor Denis Spooner invited Peter for a drink in the pub opposite Riverside Studios in Hammersmith, which was always known as Studio 3. Verity had just three weeks to find someone to play the new companion so, with Hartnell's blessing, she offered Peter the job. 'Maureen [O'Brien, who played Vicki] told me quite recently that Bill had been upset and frightened when Jackie and Russ decided to leave the show,' Peter recalls. 'When I appeared as Morton Dill, he got on well with me in the short rehearsal period, so when Maureen suggested that I might be a replacement, he visibly brightened up and spoke to Verity about the possibility. The rest is history.'

Peter played astronaut Steven Taylor, who is being held prisoner by the robotic Mechanoids. On the face of it, Steven is the archetypal action hero, although initially he does have one little quirk that adds a whole new dimension to his backstory: he has a toy panda called Hi-Fi. Steven is so fond of the little fellow that, even when the prison complex is set ablaze towards the end of his debut story, he dives into the flames to rescue it. It's only later that we discover that he's survived the inferno and stowed away in the TARDIS.

In the beginning, Peter had very little input into developing the character. Hill and Russell's departure had been so sudden that for the first couple of stories, he found himself playing roles originally written for Barbara. 'William Emms had written a very good story for Jacqueline Hill called "Galaxy 4" and I had to play her part,' he says. 'Steven was supposed to be heroic, but he spends most of that story asleep or doped! All the writer had time to do was give me Jacque's lines and make them slightly more masculine. That didn't quite work but, after that, Steven had some great parts and it was really fun.'

Much of that fun involved getting to know the rest of the cast, especially William Hartnell. Peter: 'I was really impressed to meet him because he was the Doctor. I'd seen the first ever *Doctor Who* episode and thought, "Wow what a great idea." I really did think it was a super bit of storytelling. And of course I knew his work from all sorts of things, such as the movie *This Sporting Life* where he played an elderly rugby talent scout. That was the part that got him *Doctor Who*. I remember him telling me at lunch one day, how much he wanted the part and he wasn't sure he was going to get it, but it was that movie that swung it for him.'

It's often been said that William Hartnell could be moody and judgemental, but he was also a very professional actor who took his job seriously and wanted the show to be successful.

'Bill,' Peter says, 'was a strange man. He didn't get on well with other people. He didn't get on with a lot of the directors he worked with. There were a few he liked, and if he liked them then life was easy, but if he didn't then he could make life pretty miserable. I watched him do that with other people. He was a bit of a bully in that respect. I saw all of Billy's faults – and he had a lot – but he cared about the work and the people he worked with.'

Friends & Colleagues
Hartnell took a shine to Peter and took him under his wing. 'He was,' Peter comments, 'very generous … and always very kind. He would give me little acting tips - some of them I took on board, some of them I took with a pinch of salt - and he would always take me to lunch at least

once a week when we were rehearsing in Shepherd's Bush. We'd go to Bertorelli's, which was a really nice Italian restaurant, with old-fashioned waitresses in black and white pinafores, and he would always treat me. He also taught me a thing or two about food that I didn't know. Such as how to eat a rare steak instead of having it ruined! He was very good company and I enjoyed working with Bill.'

Peter also enjoyed getting to know Maureen O'Brien, who played Vicki, although their time together came to a very abrupt end. 'She didn't know she was leaving. We did two serials and came back after the summer break to do a serial called "The Myth Makers". Maureen got the script and discovered that she was written out in Episode Four. No warning. But they did that all the time!'

Among the stories of which Peter has fond memories are: 'The Myth Makers' – 'I got to be an heroic Greek in the siege of Troy!'; 'The Massacre of St Bartholomew's Eve' – 'a fabulous story'; and 'The Celestial Toymaker'. 'Anything where you've got virtually the leading role is always fun. An awful lot of being *Doctor Who*'s companion is going, "Look out Doctor!" but sometimes there were parts you could really get your teeth into. "The Celestial Toymaker" was very strange, though, because it was the first attempt to write a serial without Bill being there. He needed a break so he only "appeared" as a disembodied hand! The Celestial Toymaker – his nemesis – turns him into a hand and he has to play this game, which he must win or we'll all die.'

Children & Animals

After 45 episodes, Steven Taylor's travels with the Doctor finally ended in a story called 'The Savages'. 'I didn't want to go', Peter says, 'but the producer, Innes Lloyd, decided he wanted a change, so I went with four weeks' notice, just like Maureen! Bill was very angry about it. He had been angry when lovely Maureen was axed, and felt confused when first Adrienne Hill and then Jean Marsh joined and then quickly departed. I think he felt undermined, and didn't in fact see the writing on the wall as far as he himself was concerned. He had created the Doctor, he was the Doctor, and he did not like change. Having been instrumental and influential in my engagement, he was very upset that I was to go. Our paths crossed only once or twice after I left the show – a couple of dinners I think – and that was it. All rather sad, but the acting world can be like that. Ships that pass ... and all that.'

Peter joined the hugely popular children's magazine show *Blue Peter* in 1967, 18 months after leaving *Doctor Who*. It was only supposed to be a temporary job. 'I knew the show and as I wasn't working I took it, literally, as a stopgap,' he says. 'I had no intention of giving up acting, but after six months were up, I was offered a further six months. I discovered that, according to my original contract, I had to accept. As you know, I stayed with the show for ten and a half years. So I never really gave up acting – acting gave me up!'

Other presenting jobs followed, giving Peter the chance to work with both children and animals. Perhaps most memorable was the motorcycle trial show *Junior Kick Start*, which was compulsory, edge-of-seat viewing for kids in the 1980s. Peter's love of dogs also made him a natural choice to be the voice of Crufts' dog show, which he's now been involved with for 35 years.

His first love, though, has always been acting. He got the bug when he just a kid, watching end-of-pier shows in his hometown of Blackpool. Later, as a student teacher, he spent most of his time in the drama society and playing in a skiffle band. 'I didn't do any real studying,' he admits, 'but teaching is a bit of a performance so I qualified with a distinction. However, I never intended teaching. I always wanted to act.' Getting his first gig was the hard part and required a lot of 'shoe leather, enthusiasm and brass neck'. So, the fact that he's returned to both acting and the world of *Doctor Who* is great news.

Peter is now recording his tenth Companion Chronicle audio for Big Finish, which means we'll be hearing more adventures for Steven Taylor. But what about that little stuffed bear, Hi-Fi? Well, he seems to have joined Steven on his travels too. As the Doctor says when describing the workings of the TARDIS: 'That is the dematerialisation control, and that over yonder is the horizontal hold. Up there is the scanner, those are the doors, that is a chair with a panda on it. Sheer poetry, dear boy …'

Peter's Top Five *Who* Moments
1. Not a Steven – but a Morton Dill moment. Actually getting the opportunity for my very first comedy cameo on TV. I loved it.
2. Enjoying the permanence of a job that allowed me to socialise with both Maureen O'Brien and Bill.
3. Meeting the adorable Jean Marsh and working with her for 12 weeks. A high-spot for anyone.
4. Playing the hero in 'The Myth Makers' and having a great role in 'The Massacre of St Bartholomew's Eve'.
5. Being allowed to enjoy the comedic elements in 'The Gunfighters'. It was understated (unlike Morton Dill) but I managed some good double-takes and played the gentle idiot.

The Gunslinger: Shane Rimmer

It's 1881 and three strangers have just arrived in town of Tombstone. A battle is a-brewing at the OK Corral and little do the TARDIS crew realise it, but they're about to get stuck slap bang in the middle. With its musical narration and epic vision, 'The Gunfighters' was perhaps one of the first Doctor's most adventurous stories. Canadian actor Shane Rimmer was there, at the Last Chance Saloon, and shares his memories of *Doctor Who*'s first Western.

What brought you from Canada to the UK?
Well, when you're in Toronto, you run out of things to do fairly soon. There are two options. You either go down to California, Hollywood, and try your luck there or you come to Europe. I went down to Hollywood but I didn't like it very much. It's total commitment down there. Anything else that you're up to takes second place, and I didn't like the sound of that. But here there's a broader sort of perspective. Plus both my parents were from over here, which made me feel sort of comfortable. So I settled in and did a lot of films both in the UK and on the continent. It was a really full deck at that time.

From your early career, which one role sticks in your mind most and why?
I liked *Danger Man*. I liked it a lot because of its star, Patrick McGoohan. I thought McGoohan was terrific and I was intrigued by him. I used to watch him all the time in the studio when I wasn't doing something. Totally Irish and a terrific fella. I got to know him quite well and we got to be very comfortable with each other.

How did you come to be offered the part of gunslinger Seth Harper in 'The Gunfighters'?
I went in and read for it, which you do most of the time. You go in and there's a big, fat, cigar-smoking producer and you read the part. If you're lucky you get it, if you're not you go onto the next one. That turned out quite well and of course once you get established, no matter how slightly, things start happening – which they did.

Did they give you any guidance on the sort of character they were looking for?
No, they just said remember the lines! It was pretty basic back then.

What was the first day on set like?

William Hartnell was very much at the helm. He came over and he said, 'Are you from above or below the Mason Dixon Line?' The Mason Dixon Line is a sort of geographical divider in America between the North and South. It's very contentious – people from the South and people from the North are constantly at each other's throats. So I said 'The North – Canada', which stumped him for a second, and then he said 'That's all right.' So I passed his pre-examination and he was fine after that.

Do you think it would have been bad if you'd been from South of the Line?

I wouldn't have dared say anything! He could be a bit of a grump, but he was very strong and he made his feelings known, so you were never in any doubt as to whether you passed the grade or not. I got to like him but he wouldn't stand fools, and that showed in his acting. Although there was a whimsical thing to *Doctor Who* at that time – still is, I guess – he held his ground very well.

As an older actor, he probably had to do that quite a lot …?

I guess. Sometimes his tolerance levels were a little low, but I got him on a good day. It worked out well and I loved the series. I thought *Doctor Who* was a real breakthrough show, but they needed someone pretty strong in the pilot seat and he did the job perfectly.

You got to work with David Graham on 'The Gunfighters'. Did you already know each other from *Thunderbirds*? Which came first?

I think *Thunderbirds* just edged it by a little. But David was great in the role. He had a backlog of voices like you wouldn't believe. They just poured out of him, which made him a very valuable member of any cast. In fact I'm still very much in touch with David. He lives over in Hampstead and I'm about ten miles away, so we get together fairly often – doddering along the sidewalk together.

What were your impressions of the story?

It has a very standout feel. It has its own atmosphere, especially with the music. But you know, it was a good story. How the writer Donald Cotton managed I don't know, because the plot was taken from a picture called *Gunfight at the OK Corral* with Kirk Douglas and Burt Lancaster. How he got all that into a studio, I don't know. There was some sort of magic he had. But it really worked. If a drama doesn't ring true, you're done for, and you can't do anything about it no matter how hard you might try.

There's a great scene in 'The Gunfighters' with Peter Purves where he's being forced to sing at gunpoint. Was it as much fun as it looked?
It was. It was very light-hearted.

Were you bothered about the occasional wobbly set?
Possibly we just turned our backs on it. But really how much that sort of thing bothers you very much depends on the atmosphere on the floor, and the lead man has a lot to do with that. Hartnell was very firm in a lot of respects and he held the thing together. He was a very good actor and had created this terrific character. We just paid attention to him, and anything wobbling was some else's problem!

British actors, especially in the '60s, seemed to really struggle with American accents. Did you offer any advice on set?
I never offer any advice to any actor! I mean, I have trouble after all this time doing an English accent! But it was pretty basic dialogue and nobody was doing anything exceptional with the language. Today, of course, British actors are top of the heap when it comes to doing different accents. They can go to America and do it – it's way beyond anything I could conjure up. Bob Hoskins is terrific at it. I did a stage play with him called *True West* and he had the accent down marvellously well. It's not just the sound; the speech patterns are different too. The rhythm is different in America than it is in England.

And in Canada?
Yes, but in North America, we were all brought up on cowboy films, so it comes very naturally.

Do you have any specific memories of working on 'The Gunfighters' that you'd like to share?
We were a bit worried that we were so confined with studio space. Something like a cowboy picture should be shot out in Wyoming, but they handled it very well. I remember the Clanton Gang came in through a side door of the studio on horseback. Well, most of us were on horseback. One of them was on a mule, which had been conscripted from the local fields, I think. That really broke us all up – when the mule

came staggering in. The Clantons are supposed to be a totally fearsome bunch and this mule didn't seem to know which door to go in or out! It wasn't in shot that often but I think somebody had to dangle a few carrots around to get it to keep going. But the whole episode was rather gently done and slightly whimsical. That suited Hartnell right down to the ground and we all took our cue from him. That was part of the success of it. In fact, during the filming there was never any pressure, or ordering about unnecessarily. You had to find your marks and you had to respond in the way you should, but I think it was all rather gently done.

You've been in some of the most famous television and film franchises. Which was the most fun and why?
You do pin me to the wall don't you? I guess the Bond picture *The Spy Who Loved Me*. You couldn't help but be impressed with the extent of the operation. There were usually two camera crews going at the same time. One was doing special effects, which there were a lot of, and one was on the ground floor doing the actual dialogue. The Bond family – Barbara Broccoli and her father – have kept a very sensible organisation there. If it were Hollywood and Vine it would have been tougher, but they gave you some slack. It was a joy to work on. A lot of the pictures over here have that same sort of quality. I don't know why. It's a slightly laid back way of doing things, which was, in some instances, the total opposite of what would have happened in America. So we all enjoyed it.

You've recently done an audio book of 'The Gunfighters' for the BBC. Was it hard to go back?
No, not really, because it was so very well written. Donald Cotton had the lingo, the language, down very well. So you weren't having to school yourself in anything that wasn't natural to you. It was fine, but it was a slog. Two days of sweat, I can tell you that! They only let you out for water every four hours!

Would you like to do more *Doctor Who*?
Sure, but these days I wouldn't be *in* Tombstone I'd be *a* tombstone! Ha!

The Man of a Million Voices: David Graham

**'The make-up when Kerensky had to age rapidly was
a major feature of the show, and the time it took to put it on
is still vivid in my memory!'**

David Graham is the man of a million voices. Since the 1950s, the London-born actor has leant his considerable talents to bringing to life both puppets and animations, from *Supercar* to *Thunderbirds*, from *The Moomins* to *Peppa Pig*. He's appeared in *The Avengers*, *Danger Man*, *Timeslip*, *Callan* and *The Tomorrow People*. He was Big Brother in the famous 1984 Apple Mac advert. In fact, David Graham has pretty much been there, done that and bought the T-shirt.

The urge 'to perform' was, David says, 'an emotional need'. At school he always wanted to recite the poem or read the extract. Later, after National Service with the RAF, where he was a radar operator, he went on to work in an office but found the environment stifling. It wasn't until he went to stay with his sister in New York that he finally got the chance to feed his 'raging acting gene', by enrolling in drama college.

It proved to be an exciting time to be Stateside. Playwrights like Arthur Miller, Tennessee Williams and Richard Nash were setting the stage alight. It was there too that the musical was experiencing its big revival with Loewe and Lerner's *My Fair Lady* and Rodgers and Hammerstein's *South Pacific* to name just two of the decade's major productions. David lapped it up, returning to the UK with his acting gene in full throttle.

Back in the '50s, most actors learnt their craft working in 'weekly rep' – performing a different play each week with repertory companies – and David did his fair share of treading the boards in the provinces. Finally, though, he made the leap to the capital, debuting with a role in the hard-hitting social drama *Bread and Butter* at the Jeanette Cochrane Theatre. Critically-acclaimed roles followed in London's theatre land. Some of David's career highs include *Filumena*, directed by Italian filmmaker Franco Zeffirelli, and *Arturo Ui* with Leonard Rossiter – 'his energy was demonic,' David recalls. David was also with Laurence Olivier's company at the National Theatre when the whole cast corpsed during a production of *Saturday Sunday Monday*. During a scene where they had to eat a meal, they discovered that the meat was off. 'Much mirth ensued,' David says.

Unfortunately Olivier didn't appreciate the humour of the situation!

A Good Ear

Flexibility and talent are two great requisites for any successful actor and David fortunately has both. 'I was lucky,' he says, 'to be born with a good ear,' and it was this ability to pick up voices and accents that ensured him a steady stream of work both in the theatre and the 'new' medium of television.

David's first appearance on the small screen came in 1952 with *The Portrait of Peter Perowne* co-starring Roger Delgado. However, in 1960, David's incredible voice talents came to the attention of Gerry Anderson, whom he met while working on a film in Elstree. 'We just got talking in between takes and he said he was going into puppetry. I'm not usually forward in coming back or backward in coming forwards so I said, "I do puppet voices," and six months later he called me up and said he was doing this show *Four Feather Falls*, which we made in a house in Maidenhead with dear Kenneth Connor.'

That show was the first on which Anderson worked with puppets, and would ultimately spawn *Supercar*, *Fireball XL5*, *Stingray* and *Thunderbirds* and ensure David Graham the adoration of kids everywhere as the voices of Brains and Parker. As if that wasn't enough to ensure him a place in the Geek Hall of Fame, David also has the distinction of working on six *Doctor Who* serials.

Along with Peter Hawkins, David was one of the original voices of the Daleks. Peter Hawkins, was, as David comments, 'a great voice artist and a close friend for many years.' While David was busy providing the voices for Gerry Anderson's AP Films, Peter was breathing life into the likes of *The Flower Pot Men*, *Captain Pugwash* and the characters Zippy and George from the children's show *Rainbow*. He was so much in demand that 'he was able to amass a valuable collection of impressionist paintings.'

Men & Monsters

David played the voice of the Daleks in four William Hartnell stories: 'The Mutants' (aka 'The Daleks'), 'The Dalek Invasion of Earth', 'The Chase' (where he also provided Mechanoid voices) and 'The Daleks' Master Plan'. The process was deceptively simple, although it wasn't just a matter of running the actors' voices through a ring modulator. It was all about tone and timing. 'We pre-recorded the Dalek voices in a studio in Lime Grove,' David says, 'and the voices had to be menacingly stylised.' This meant that David and Peter would have to vary the pitch and speed of their lines according to the dramatic impact of the scene. Their voices would then be processed by the BBC Radiophonic Workshop to create the distinctively grating Dalek voice.

However David is one of the few actors in *Doctor Who* to have played both monsters and men. He played the barman Charlie in 'The Gunfighters' in 1966. 'It's shrouded in the mists of time now,' David comments, 'but I do remember that as Charlie I put a small wad of cotton wool behind my lower lip to accentuate the character. I also met a great friend, Shane Rimmer, on set and we subsequently worked on the famous Gerry Anderson series *Thunderbirds* together.' David also appeared with Tom Baker's Doctor, playing time-dabbling Professor Kerensky in 'City of Death' (1979). Oddly both roles earned him a gruesome death!

Does he have a favourite? 'I have no particular favourite story,' he says. 'To use your talents is always a joy, but I found William Hartnell really pleasant to work with, and he once said to me, "We'll have you back". I also enjoyed playing Professor Kerensky in "City of Death". Tom Baker was a larger-than-life character and very pleasant to work with. The atmosphere was good on set too, which always helps actors, because work always involves pressures. The make-up when Kerensky had to age rapidly was a major feature of the show, and the time it took to put it on is still vivid in my memory!'

Much of David's most famous work has been in sci-fi or fantasy shows, but surprisingly he has 'no particular love' for either genre. 'My career just seemed to point in that direction for a while and I was grateful. At my age I am thankful for any opportunity that arises. Actors don't retire, they just fade away!'

Thankfully David shows no sign of fading. When he's not working he's 'addicted to music – mainly classical – along with the company of friends, good food and literature.' He's still very much in demand as an actor too, and has just started work on a new *Thunderbirds* series, which will be out in 2015. 'To try and experience life to the full and pour it into one's work, that is,' David believes, 'what life's all about.'

The Doctor's Most Faithful Companion: Bernard Cribbins

Doctor Who, Carry On …, Fawlty Towers, Coronation Street. Over the last 50 years, Bernard Cribbins has appeared in some of Britain's most popular films and television series. Now in his eighties, he was made an Officer of the Order of the British Empire in 2011 for his services to drama. But it's his association with *Doctor Who* that's earned him some of his most loyal fans. Bernard appeared in the 1966 *Daleks – Invasion Earth: 2150 AD* movie, playing PC Tom Campbell opposite Peter Cushing's human Dr Who. In 2007 Bernard made it a double. He appeared in both the *Doctor Who* radio play *The Horror of Glam Rock* and made his first appearance in the television show as Wilfred Mott in 'Voyage of the Damned'. No wonder that executive producer and showrunner Russell T Davies dubbed him the Doctor's most faithful companion …

How did you get started?
My God! How long have you got! It was during the War. I'm from Oldham in Lancashire and they were having a collection for a warship, which I think was called *HMS Onslow*. We had a drama festival to raise money and I went along with my school. I was about 11 years old and I played a small part in a play. The producer of the local repertory company noticed me and thought that I could be useful, so I was offered some other small parts with the company, which I did while I was still at school. Then I left school at 13 and I was offered a job as assistant stage manager/small part actor, which I took. That was in 1943 and I've been at it ever since, apart from doing my National Service with the Paras, which I loved.

What was your 'big break'?
Well, I was in rep for eight or nine years altogether, but I got my first job in television – live television in those days – in *David Copperfield* for the BBC, playing Tommy Traddles. My first film was the same year, in 1956, called *The Yangtze Incident*, with Richard Todd. I've been ducking and diving ever since!

Which do you prefer: film, theatre or television?
I've done mainly theatre because it's what I know best. In the theatre, you have some sort of control. Once you get on, the only thing that they can do to stop you is either drop the curtain, turn the lights out or shoot you! I suppose next to that, films. I love making films. Television comes sort

of third for me, unless it's filming for television, which is quite a different experience. But working in a studio used to be very restrictive – it's different nowadays – but way back, live television was very tricky. Very tricky indeed.

You've appeared in dozens of classic British comedies including *The Two Way Stretch* with Peter Sellers, which has a great fan following. What do you remember about that?

It was wonderful and unique in its own way, because we started off on the first day of our filming in the prison cell – Peter, David Lodge, Lionel Jefferies and me – and we started on the second page of the script and we went through for a fortnight chronologically, which is a highly unusual way to film. But it was great fun, working with Peter and David – and especially Lionel. Great fun! Of course Lionel was instrumental in another of my films, *The Railway Children*, which he wrote and directed so well.

You worked on the unofficial Bond movie *Casino Royale*, which has the reputation for being a 'difficult' film. Was there really a feud between Orson Welles and Peter Sellers?

Well, there were tensions on set. In fact, Orson and Peter never met ... There was some fracas and they had to do their scene, the one where they meet across the table, with a stand-in on one side and Orson doing his lines, and then the reverse with Peter. Acting is a funny old game sometimes, I can tell you!

What's been your favourite role so far?

My favourite job, I think, was doing *Guys and Dolls* at the National Theatre, which was an absolutely wonderful experience. They had one of the best ensemble companies you could ever wish to see, and it's a great book – wonderful music. Superb production all round. It was 99.9 percent right. Terrific job. I've done so many things that I've enjoyed but the jobs that I've done just for the money, I haven't enjoyed.

Can you mention any of the ones that you didn't enjoy?

No, I can't remember any now. Honest! But I've enjoyed the *Carry On*s, *The Railway Children*, *She*, *Fawlty Towers* ... All lovely jobs.

Many actors have bad memories of working on the *Carry On...* films because of the bad pay and bad conditions ...

Well, you shouldn't do the job if you don't like it!

But you did?

Yes, I did. *Carry On Columbus*, which was the last one, felt a bit sort of grey, you know? It wasn't the best film in the world. But *Carry On Jack* I loved! *Carry On Spying* was all right, but *Carry On Jack* is my favourite.

What was it like working on *Daleks – Invasion Earth: 2150 AD*?

Smashing. Great fun! I did get into trouble with the Daleks though. There was an Australian guy in one of them and they had to read the lines out so that we could work the scene out, and this little Australian voice used to come out of this tin pot saying: 'You will be extermaanaated!' It always made me laugh, and whenever I was laughing, Gordon Flemyng [the director], God bless him, used to get very cross!

You've worked on quite a bit of *Doctor Who* over the years …

I've actually worked with Peter Cushing as a Doctor, David Tennant, most recently, and Paul McGann on *The Horror of Glam Rock*, which was a radio play. I've also worked with Peter Davison on *Dangerous Davis* and Jon Pertwee in *Worzel Gummidge*. So I'm collecting Doctors. I've got five so far.

Did you ever fancy being the Doctor yourself?

I did. In fact I went along to an interview just after Jon Pertwee left, but I don't think I was seriously in the running.

Is it true that you wore some of your own clothes for the role of Wilfred Mott?

It is! The parachute regiment badge I have on Wilfred's hat is mine from my army days. But Russell T Davies is so clever like that. That speech I give in 'Voyage of the Damned' about being in Palestine; that's all me. I spoke to Russell about my experiences during National Service and he incorporated it almost word for word.

The last time we saw you on screen in *Doctor Who* was in 'The End of Time'. There are persistent rumours that you'll be back …

I'm not telling you anything! If I did, I'd have to kill you! My lips are sealed!

Finally, you must have had a lot of strange requests from fans over the years … Anything you can admit to?

Err … I have signed ladies' chests and things like that! I mean, you know, high up on the chest. No dotting the 'i's!

The Highlander: Frazer Hines

**'… if we hadn't had those two women nagging us,
we'd still be there now, because we were having so much fun!'**

I really hate being late. However, two weeks of nearly constant rain has almost brought London's traffic to a grinding halt. Finally, I decide to abandon the wheezing, groaning red double-decker and continue my journey on foot. I'm heading for Covent Garden – one-time flower market – now a trendy place to hang and meet friends. The trip takes me past the grand old BBC building Bush House at the end of Kingsway and down the Strand. The street is just over three-quarters of a mile long, starting at Trafalgar Square and running east to join Fleet Street. In the 11th Century the street was known as strondway, 'strond' being the Old English for riverbank. Today, it looks very much like the River Thames is trying to reclaim lost territory. I'm wading ankle deep in muddy rainwater, my clothes are sodden and I'm now an hour late. I keep looking at my watch like the White Rabbit on speed but it really doesn't help. When I finally arrive at a discrete basement bar, just behind the Adelphi Theatre, I'm breathless and bedraggled. There's no sign of my interviewee. I head outside to get a better signal on my phone and just in front of me is the man I've come to meet. 'Hello,' he says in a soft, Yorkshire accent. 'I'm Frazer.'

It's hard to believe that it's been 47 years since Frazer Hines first stepped into the TARDIS. In real life, the man who was Jamie is a trim, athletic 60-something with peppered grey hair and the slightest hint of a tan. He's just returned from a five-week stint in Australia where he's been doing 'a bit of business' and having a lot of fun. That fun included 'a couple of *Doctor Who* conventions' and 'playing cricket for the Over 40s World Cup'. In fact, although acting still pushes Frazer's buttons, he's always had two other big passions: horses and cricket. 'If I hadn't have gone into acting,' he muses, 'I'd have loved to have been a cricketer. I've played cricket now for 40-odd years. I've also ridden as a jockey for about 20 years, which I love. The only trouble with that is you have to keep losing weight. But being a cricketer would have been really good fun.'

So, what was it that made Frazer set his sights on a life on stage? 'Well, my parents were in the operatic society in Harrogate, Yorkshire and I used to go to Saturday morning dancing lessons and singing lessons when I was seven. One year, the person who ran the drama school put on a show and I did a Maurice Chevalier impression. Somebody in London at the Corona School saw this newspaper article that said: "Seven-year-old stops show." So I ended up going to there.'

Frazer was nine when he started at Corona and it turned out to be a good time to join. Dennis Waterman, Francesca Annis, Richard O'Sullivan and Susan George were all schoolmates. However, Corona was a far cry from the *Fame*-style stage schools we might imagine. 'We had a fairly normal childhood,' Frazer says. 'You weren't allowed to play cricket or football in case you got a cricket ball in the face or a broken arm or something like that. But you got the Three Rs in the morning – reading, writing and 'rithmetic – and then in the afternoon, depending what grade you were in, there'd be tap on Monday, ballet on Tuesday, Shakespeare on Wednesday, stage craft on Thursday and whatever play we were reading on Friday.'

At the age of 11, when most schoolboys were reading comic books and swapping cigarette cards, Frazer made his professional debut in a short film called *On the Twelfth Day*, which earned itself an Oscar nomination. A year later, he appeared with Dean Jagger in the Hammer Horror classic *X: The Unknown*, followed by a part in Charlie Chaplin's *A King In New York*. It was all pretty heady stuff and, even today, Frazer still has great memories of those early years. 'That's the great thing about this business,' he says. 'I've had such a varied career. I can be at a dinner party in England and some actor might say, "Well John Gielgud said to me ...", and I go, "Well Charlie Chaplin once said to me ...", and the knives and forks go down! It's a great leveller. In fact Chaplin was a lovely man. I got on very well with him because he asked me if I could sing opera, and the next day my mother made me learn "The Stars are Brightly Shining" from *Tosca*. So I went back to Mr Chaplin and I started to sing and he realised that this little boy hadn't just gone home and played football, he'd actually done his homework. So he took quite a shine to me. So much so that, later in the day, I suggested a bit of comedy business to him. And instead of him smacking me around the ears and saying, "Look I'm Charlie Chaplin, I've written, produced, and star in this film," he listened to me.'

Hard Work, Good Fun

By the time that Frazer was in his teens he'd moved onto the small screen as a regular in Shaun Sutton's children's Sunday serials for the BBC. Does he wish now that he'd stayed in film, or was TV just too good an opportunity to miss? 'I started out in film because television was very much in its infancy back then,' Frazer says. 'But you always went where the next job was, to be honest. I suppose if I'd done a Michael Caine – he was offered *Z-Cars* and turned it down because he wanted to be in movies – then things might have been different. But then I went into *Doctor Who*.'

Despite the passage of time, Frazer clearly has deep affection for the show and for the character of Jamie, the Highland Scot with the lowland accent ... 'Well,' Frazer laughs, 'I was originally only supposed to be in four episodes [in the story "The Highlanders"], so I gave him this very up and down Highland accent. Then, when the producer, Innes Lloyd, asked if I wanted to do another year in the TARDIS, I realised that the Highland accent is not very dramatic. So I sort of watered it down to what I call a TV Scottish accent.'

As he speaks, Frazer slips without pause from accent to accent. It all sounds very natural, but is he a Scot? 'My mother was Scottish and I spent most of my holidays up in Port Glasgow. In horse-breeding you always take from the dam's side, so I'm more Scottish than English, and when England play Scotland at cricket or football or rugby I always root for Scotland!'

Frazer stayed with *Who* for three years, and Jamie eventually appeared in more episodes than any other companion. But if Frazer had had his way, he would have stayed even longer. 'Someone said the other day that one year we did 46 episodes – wasn't that hard work? And you know, I don't remember ever thinking "God, this is hard work!" We'd record a few episodes and have a summer holiday. Then we'd record a few episodes and we'd have Christmas off. I never felt it was hard work at all. Wendy Padbury, Patrick Troughton and Deborah Watling were a great crew. Nobody ever fell out. I can't remember any raised voices in rehearsal rooms. I never felt "Oh God, I hope he's in a good mood today" or "I hope she's not drunk again". We just had a ball, but my agent said, "You must go back and do more movies, darling," and Patrick's wife was saying, "You must do better television then children's TV." So I always say that if we hadn't had those two women nagging us, we'd still be there now, because we were having so much fun!'

How much of a say did he get in developing Jamie's character? 'Quiet a lot, actually. Because Jamie was from 1746, I was able to do what I called Jamie-isms and change the script. The lovely thing about Jamie's character is that he could ask all the questions that the kid at home watching would ask his dad. If you'd got the Doctor and two professors in the same room, they'd all know what they were talking about, but Jamie could ask: "Why does that work?", "What's that doing there?"'

Was there anything about the character he'd have liked to have changed? 'No. He was loyal and strong and tough. He was a great character and it was so easy to slip straight back into how I played him in "The War Games", 16 years later in "The Two Doctors".'

In between those two cracking stories, Frazer was busy working on another British TV institution – the soap opera *Emmerdale Farm*. Frazer played the role of unlucky-in-love farmer Joe Sugden on and off for 22 years: a feat that recently won him a place in TV's Top 100 Greatest Soap Legends. It also makes him something of a rarity, having appeared in two of Britain's longest-running television shows. Does it bother him that he's done so much work but is mainly remembered for just two characters? 'I can't understand actors who try and erase their past. I'm very proud of the two shows. I don't mind if people say "I loved you in *Doctor Who*." Thanks to those four episodes of "The Highlanders", I have now seen all parts of America and all parts of Australia. All on the back of something I did 40 years ago! No, not at all.'

Raring to Return

The sad thing for many fans is that some of the Jamie-era *Doctor Who* serials are missing. The original tapes were wiped by the BBC mainly because the rights to repeat the shows had expired. Although a number of episodes distributed as film prints to overseas broadcasters have recently been recovered, at the time of my interview with Frazer that wonderful news had yet to become public knowledge, and he told me that he shared the fans' frustrations at the gaps in the archive. 'I think eight or nine complete stories of mine still remain, but I'd love to see my first story, "The Highlanders", again. I wish they could find it in Nigeria or Australia, because that would be nice. They've found episodes of "The Underwater Menace", which was my next story, in which I wear the old Highlander rough kilt outfit. So you never know, one day …' he adds with a wistful look that many *Who* enthusiasts will appreciate. How did he feel about the missing episodes of 'The Invasion' and 'The Ice Warriors' being animated? 'We didn't like that,' he jokes. 'The animated characters were much better actors than we were!'

Since officially leaving *Who*, Frazer has actually returned to the series twice, in 'The Two Doctors' and 'The Five Doctors', as well as performing in a run of Big Finish audios. He also does a one-man show called *The Time Travelling Scot*, where he comes on stage dressed as Jamie and talks about every story he's ever done. 'I tell little stories and point out things that you may not have noted before,' he explains.

In fact, he's a pretty busy man. 'I've also got another show, which I call *My Life in Showbiz*, in which I talk about all the films I've done and all the people I've worked with. I have an interest in a record company, Red Record Discs in Australia, and a horse-breeding company in Newmarket, and we're negotiating for a TV show a friend of mine's written for me called *The Mild Bunch* with Colin Baker, Vicky Michelle and John Challis.' This year, he's so busy that he's had to break with a 30-year tradition and miss panto, which he adores.

As if that wasn't enough, rumours abound about whether or not Frazer will don the kilt one more time. 'Before Sylvester McCoy became the Doctor,' Frazer says, 'the *Sun* newspaper had a list of people who had been approached about the part and I was one of the names. I hadn't in fact been approached, but I'd have loved to have been the Doctor. However, I liked Matt Smith. He's very like my Doctor, with the hand movements and the bow tie, and his favourite show is "The Tomb of The Cybermen" apparently. Well, I'm in that one. Patrick was in it. Patrick is no longer with us, so why doesn't he suggest that Jamie pops back? But I haven't had a call yet.' With a new Doctor stepping into TARDIS, we can only guess what will happen next, but the key phrase here is 'yet'. Here's hoping!

The Storyteller: Victor Pemberton

An eerily memorable theme tune. Great monsters. Innovative effects. Cool costumes … and actors who really make you believe it. *Doctor Who* has it all. But the most important part of the mix is the one that is so often ignored: the writing. Even if the monsters look laughable and the costumes are silly, a good writer can turn the germ of an idea into a story that people will still talk about 50 years later. Victor Pemberton is one of that rare breed who have made their living making the world – and *Doctor Who* – a lot more interesting. And yes, he really did invent the sonic screwdriver …

Many artists say that they were born with the compulsion to 'make marks'. Is it the same for writers? Have you always written stories?
I have always wanted to make up stories. The reason for that is, I love the movies. I was brought up during the War and cinema was a great form of escapism. It taught me a great deal about storytelling and allowed me to escape from the grim realities of a very grey War. It taught me about ways of living, and how to observe. It taught me about death, which I saw for the first time in the rubble of Blitzed houses and in my own family. So yes, I always wanted to write, but it lay dormant for a while.

Writing's not an easy profession to get into. What was your big break?
Myself, my friend David Spenser, and another actor shared a flat. I used to criticise their criticism of plays, and because I worked in a travel agency they said, rather grandly, 'You have nothing to do with this business! If you think you know so much, go and write a play yourself.' So I got all hoity-toity, had a little tantrum, locked myself in my bedroom and did exactly that. At the time, my father had been working as a ticket collector on the London Underground. After 47 years he had to leave because he had the first signs of cancer. London Transport wouldn't give him a pension because he was a year and a half short of the age. So I thought I'd get my own back and I wrote a half-hour play for radio about it. I gave it to the two lads, who read it rather snootily, but then their attitude changed. They thought it wasn't bad, and David showed it to a producer. She loved it but wanted a happy ending. So I wrote an ending that couldn't be more clichéd if you tried. I wrote that he won the football pools! It

went back and she loved it. She said, 'That's it, chum, that's the way to do it!' I thought it had finished me as a writer, but it went out as a half-hour Saturday afternoon play on BBC radio. Well, I was so nervous that I went home to listen to it. It went out at two o'clock, and at five, my mother called to tell me that my father'd won the football pools!

I notice you're often credited as an actor ...
People do keep referring to me as an actor, but I'm not. In fact, there was nothing on Earth I wanted less than to be an actor. The thought of acting absolutely destroyed me! But I started working in television because of a dear friend of mine, Frederick Messina. He used to produce *Play of the Month* and he said, 'Get out of that travel agents and come and be an extra for me. I'll give you £5 a day and you'll learn your craft.' So I did. My God, I learnt a lot too! I didn't play cards with the other extras, I just noticed what was going on, and that really helped me ... but it's haunted me ever since.

So that's how you ended up working on the Patrick Troughton story 'The Moonbase'?
Yes. I'd done another show, which most people have now forgotten, called *Quick Before They Catch Us*. Morris Barry was the producer of that. I had an extra part with a couple of lines, and he remembered and asked me to be in 'The Moonbase', which he directed for *Doctor Who*. It was only a line and a half, but those ghastly pictures of me from it still keep cropping up!

Was it fun?
It was fun because I teamed up with a guy who was my fellow astronaut and we had a lot of giggles. Pat was a great friend of ours anyway and I loved Debbie and Frazer, so it was all good. I said my one and a half lines, took the fee and went off!

Was there ever a hint that you might go back to *Doctor Who*?
No, none whatsoever. What happened was that Peter Bryant was taking over as producer of *Doctor Who* and asked me to come and be his junior script editor. So off I went to the BBC's offices on Shepherd's Bush Green, and the first thing I seem to remember being there for was 'The Evil of the Daleks', then 'The Ice Warriors'. Then Peter mentioned that we'd be doing a new thing with two writers and asked if I'd come in and be the full script editor on it. The writers were Kit Pedler and Gerry Davis and the story was of course 'The Tomb of the Cybermen'.

What do you remember about the evolution of the story?
Kit and Gerry were fascinating but two very different people. Kit was the technician, the academic, and Gerry was the dramatist. So they fused fairly nicely. They used to row and quarrel occasionally and I used to mediate, but not a lot – just occasionally. They were both determined to do things their own way! I didn't interfere too much but, of course, I made a few changes and a few suggestions as the story developed. Initially when the Cybermen came out of those awful coffins, they just came straight out, and I thought it should be spookier. I said to Peter and Morris [who was directing again] that we should put some dry ice in there, so that when the things start to open up, it looks as though they're emerging from something sinister. It turned out to be a quite fascinating effect and a rattling good story. What I loved about it, was that I was able to be there all the time and see how the whole thing came together. It was a terrific experience.

Any specific memories?
Well, there would always be someone making comments about the Cybermen costumes, like 'Has anyone got a tin opener?', and there was always the teasing that went on between Pat, Debbie and Frazer. Frazer is one of the greatest jokers of all time. He'd play the most awful pranks on you – he'd put itching power in your shoes. He was a rotter! We all used to tease Debbie. She was beautifully teaseable. Still is!

Did you have any problems bringing the script to life?
No, it came alive quite well. Gerry knew what he was doing and Kit made sure that the technology was authentic and feasible. They kept a close eye on things, but when it came to filming, they didn't interfere at all. Morris, the director, was lovely – very memorable. He used to go around in plimsolls all the time in the studio. But he was quite temperamental and everyone knew that. He had a very quick fuse and got rather cross at everybody, but he had a vision of how it should be, because he took it very seriously. I think you can always tell which directors take *Doctor Who* seriously and which ones treat it as just another job. Later on, I found there were some directors who were just there to have a good laugh – an in-house laugh as it were – and I didn't like that at all. It doesn't matter how preposterous something seems. Those old B-movies were silly, but you had to take them seriously because the best drama is something that's treated realistically. All of the shows we did, even though the sets did wobble and it was in monochrome, were treated seriously.

When you came to write your own *Doctor Who* serial, 'Fury from the Deep', how did you find the experience?

It was troublesome! Peter asked me to write something and I didn't want to write intergalactic stuff – space stories. I was brought up on science fiction that took place on planet Earth and I've always found that more realistic. I had the germ of an idea for a story like that so I did a synopsis. Then Derrick Sherwin took over as script editor and he wanted to change everything, including the title. Peter had loved it but when I got the script back from Derrick he'd virtually rewritten the whole thing. So I said to Peter, if you take the script like that, then take my name off it. Luckily Derrick hadn't consulted Peter about the changes, so it was all put back as it was. The only thing I did allow them to change was the title, because it was more filmic. But when *I* was a script editor, I helped, I never took over!

'Fury from the Deep' was Debbie Watling's last story. Did she speak to you about how she would like to go out?

No. In fact, she sprang it on us so quickly, that I hardly had time to work out just how she would go!

There's a Doctor for every age. What sort of Doctor is yours?

There are several sides to the Doctor. There's a dark side that has never really been explored. It's almost a Jekyll and Hyde thing. That's what I always had in the back of my mind when I was writing for it or as a script editor.

Were you able to bring those ideas to the fore in your own story?

Yes. What I did was to make sure that he doubted some of the things that he did himself. He didn't just know all the answers automatically. He had to work them out first and they didn't come immediately, unless there was a crisis. For me, that was because the other side of his brain was telling him, 'Beware'.

It sounds like you really got under the skin of the character. Would you have liked to have carried on working on the show?

No. My turn as script editor came to an end after three months and I didn't want to go on with it because I wanted to write my own stuff, and in those days – typical BBC – you weren't allowed to write and be a script editor at the same time. Terrance Dicks was brought in then, and he's made a career out of it. But I didn't want to get stuck in one thing. My career has been very varied, which is what I wanted.

In the early 1990s, there was a celebration at the BFI in London after a copy of 'The Tomb of The Cybermen' was returned to the BBC from Hong Kong. How come you weren't involved?

I wasn't asked! It was extraordinary as I'm the only member of the production staff left. They gave the excuse that they couldn't afford the air fare from Spain. I think they thought I might have sued them 90 billion pounds for my sonic screwdriver!

Other people have claimed that they invented the sonic screwdriver. Presumably that's not true, as it first appeared in your scripts for 'Fury from the Deep'?

No, but isn't it typical? You always find somebody doing that. But fans have written to me from all over the world about the screwdriver, saying 'Why haven't you claimed it?' The *Sun* newspaper even did a big article and phoned me to ask why I didn't take action, and I said, 'If you give me the money to do so, I will!' But as for people claiming it for themselves, they should be careful, because I have all the correspondence and paperwork!

Are you writing your autobiography?

Several people have asked, but it's not an easy thing to do. But I will do it and there will be a lot of revelations about *Doctor Who* and other shows that I worked on like *Black Beauty*, *Fraggle Rock* and all that.

Finally, you have a huge archive of your work ... you don't happen to have a copy of 'Fury From the Deep' in the garage hidden away?

No, I'm afraid not! There wasn't the means to tape television back then and, in any case, I was at the studio during it all. However, I do think that somewhere in my archives I've got some Super 8 film from the location. My archive is so full, it would be quite a job to dig it out – it would take forever. But everybody wants it!

The Victorian Miss:
Deborah Watling

'Working with Frazer and Pat, you had to prove yourself ...'

First impressions are funny things. When you meet Debbie Watling, it's hard not to be reminded of the character she made so famous – Victoria Waterfield – companion to the second Doctor. Like Victoria, Debbie is pretty, petite, and seems a little reserved and ever-so proper. It's only once we start chatting that I get a glimpse of another Debbie. Intelligent, witty and with a backbone of steel. But then, this is a woman who's survived in the showbiz world of chew 'em up and spit 'em out for 55 years and is still smiling.

Acting is in Debbie's blood. Her father Jack, mother Patricia Hicks, sister Dilys and brother Giles all 'went into the business'. A younger sister, Nicky, didn't. 'She tried it and didn't like it. I think she found God, so that was it!' Debbie laughs. Her first television role came in 1959 when she was just nine years old, in the ITC show *William Tell*. 'My godfather rang my father and told him that there was a part going that would really suit me. Father said, "But she's only nine years old," and he said, "Well, go to Elstree and have a see." So I met the director, Ralph Smart, and he was this rather large, imposing man. Being only nine I thought, "Oh dear, I don't like the sound of this." Anyway he asked me to read the script and I said, "No I can't read," and my mother said, "Of course you can!" So I did it and I got the part.'

A reoccurring role followed in another Ralph Smart-produced ITC show, *H G Wells' Invisible Man*, and then Debbie returned to school to do her O Levels. After exams came drama school but, frustrated by the tutors, she left after just three weeks to get herself an agent.

A part in *The Wednesday Play* about Lewis Carroll, in which Debbie played Alice, put her on the cover of the *Radio Times*, and it was that cover that attracted the attention of *Doctor Who* producer Innes Lloyd. 'I was invited up to see Innes Lloyd,' Debbie remembers, 'and he said that he'd seen me and believed I'd be absolutely right to be in *Doctor Who*. We both agreed that I should go away and get a bit more experience. So I went away for a year, and then in 1967 I got the call and he asked if I was still up for it and I said yes.'

Over the next year, Debbie was to work on some of the most memorable serials of Pat Troughton's era, meeting Daleks, Yeti, Cybermen and Ice Warriors. Her character, Victoria, may have been young, unworldly and vulnerable but she was also surprisingly strong-willed. How much of that came from Debbie and how much from the script and direction? 'It was a bit of both really, because the clue is in the name Victoria. She is a Victorian miss – rather prim – but she's got a head on her. She knows exactly what she wants. However the way the character developed, that was all Watling.'

Someone Else's Shoes

They often say that being an actor means being able to stand in someone else's shoes, and for Debbie that's absolutely true. 'Getting the character of Victoria is all about the way she sits,' she says, and suddenly her whole body language changes. 'She is always upright, and then there's the walk as well. You always have to put on your shoes first of all, then you get the character. Shoes first, get the walk, then the voice and the character emerge.' And the clothes? 'Yes, but the funny thing was that in *Doctor Who*, for my first story I had a very long Victorian frock on. That was fine. Then, throughout the year I was there, my skirts got shorter and shorter and shorter, and eventually they ended up like a curtain pelmet. Tiny!'

Debbie's first story was 'The Evil of the Daleks', and she found it a nerve-wracking experience. 'It took me about a week to settle in, because I was really quite nervous, but Pat and Frazer made me so welcome. In fact they always used to go to the BBC Club at lunchtime and I always sat in the rehearsal room with my sandwiches and a flask of coffee, and they got fed up with this and one day they said, "Debs, you're coming with us. We're taking you to the BBC Club." So I went there and they gave me a glass of wine and I've never looked back since! It really was an absolute dream. A lot of fun.'

Had she seen the Daleks before? 'No, I hadn't, and on my first day of filming, in this big old house in Harlow, I thought, "What am I doing here?", because my co-stars were these strange creatures with bumps all over them and a plunger sticking out of the front. But we were introduced and they saw that I was slightly nervous, and I was just standing there minding my own business waiting for the shot to be set up, and they came up behind me with their plungers! I shot to the ceiling. I laughed a lot, so that broke the ice.'

'Fun' is a word Debbie uses a lot when talking about *Doctor Who*. Frazer and Pat were famous practical jokers and there was clearly a lot of laughter on set. When Debbie's dad made his first appearance as Professor

Travers in 'The Abominable Snowmen', it took five takes to stop laughing because, she recalls, he looked 'so silly' in his costume. In 'The Ice Warriors', she had the hysterical experience of whispering directions to an Ice Warrior. He was supposed to be dragging her away down a polystyrene tunnel but, because of the costume, he couldn't see a thing and Debbie had to lead him. Then, in 'Fury from the Deep', she was dumped into freezing foam on the beach by Frazer and Pat to 'celebrate' her birthday!

In addition to the fun, there was also a lot of work. During her time with *Who*, Debbie appeared in seven serials. That meant a six-day week, including location shoots, although those locations were rarely as glamorous as they seemed. 'The Evil of the Daleks' included night filming at Grims Dyke House; 'The Tomb of the Cybermen' saw the cast decamped to Gerrards Cross Sand and Gravel Quarry; Nant Ffrancon Pass in Snowdonia stood in for Tibet during 'The Abominable Showmen'; Climping Beach in Littlehampton became Australia for 'Enemy of the World'; and Debbie's final story, 'Fury from the Deep', took her to Margate.

Just For The Fans
Debbie was just 19 when she got the role in *Doctor Who*, 'but I looked about 15, not even that,' and along with the workload came the pressure to deliver. 'Working with Frazer and Pat, you had to prove yourself to a certain extent on screen, otherwise you'd be dismissed – and I wouldn't allow that,' she says with a flash of that steely resolve.

Like Frazer Hines, Debbie laments the fact that some of her *Doctor Who* episodes are absent from the BBC's archive. 'It's awful,' she says with genuine passion. 'It gets me very uptight.' If her surviving episodes are anything to go by, we're missing some cracking stuff. For instance, there's a wonderful moment in 'The Tomb of the Cybermen' where Victoria and the Doctor are talking about family. It feels so real, and it's more like we're eavesdropping than watching a performance. Did she feel that too? 'Yes, it was just like me talking to Pat. It was extraordinary. I remember that day I had terrible flu and it didn't show, thank goodness, but I thought I was dying! People always say that scene is absolutely brilliant, they love it. The stunned gentle thing, they called me!'

All good things come to an end and Debbie decided to call time on *Who* after a year travelling in the blue box. What made her decide to leave? 'In those days you didn't have much say in the character and the way it was written, and I thought I couldn't really do any more with Victoria. But she's always been a part of my life. I've done spin-offs – she's older, of course, but she comes straight back to me.'

That last story, 'Fury from the Deep', is also her favourite. ' Not because I was leaving,' she's keen to point out, 'but because it was so well done. It was about a seaweed monster. You didn't see the actual monster until the fourth episode, but you knew it was around, and the way you knew was that it had a heartbeat, and as it got nearer and nearer it got louder and louder … der dum … der dum … der dum. Terrifying! I loved it.'

After *Who*, Debbie went on to do more film, television and theatre as well as becoming a regular on the *Doctor Who* fan circuit; something that has brought even more laughter. 'I was once asked to sign a pair of boxer shorts!' she says. With a man inside? 'Well, that's what I thought! I've had things in the post too, but we won't go down that road! To be honest when I was first in *Doctor Who* I thought: it's a children's programme, fine, this will do for a year. That's all any actor wants – a job for a year. I never thought, after all these years, I'd be back talking about the character. But I am, and I'm very proud of it, because she's a huge part of my life and I'll never forget her. It is,' Debbie says, seriously, 'all about the fans – that's what keeps us going.'

So, I have to ask, did she ever get her own back on Frazer for being dumped in the sand and foam? 'Not quite, but I will one day!' I suggest that she should set something up for a long, slow burn. 'I think I will,' she says in a way that makes you really believe it. Like I said, backbone of steel.

The Triple Jumper: Peter Craze

Peter Craze has appeared in *Doctor Who* three times, in 1965, 1969 and 1979, and with three different Doctors. His brother Michael played the companion Ben Jackson opposite William Hartnell and Patrick Troughton. However it seems that the actor and director simply can't get enough of the wonderful world of *Who* …

Tell us a little about yourself.

I was one of a large family. My brother Michael, who became Ben Jackson for a year with Pat Troughton, was very, very keen to go on the stage. He had a 'Sign from the Heavens' as he called it, the day James Dean died. That was in 1953 and he said, 'Right, that's it. I'm going to be the new James Dean.' So at the age of 12 he started to pursue an acting career. I was about four years younger than him and I thought, 'This is money for old rope,' so I followed him. There was no ambition, but for a kid from a big, fatherless family, acting was a way out of a lot of the problems and difficulties. I had a golden period from aged about 15 to 25. Then, in my mid-30s, I started directing, because I got very bored with bad directors. I mixed it up for another ten years directing and acting. Then I joined the Drama Studio, London, which is quite a famous drama school. I went with my family and lived in San Francisco for two years and ran the school and directed around the peninsula in San Francisco. By that time I was completely committed to directing and that's really what I've done for the last 30 years. Eventually, I became principal of the school for nine years. I finished that last year and now I'm back as a freelance director.

Why acting? Was it in the family?

We came from this rather tough, working class area of Brixton and I think my brother wanted to have some dignity. Also, he was a very natural actor. Judgement might say I was the better actor, but I didn't really make any choices. Success was sort of foisted on me.

In the '50s you needed money to go to drama school. Was it tough to get into the business coming from a working class background?

Not as a child actor. Back then, not many kids went into it. The upper middle class who were going to RADA were known as Barnes Babes. It was like a finishing school for young ladies. But if you were working class, acting was like boxing or football. It was a way of breaking out of your class.

What one role cemented acting as the right decision for you?
I think when I was in *Peter Pan* on stage in the West End. I played Michael Darling, and Sarah Churchill [Winston Churchill's daughter] was Peter and Julia Lockwood [Margaret Lockwood's daughter] played Wendy. I was with ten or so London acting boys and having a blast. There was complete equality. I discovered that acting had nothing to do with class. I felt very comfortable, and I've always felt very comfortable in the theatre, but not so much in society where class still seems to be very important.

What was it like – being young and famous?
We hadn't had people like David Bailey and Terence Stamp yet. So those working class boys who broke out were not so much celebrities, but they were somewhat elevated in their own communities. My older brother, Tony, became quite a well-known playwright, and my sister was an actress too. We had quite a stern mother and we were all kept well grounded – there was no getting above yourself. However I did know a lot of the kid actors at the time who were completely led astray by early drugs and alcohol. If you were even a minor success in the '60s, it was easy to be sucked into that world. On one job, I was earning £125 a week, which was a fortune. [The average wage at the time was £12-14 a week.] Money was pouring in and you're hanging out with famous people. It was bloody marvellous, but dangerous too.

Your first appearance in *Doctor Who* was in 'The Space Museum' in 1965. How did you find the experience?
It was a new show and still finding its feet. There were three young actors in that story: myself, Jeremy Bulloch and Peter Sanders. Verity Lambert, the producer, was a very strict disciplinarian and Bill Hartnell, I have to say, was a bit of a miserable old git. Being a classic grumpy old bugger, he didn't like youngsters, and we were all 17. We thought this *Doctor Who* thing was bit of a lark and he sensed that we weren't quite taking it as seriously as he did. We'd had our eyebrows soaped off and I remember our costumes getting caught up in the fake eyebrows. Jeremy had a piece of cotton caught on his eyebrow and I couldn't look at him without laughing. Hartnell got very, very cross and said we should all give up acting immediately! The most memorable thing, though, was the director, Mervyn Pinfield. He had a sort of tin box fitted with mirrors on a tripod and he would follow you round with this thing. You'd be acting and you'd look out front and see this giant eye, reflected by all these mirrors! He was

very weird. He actually made Hartnell seem jaunty and young.

'The Space Museum' marked the start of a long relationship with *Doctor Who* for you. How did your next serial, 'The War Games', compare?
Bill was superb actor and had a great career, but Pat Troughton was much more of a classical actor. Pat was lovely but I did only one episode on that story. I played a Frenchman [Du Pont], and just before the recording, someone came down and told me I was pronouncing one of the words wrong. That just set me off worrying. I remember thinking, 'Oh God, what if they're *all* wrong!'

Your third appearance was with yet another Doctor, playing Officer Costa in the Tom Baker serial 'The Nightmare of Eden' ...
Tom was just wonderful, and 'Nightmare' was a crazy time. He was a passionate and committed actor. I did a thing with Lalla Ward last year and I reminded her of this anecdote but she denied it, of course. We were doing a run through of Episode Two of the four-parter and Tom burst out at the director: 'You don't even care about *Doctor Who*! Get out of this rehearsal room. Go in the other room and play with your silly camera script. We're going to get on with the acting!' – and he threw him out! The director was a guy called Alan Bromly, and I announce his name handsomely, because I think he was a disaster. But Tom was just so passionate and devoted and crazy and dangerous. His Doctor was very exciting. He brought a lot of humour – dark humour – to it as well. He was lovely. I liked him a lot, and I liked him as an actor too because he brought danger to his performances when things on television were starting to become very formulaic. Tom kept it buzzing.

Obviously Michael was in *Doctor Who* too. Was there ever the possibility that you'd be offered the role of Ben rather than Michael?
No. I've had too broad a career, really. Michael got entrenched at the BBC and they loved him and he did lots and lots for them. It got to be a bit of a club. In fact there literally was the BBC Club and, when you were in it, people would come across with a pint and offer you work. Sadly Mike's career faded and he became a bit of a *Doctor Who* acolyte. He'd got to the point where all he did was go to conventions.

Did he enjoy them?
Loved them. Unfortunately it became his life, and there's a great danger

in that. I've only done a couple and enjoyed them enormously but that was his world, and although he died 15 years ago, his shadow still falls across the convention circuit. When he died, I was in Miami directing *Into the Woods*, and I came back home for his funeral. I didn't recognise any of the people at the crematorium, and when the music started for his coffin to enter the furnace, it was the *Doctor Who* theme. It was then that I realised that all these people were fans who'd come from all over the world to say their goodbyes. They went off to a hotel and I went along to say hi. I realised that he'd formed his own family in that *Doctor Who* world. It was very lovely and very moving, but also very dangerous. Anneke Wills is very clever, because she dips in and out of it, but Mike began to rely on it as his energy and his force. He was also drinking like a fish, and those conferences are not helpful when you've got a problem. Great fun – but you can't do it regularly.

As a director who's also acted, do you ever feel the urge to tell an actor they're doing it wrong?
No. You can never do that – but you do have to keep reminding yourself!

Do you miss acting?
No. An actor's experience is just a small part of a production, whereas a director's input is huge – and a lot more fun! I started acting too young and, when I reached a certain age, I became aware of what good acting was and was disappointed not just in myself but in the directors who should have been helping me and weren't.

Being so involved in training today's new actors, how would you say the business has changed?
You can't really break into this industry now unless you've been to drama school, and many people can't afford it. Plus, expectations are different. Kids want to be stars. They're not interested in acting. Some schools don't even do theatre – they just do 'media'.

What's been your most memorable job?
I played Pip in *Great Expectations* with Donald Sutherland. I remember that being haunting and brilliant. But usually it's been theatre work and directing – when I feel that I've really got to the heart of what the playwright intended.

What's next for you?

I'm going off to direct *Blithe Spirit* in a new university in the American Mid-West. I'm looking forward to re-establishing my freelance directing career. What I would like to do, though, is another episode of *Doctor Who*!

What sort of character would you like to play?

I'd be happy to sit at the desk and answer the phone. I'd love to do it as a cyclical thing. So that I can say I've been right through the show, from the first to the most recent. I think that would make a great story!

Chapter Two: The '70s

'Do I have the right? Simply touch one wire against the other, and that's it? The Daleks cease to exist? Hundreds of millions of people, thousands of generations, can live without fear, in peace, and never even know the word Dalek ... But if I kill, wipe out a whole intelligent life form, then I'd become like them. I'd be no better than the Daleks.'
(The Doctor, 'Genesis of the Daleks')

It's been called the decade that taste forgot. Yet there was more to the '70s than frilly shirts, velvet jackets and big, big hair. More than any other post-War era, the '70s was a time of social revolution. A period of people power, when trade unions flexed their muscles, women burnt their bras, and gay issues came firmly out of the closet. Despite massive unemployment, power cuts and a three-day week, it was also a time of enormous creativity and optimism. This was the era of inventions like the word processor, the domestic videotape and liquid crystal displays. It was the decade when the Office of Strategic Operations taught us you could rebuild a man for six million dollars and when *The Tomorrow People* taught us how to jaunt. From glam rock to punk rock, from Starbuck to Buck Rogers, the '70s had it all ... But it almost didn't have *Doctor Who*.

In 1969, *Doctor Who* was teetering on the brink of cancellation. The show was simply too expensive to continue in its current format. To cut costs, the decision was made to limit location shoots and exotic props and costumes. The Doctor would, it was decided, be Earthbound. The decision could have spelt disaster for the show. Fortunately, when Jon Pertwee fell from the TARDIS on 3 January 1970, he brought all the flare and flamboyance of the era with him.

The popularity of spy-fi shows such as *The New Avengers* almost certainly influenced the storylines. So too did Pertwee's own dapper style and love of gadgets. The third Doctor was very much a James Bond wannabe with a sonic screwdriver rather than a Beretta and an Edwardian roadster in place of an Aston Martin. He even had an evil nemesis and a glamorous babe on his arm. Combined with the development of the UNIT 'family' and the show being made in full colour for the first time, *Doctor Who* was back with a vengeance.

Four years later, when Tom Baker took up mantle of the Doctor, the scriptwriters again responded to the mood of the age. Early stories had a strong gothic element inspired by the Hammer horror films of the late

1970s. In came more independent, more rounded companions in the form of Sarah Jane Smith, Leela and Romana. And in too came a more complex Doctor. Tom Baker's incarnation appears on the surface to be a comic and bohemian figure. But behind the mile-wide smile and love of jelly babies there's a dark, brooding personality. It was an incarnation that proved increasingly popular with adult audiences. During Tom Baker's tenure, the show averaged between nine and 11 million viewers. That was around a quarter of Britain's viewing population.

Since the show began 1963, it had slowly moved away from the initial BBC expectations of a semi-educational series, and by the mid-'70s was increasingly relying on good stories and character development. In the capable hands of Pertwee, the show blossomed. With Tom Baker at the helm, it reached its zenith. *Doctor Who* had never been more popular.

The Captain: Richard Franklin

'We didn't call him Mr Pertwee – we didn't go that far – but he came from that background and he did expect you to treat him as six foot three with a lot of white hair and a white ruffled shirt!'

Just around the corner from that magnificently ugly tribute to '70s architecture known as the Barbican are some of London's most discreet residences. Tucked away in a secluded courtyard, built around the remnants of a medieval monastery, is the sort of place you might expect to find ex-MI5 types whiling away their genteel dotage. If Captain Mike Yates, late of UNIT, ever decided to retire and write his memoirs, then this is probably the place he'd do it.

So it seems appropriate that it's here that Mike Yates's *alter ego*, Richard Franklin, has chosen to make his home. Fortunately though, unlike the redoubtable Captain Yates, Richard has no plans to retire. He's still busy doing exactly what he loves: acting and directing.

'I had the desire to be somebody else from the age of about four or five,' Richard says. 'Looking back on it, the times when I really felt I'd come alive were when I wasn't being me.' It's a surprising statement, but then Richard's a surprising man: quietly spoken and thoughtful, with that natural reserve many actors seem to have when they're 'off duty'. In fact, the man behind the mask has none of Mike Yates' brash confidence or military stiffness, but all of his charm.

Richard first got his chance to indulge his passion for being someone else in school, although his stage debut wasn't exactly auspicious. 'The very first play I ever did was called *The Ghost of Jerry Bungler*,' he laughs. 'It was written by a master at my prep school and all I really remember was that we all rushed round in white sheets and scared each other absolutely senseless. Great fun, but probably dreadful! Then I went to Westminster School; and of course there were no girls there so, on one famous occasion in *Julius Caesar*, I was Portia in the first half and General Titinius in the second half. I expect I probably played both parts exactly the same!'

Sadly Richard's ambitions to make a career of acting were initially quashed. 'My father and I were on a different wavelength. He was a famous surgeon and he wanted his son to be a famous surgeon. So, when I went to university at Oxford, I was told not to have anything to do with drama.'

After National Service – he was a Lieutenant in the Royal Green Jackets – Richard joined an advertising agency, which turned out to be a successful if unfulfilling career move. 'I'd have been a director of the firm at 26 and probably incredibly rich by now, and not living in this small flat …' he muses, 'but then a life-changing moment came, as it so often does, out of a tragedy. My younger brother was very ill, which was a great shock, and the shock let the cork out of the bottle. What I really was and wanted to be, came to the surface. The circumstances that drove me to the stage could not have been worse, but the decision to go into the theatre was like a new life.'

Blue Boxes

That new life began, oddly enough, with a blue box – or rather a series of blue boxes. These days if you visit Century Theatre in Derwent Water, you'll find a lovely little 400-seater playhouse down by the lakeside. It's still Britain's most remote theatre but, back in the '60s, Century were a touring company of idealistic actors looking to bring theatre to the arts-starved provinces. The cast lived and performed out of three blue metal caravans that could be converted into a raked, 225-seat covered theatre known familiarly as the tin box. For Richard it was the start of a lifelong love affair with the stage. After 18 months with Century, he moved onto repertory. Over the next six years, he honed his stagecraft, appearing in productions in Bristol, Ipswich, Manchester and Birmingham, before making his West End debut as Corin in *As You Like It*.

It was then that TV came a-calling with roles in classic British dramas such as *Dixon of Dock Green*, *The Saint* and *The Pathfinders* before Richard landed the part that made him a household name.

'My agent was a thrusting young agent – which is what all agents should be – and he was at a first night in London,' explains Richard. 'By accident, he was sitting next to Barry Letts, who was the producer of *Doctor Who*. And being a thrusting young agent, he asked Barry if he was casting anything. Barry said, "Yes, we're going to introduce a love interest into *Doctor Who*. We've got Katy Manning and we want someone to be her partner."' His agent asked if Barry had anyone in mind, and by coincidence Richard's name was mentioned. 'My agent rang me from the theatre in the interval and said, "Barry wants to see you at 9.30 at the BBC tomorrow morning." So I went along and had three interviews. The fashion then was to have quite long, Beatles-type hair and I remember on the second interview Barry lent forward and pushed my hair back and said, "Oh good, you've got ears." Then, on the third interview, I was confronted with Katy Manning, who is still a great friend, and we read a scene together.'

UNIT Unites

Those who are familiar with Jon Pertwee's era will remember that Katy Manning's character, Jo Grant, does indeed mention going on a date with Mike Yates in the first episode of 'The Curse of Peladon', but then that plot line seems to fizzle out. What happened? 'That was Jon Pertwee. He put his big foot in there!' Richard laughs. 'And I think he had a point. There's only so much that you can put into a programme, and the focus needed to be on this two-hearted Time Lord and his lab assistant. There may have been some personal reasons – not animosity toward me – but perhaps Jon might have felt that it was rather nice to have a pretty young girl on his arm! Whatever the reason, it didn't work in my favour and a nice love story was lost.'

Back then *Doctor Who* was notorious for its tight budgets. As a newcomer to the show, what that something that he noticed? 'Oh yes! Nowadays *Doctor Who* has a million quid budget. When we did it, they had £2,000 to do the studio days, and if you overran it was very expensive. The budget was deducted by the minute! So you were allowed to make a mistake and have a second take, but anything more was frowned upon. I remember Jon had seven takes on one shot and you could have cut the atmosphere with a knife! He was a great man, Jon. I liked him very much indeed and he was very good company. Very urbane but very much the star, in the old-fashioned theatre way. We didn't call him Mr Pertwee – we didn't go that far – but he came from that background and he did expect you to treat him as six foot three with a lot of white hair and a white ruffled shirt!'

Richard's character might not have got the girl, but he did get a very warm welcome. 'I have one strong memory of going into a very large room with a great number of people in it … and a general feeling of not feeling intimidated. We certainly had a first meeting in the Acton Hilton [the nickname for the BBC's rehearsal rooms]. We probably had a look at what we were going to film and then went off filming. But it was a very good welcome … Jon knew how to look after the great and the small in the company. The combination of him and Barry Letts – who couldn't have been a nicer person to work with – made my first day great.'

Ice & Fire

The welcome may have been warm but Richard recalls location filming as being something of an ordeal of fire – or rather ice. 'It was January on Dungeness Beach during a cold snap filming "The Claws of Axos". It was so cold that the Wardrobe Department gave us all pink long-johns to wear underneath our uniforms. The make-up was Caribbean, because we were so pale, and when we got into the studio we had to cut because we found we were 25 seconds over. The muscles had frozen up, so unconsciously we'd been speaking slower!'

To fans, the relationship between the characters of the Brigadier, Benton and Yates always seemed very warm and spontaneous. Was it? 'It was,' answers Richard. 'Initially that came from very good writing. Comedy's only funny if it's rooted in truth, and the army set up of the senior officer, the responsible junior officer and the sergeant is a very vital triangle; and the writers got it spot on. The Brig is a bit of a buffoon, the Captain is the image of the great British officer, and the Sergeant is the one who does all the work! Of course, as the writers get to know the actors, you find that the characters become closer and closer to yourself. In one story I was put on a motorbike, because they saw me coming into rehearsals on a Honda 50 Step Through and they imagined that I was able to cope with a 650 Triumph Bonneville. They were wrong though,' he adds, in mock alarm.

Richard is referring to the motorbike chase sequence in 'The Daemons' – a serial that also featured one of the show's most memorable final lines. However, as Richard explains, it was never actually scripted. 'The Brig and I were standing watching everyone dance round the May Pole and I said to Nick Courtney, playing the Brig, that I thought we ought to have a close-up here and a line. I asked Barry Letts who said, "Yes by all means. What do you want to say?" So I said, "Well I'd like to look at the people dancing, turn to the Brig and say, 'Fancy a dance, Brig?'" And Nick, who had a rather fine comic sense, said, "Rather have a pint, Captain Yates!"'

Friends & Colleagues

Richard speaks with warmth and honest affection about both Nicholas Courtney and Jon Pertwee. Clearly, both made a lasting impression on him. Can he share any specific memories that conjure up his time working with them? 'I can! Nick Courtney was a very good friend. He was very loveable and had a very nice quality that many actors – particularly successful ones – don't have, in that he wasn't thrusting at all. He wasn't always trying to talk to the most important person or putting himself forward as something special. He was just a very good traditional actor doing a job. He was also a good Christian, which he didn't thrust down your throat, but you can tell by that the sort of person he was.'

Nicholas Courtney was well known for his love of an ale or two, but Richard also reveals that they shared a passion for racehorses. 'He used to disappear at lunch hour to put a bob or two on the horses. In fact, I like horseracing as well, which is why I'm now living in a two-roomed flat! I had six racehorses up in Yorkshire – though only two at a time – and the only one that was really any good was a horse called Glenougie, which I part-owned with Frazer Hines. It won so many times that it didn't actually cost us a penny. We didn't make any money, but not to have spent anything is really an achievement!'

And Jon Pertwee? 'Well, Jon was one of those people who would sweep into a room and the charisma would knock everyone flat. Even in a field in Aldbourne [filming "The Daemons"]; I remember he arrived a little bit late one day and we could see him walking across the field, and the closer he got, the more the atmosphere rose. He was just one of those people who commanded attention, and of course he was a very good joke-teller. I remember when we were rehearsing in Acton ... on the seventh floor was the restaurant, and at that time Eric Sykes, Hattie Jacques and the Two Ronnies were all doing BBC shows, and they'd all be waiting for their food in the queue. Now comedians are very competitive. If one tells a joke, the next one has to be funnier. It was life or death to them, but what I took a little while to learn was that you didn't cap a comedian's joke, nor did you produce a funny witticism as the result of something he'd said. You just laughed!'

Moving On
During his time in *Doctor Who*, Mike Yates underwent a dramatic transformation. Over two stories, the Brig's by-the-book adjutant became an eco-activist. Was that fun? 'Yes, absolutely. It gave an extra dimension to the character; though, at the time, none of us liked "Invasion of the Dinosaurs" at all. However, looking back, I think it's a very good story and very well shot. As for "Planet of the Spiders", the Earthbound stuff is very interesting. Of course it's got a lot of writer Barry Letts's beliefs in Buddhism in it. But the actual planet stuff to be honest makes me cringe. The dialogue is awful. It's pseudo hippy stuff, the sets are terrible and the spiders sitting on shelves are awful. But having said that, I do like the story. It stands out.'

It did seem that, having released Mike from the confines of UNIT, he might go on to become a companion. Was that his expectation? 'What happened during the making of "Planet of the Spiders", Richard says, 'was that I got another job. I wanted to go into directing. I was actually directing a very large youth theatre up in East Yorkshire, and from that I got an associate directorship at Ipswich. So I was moving on, otherwise I'd have had a lot more to do in the end stories. In fact the writers had it in mind to end my *Doctor Who* career by blowing Yates up in "Invasion of the Dinosaurs" and Barry Letts wouldn't have it. He saved my character.'

Today, Richard is still actively involved in the Whoniverse, and very much admires the new series. 'I think is has been very cleverly brought up to date by Russell T Davies. He hasn't lost any of the essential *Doctor Who*-isms, but he has made it acceptable to young adults of today. I do find it extraordinary though how much, in the relatively short time that the show was off the air, society changed. When we were doing *Doctor Who*, somebody with grey hair was respected. Now at 30, you're too old for the role! It's actually awful, and it's fanned by a media who would rather print pictures of half-naked 21 year-olds.' Here Richard pauses to laugh self-deprecatingly, aware that he may sound like an old fuddy-duddy. 'Matt Smith, though,' he continues, 'is great. By far, head, shoulders and knees better than any of the other new Doctors. He's not acting it – though he is a very good actor – he just inhabits the role.'

If he could return to *Who*, what character would he like to play? 'Actually,' he says with a twinkle in his eye, 'I've already cast myself in the remake in the role of former Lieutenant General Yates, Sir Michael Yates, Black Rod in the House of Lords!'

Richard has reprised his role several times in audio plays from AudioGo and Big Finish. He's also written his own Mike Yates-esque adventure called *Operation HATE*, which picks up where 'Planet of the Spiders' ended. So not only do fans now have some degree of closure on what might have happened to Mike, but also the wonderful combination of Roger Delgado's Master ('the best' comments Richard) paired with Tom Baker's Doctor.

So are there any other similarities between himself and Mike Yates? 'There are qualities in Mike Yates that I admire and would like to aspire to but, in my book, I'm able to make him seem like a cross between James Bond and Biggles. Not true to life of course!' He pauses before adding with a smile, 'Mind you, there are autobiographical elements in the story ... but I'm not saying exactly what is true and what is exaggerated! You'll have to read it.'

The Director: Michael E. Briant

Michael E Briant – the E stands for Edwin – joined the BBC in 1964. He started his climb up to the heady heights of the director's chair working 'the floor', assisting on stories such as 'The Crusade', 'The Gunfighters', and 'Fury from the Deep'. He gained his first of six *Doctor Who* director's credits with 'Colony in Space'. 'The Sea Devils', 'The Green Death', 'Death to the Daleks', 'Revenge of the Cybermen' and 'The Robots of Death' all followed. These days Michael likes nothing better than messing about in boats, and has recently written an autobiography called *Who is Michael E Briant?* (see www.classictvpress.co.uk). But while semi-retirement in Andalusia may be lovely, it all seems a little tame for a guy who spent a good chunk of his career locking horns with Daleks, Sea Devils, Cybermen, killer robots and giant maggots …

You started out as an actor before heading to the other side of the camera. Do you think having acting experience helps when directing?
Just the fact you have been in the business for years outside of television, both at drama school and as an actor and stage manager, must help. Working in the theatre is a wonderful experience and probably the best preparation possible for a young TV director. Making little silent movies from the age of 13 also really helped!

What's your directing style? Do you sit back or are you hands on?
I love actors and I tend to let them take the lead. The actor knows more about their character than anybody else. Writers and directors are always concerned with the big picture but the actor is interested solely in their character, and how they live, breathe, behave and react. The actor offers that interpretation to the director, whose job is to either accept it or ask for modifications in the interest of that 'big picture'. Cast the most intelligent person, with the most ability to play the role, and 90 percent of your work is done.

Your involvement with *Doctor Who* spans four decades, four different Doctors and six stories. Do you have any favourites?
For me, Jon Pertwee was the best and most successful Doctor ever. He was a real pleasure to know and a delight to work with. Of my own shows, I probably remember 'The Sea Devils' and 'The Robots of Death' with the most pleasure because I think my ideas made them better than they might otherwise have been – plus both were so much fun to work on.

Those are both great stories with some superb moments, especially that classic sequence of the Sea Devils emerging from the sea. Was that your idea?

It was. I had put aside most of one afternoon to do lots of shots of Sea Devils coming out of the sea, so that it would look like an army. In the end, we were so far behind schedule that I could only have one take on two cameras. That, and the actors almost drowning, severely hampered the creative process!

There's been much debate about Malcolm Clarke's very quirky music, which was used in 'The Sea Devils'. What did you think of it?

The producer Barry Letts wanted to try somebody new and give Malcolm a chance instead of our usual composer, Dudley Simpson. I think, all in all, Malcolm did a good job with the facilities available at the BBC Radiophonic Workshop.

Almost everyone involved in classic *Who* has complained about the tight budgets. As a director, can you give us one example when you had to come up with an especially innovative way of telling a story without the budget to do it?

Doing the invasion of Earth by six Sea Devils against the might of the Royal Navy!

'The Robots of Death' is a wonderfully tense piece of storytelling. What tricks did you use to build and keep the tension over four episodes?

The main thing about that story was that the script was a pure, slow-burn whodunit. Chris Boucher wrote it so well and did a good Agatha Christie job of it.

It also looks incredible ...

It was intended to be a sort of *I, Robot*, with good-looking men and women and clunky robots, like Will Smith's movie. What the designers and I did was to 'send it up', with camp costumes and over the top make-up to suggest a very different future world.

'The Green Death' was Katy Manning's last story. How was the atmosphere on set during those final days?

There was some tension on the last rehearsal days and, at the end of the recording, a special party atmosphere. She was a popular actress with both cast and crew.

Some people may not be aware that Stewart Bevan, who played Cliff Jones in the story, was Katy Manning's real life partner at the time. Did that create any problems or generate any unexpected plusses?
Not really. Lots of married and unmarried actors work together. They are both professionals.

During the location filming for 'Revenge of the Cybermen' there were broken legs, unexplained illnesses and actress Elisabeth Sladen almost drowned. Crew members attributed it to the 'curse' of the witch of Wooky Hole. Did you believe in the curse?
I think if you believe in fate, good or bad luck, then – even if you are an atheist – there are things out there that are very hard to explain!

Interviewees have said the following to me. As someone who has worked with all four actors, which statements would you agree/ disagree with and why?

William Hartnell could 'make life pretty miserable' if he didn't like you.
No, I always found Bill Hartnell to be a pleasure to work with.

Patrick Troughton 'was all fun and giggles'.
Patrick was a delightful man but had health problems, so sometimes was not all fun and giggles. But he was always professional and charming.

Jon Pertwee 'had to be the star of the show'.
Jon was the consummate professional. He wanted to look good – and there is nothing wrong with that. So if you worked with him to achieve that, he would be kind and generous to all the other actors.

Tom Baker 'took it all very seriously'.
Tom had his own ideas of how the Doctor should be portrayed and was so very serious about the series and the character. In the end, he believed his own publicity!

The Golden One:
Bernard Holley

**'...That naughty Katy Manning has talked
in slightly glowing terms about my anatomy ...'**

It's mid-January and I'm heading for a coffee shop on London's bustling
Charing Cross Road. Once the area was the preserve of antiquarian
bookshops but now the mighty bean has arrived in force. I've chosen a
little independent place, touted by the board outside as selling 'London's
best coffee'. The street is full of window-shoppers and, as I push and shove
my way down the street, I'm starting to wish my umbrella was a cattle
prod. Finally I fall into the shop and, after ordering enough caffeine to set
my teeth waggling, I take a breath and look around. There by the window
is the legendary Bernard Holley. I was wondering if I'd recognise him
with his clothes on.

It's 2013 and, as the Whoniverse braces itself for an anniversary of epic
proportions, Bernard Holley is about to have an anniversary of his own.
In August 1963, he was a 'frightened young actor' going up to Lincoln
Theatre for his first professional job. So his fiftieth anniversary is coming
up too – and he's wearing it unbelievably well.

'It's really nothing to do with me, though,' Bernard says. 'It's all because
I've got this dreadful portrait in the attic! No, seriously, it's the genes. My
mother died when she was 85 and still had skin like a babe.' It's easy to
believe. With the Devil's own charm, and a voice like melted chocolate,
if you ever need someone to play James Bond's dad, Bernard's your man.

Was acting in the genes too? 'No,' he replies. 'It might sound strange,
but as a kid I always felt like there was a camera following me. No idea
why. Nothing to do with having any bug about the theatre. I just had this
feeling that I wanted to be on film of some sort.'

After flunking his O Levels – 'I larked about too much.' – Bernard did
his re-sits then drifted into a job as a management trainee. He enjoyed
the work but still hankered after 'something else'. Eventually, he took
the plunge and joined the local drama society. 'They had a competition,'
Bernard recalls, 'and I did a bit of verse-reading and a little bit of Jimmy
Porter from *Look Back in Anger*. I came first in the verse reading, because
I was the only contestant. I came second in the acting category, because
there were only three of us!'

Becoming a Legend

Bernard is quick to laugh off his achievements, but those certificates gave him the confidence to go on to drama college – and he's barely been out of work since. 'You hear about actors being out of work for months, but until I was about 60, 65, I never stopped,' he says.

With him having had such a varied and prolific career, the chances are that you've seen at least some of Bernard's work. On stage he's played roles as diverse as Horatio in *Hamlet* and Norman in *The Norman Conquests*. On TV he spent three years in *Z Cars*, four in each of *The Bill* and *A Touch of Frost* and two in *The Gentle Touch*. He's done comedy too – including *The Dick Emery Show*, *Please Sir!* and *Birds of a Feather*. But it's *Doctor Who* that made Bernard Holley a legend.

'I got a tweet the other day saying "I'm doing my washing later tonight watching 'The Claws of Axos', featuring the legendary Bernard Holley!" I know one tweet does not a legend make, but an Irish *Doctor Who* blog recently called me "the legendary Mr Bernard Holley". That's twice,' he laughs, 'so it must be true!'

Bernard's first *Who* role came in 1967 when a drama school chum, Gareth Gwenlan, put him in touch with Morris Barry, who was casting parts in a new *Doctor Who* serial, 'The Tomb of the Cybermen'. By then Bernard and his wife, Jean, had a little boy, and although television wasn't exactly a cash cow, it was a lot better paid than theatre, which made it attractive – especially with mouths to feed.

'The Tomb of the Cybermen' was only Bernard's second television role and he admits that when he watches his performance now, all he sees is 'this young bloke hanging around the back not quite knowing what he was doing.' Fortunately the part of Peter Haydon, who is gunned down on a cyber testing range in the first episode, had some unexpected perks. First was the revelation that he would get paid for two episodes, even though he only played a corpse in the second. Then there was Debbie Watling: 'She was gorgeous, just very nice and good fun, and so was Frazer. Frazer was a little Scottish joker, but all of them were. I don't remember having any social intercourse with Pat Troughton. Not that he was aloof. He wasn't – just another one of the boys – but he was just the next generation up from me really.'

A Well-Oiled Machine

Back in the '60s, London may have been swinging, but Auntie Beeb was still a fusty old bird. As Bernard explained, even in the arts, there was a quaint formality about the proceedings. 'All the technicians wore ties and the actors often went into rehearsals wearing ties, certainly on the first day.'

A show like *Doctor Who* took a week to rehearse and record an episode, with plenty of time to hone a performance. 'Nowadays it's just rehearse and record. You get your script, and you hardly meet the other actors or the directors. You do it and you go, but back then with *Doctor Who*, there'd be some location filming a few days in advance and then you'd start rehearsals. On the Friday, there'd be a technical run, and then on the Saturday you'd be in at whatever time they wanted you for make-up. Then there would be a couple of dress rehearsals. You had breaks between 6.00 and 7.30, and then at 7.30 on the dot you'd go in and start recording. Quite often, especially on *Z Cars*, we'd do the whole thing in one take. There would be four cameras moving around. It was all very well planned and co-ordinated. Morris Barry was very good at that on "The Tomb of the Cybermen". In fact he was an old-fashioned bloke in many ways. He had a music stand and, when we were rehearsing, the script would be on it and movements would be marked out, from A1 to B2 and so on, in squares on the studio floor. Well not quite – I'm exaggerating to make a point – but a bit like that.'

It wasn't all hard graft though. 'You had lots of laughs, lots of fun,' Bernard recalls. 'The directors had a great deal of trouble getting us away from the snooker table or the poker school. It was pretty outrageous. You'd never get anything like it now!'

The BBC Club – a bar in Television Centre – was also a popular retreat, as well as a good place to pick up work. Bernard takes up the tale: 'Michael Ferguson, the director of "The Claws of Axos", came up to me in the famous BBC Club with a pile of scripts in his hand – six I think in the beginning, but four eventually – and he said to me they were looking for someone who was quite presentable-looking and would be all right in a leotard. He didn't entirely go into details. He didn't say that I was going to have gold paint sprayed everywhere! He just handed the scripts over. So I read them and thought "What can I do with this?"'

Despite my earlier comment, I should point out that I've never actually seen Mr Holley in the buff, but that leotard did leave little to the imagination. 'Well, I had an operation of course and had everything removed surgically and then they sewed it back later!' he chuckles. 'That naughty Katy Manning has talked in slightly glowing terms about my anatomy but really, I don't remember being uncomfortable. I didn't like walking out into the green room – I had dressing gowns standing by for that – but I was young and slimmer, and whenever you're doing something like this you're always looked after. The only real problem was getting rid of all the gold. It was only my hands, face and neck that had the gold make-up on, but it used to lurk around for ages. Flecks of it would just keep appearing. In fact at the time the show went out there was a picture of me in the *Radio Times* and an article talking about the making of the story. A man wrote to me saying that he frequently modelled naked wearing gold or silver paint, and he went into great detail about how I should scrub my body down to get into every crevice. Very strange!'

Tombs & Claws

The Axons are one of *Doctor Who*'s most innovative aliens and, combined with Michael Ferguson's characteristic low, tight angles, the story has a wonderfully claustrophobic feel. It's a cracking tale, but how did it compare to 'The Tomb of the Cybermen' in production?

'On "The Tomb of the Cybermen" – although I can only really relate this to my own scenes – if you put your hand out, things on set wobbled a bit. But by "The Claws of Axos", things were much better – and in colour of course. But what was really clever about that latter story was Michael Ferguson's input. It was all beautifully done. There were bits and pieces that looked like a pantomime … those monsters with creeping spaghetti arms … but they worked.'

When it came to Bernard's character, Michael Ferguson had a lot of input too. 'I seem to remember,' Bernard begins, 'that one of the writers said to me: "We envisage an emotionless figure, especially at the beginning. Not nice, not charming. Just somebody who's stating what's going on. You then get nasty later on, so it comes as more of a surprise." I based the character roughly on that. But the subtleties came out of rehearsals and thanks to Michael's input, because he was a very good director.'

A good cast was also an essential part of the mix and Bernard enjoyed getting to know the third Doctor, Jon Pertwee. 'We got on very well. He liked me, but he was a bit like all comics. I worked with Kenneth Williams, and if you didn't interrupt him, he was fine, but if you interrupted his latest joke, he'd be a pain in the arse. Jon wasn't quite as bad as that, but he would get upset about the smallest things. One time I was in the dressing room getting the gold tarted up and he said: "I've got a feeling things are going to go wrong today." Just like that. And they did, because he made them go wrong! But we got on very well together. To him I was a pro, I knew what I was doing.'

Bernard also enjoyed the chance to work with Roger Delgado, playing the Master, and, like everyone else I've spoken to, found him totally charming. 'Although,' Bernard adds, 'he did actually lose his cool during the filming of "The Claws of Axos". At one stage, he had to be handcuffed. Well, they cuffed him to a radiator and lost the key. He wasn't happy! I can still hear him, pulling at this metal bar cursing. We'd all gone for a break and he was stuck there. They told one of the prop boys to take him a sandwich and a cup of coffee and sit and talk to him. He was irate!' You can imagine the language!

Forty years later, Bernard Holley is still busy working, and using his famous voice to good effect. He was the storyteller for 13 years on the children's show *Jackanory*, and has also lent his voice to various television advertising campaigns. 'For 12 years I did Just for Men, until they decided they needed a younger image. Don't know why, because it's only old men that get grey hair! Over Christmas I did a voiceover for Barclaycard. All I had to do was say, "I'm a car, I'm a robot," about 40 times. Great fun.'

Bernard has also worked for Big Finish on their Bernice Summerfield audios and, more recently, gave a fabulous return performance as the voice of Axos in 'The Feast of Axos'.

I ask if he would like to return to the world of *Doctor Who* on TV. Like a shot he replies: 'Yes please!' Who would he play? 'Lord of the Universe. Got to aim for the top.' What about having a crack at the Doctor himself? 'Well, you know', he says, 'it was mooted before ...' With Peter Capaldi currently making waves as the Time Lord's newest regeneration, it seems that more mature Doctors may be back in vogue. So *Who* knows?

The Cyber Controller:
Michael Kilgarriff

It's impossible not to like Michael Kilgarriff. At six foot six-and-a-bit he's very much the gentle giant, with a deep, resonant voice, infectious laugh and easy manner. He's also something of a surprise. As well as acting, he's an accomplished musician, has a passion for old time music hall and a thriving sideline as an author, with numerous books and radio plays to his credit, including the best-selling dramatisation of J R R Tolkien's *The Hobbit*. Having appeared in four *Doctor Who* serials, with four different Doctors, he also has a wealth of tales to tell about the sometimes bloody experience of being the man behind the mask …

Did you always want to be an actor?
Oh Lord! Well, if anything, as a child, my great interest was classical music. I wanted to be a classical pianist and I was pretty good. I'm talking about the 1940s – I'm such an old man now. But back then lots of children learnt the piano. However I realised by the time I was 14 that I may have been Cock of the Walk in my school, but at music festivals, I was pretty average. I knew I was never going to be good enough to make a living at it, but then I started doing amateur dramatics. That was the spark.

Was it a tough business to get into?
Yes, really because I had no connections and no possibility of going to drama school. I was working for Barclays Bank. I was a junior clerk and it was a terrible job. But I'd come home on the bus, have a quick tea, then rush off to rehearsals. I remember once, I had six different shows on the go at the same time. I rushed around like a blue-arsed fly. Sometimes I'd have two productions in an evening. Everybody seemed happy with that though, because I was tall, good-looking, young and male. They were pleased to have me because it wasn't very fashionable for young men to do amateur dramatics then. Anyway, the more I did, the more I thought this was what I want to do professionally. So I started answering adverts in the *Stage* newspaper and I got into a schools version of *Alice in Wonderland*. They had a fit-up set you could put in a classroom and we all travelled round in a van. Oddly, though, I got that job because I could play the piano, so you never know! Nothing's ever wasted in life.

What was your big break?

I suppose there was one role that was important to me, although I didn't realise it at the time. By chance I'd bumped into a friend whose agent was looking for a chap like me. A lot of the very tall people in the business tend to be ex-wrestlers and bouncers – not very articulate! This meant that when they wanted tall people who could speak, I was in with a chance! So I went to see this agent, and to my surprise she didn't ask me to audition, she just accepted me. Through her, I went on to play the ogre in a pantomime at the London Palladium. That opened a lot of doors for me. It also meant that, for the next 30 years, no matter how bad the year might have been for me as an actor, I could always look forward to a really well-paid panto; because the money was sensational – at the Palladium, more than twice what I'd ever got in rep or anything else.

You first TV roles were in the early 1950s. TV was pretty primitive in those days …?

It was pretty hairy too, because it was live. There was no recording and it was alarming to know that the camera was going to come over to you and the entire nation would be watching. I do remember the producer of one show was very grateful to me. There was the sound effect of a distant cannon, which my character was supposed to hear and react to. In rep, things are constantly going wrong, and you get used to busking round them. So, even in rehearsals, I knew I had to be ready in case the sound effect didn't come. Sure enough, on the live transmission – no bang. So I ad-libbed a line or two, and then came the effect, so there was no nasty pause. After it had finished, the producer literally had tears in his eyes. He was practically on his knees, crying, 'You've saved my show!' Ha ha!

How did you come to be offered the role of the Cyber Controller in 'The Tomb of the Cybermen'?

I'd done a few tellies by then and heard they wanted tall people who were reasonably articulate. The daft thing about the dear old BBC was that you'd start off on a pretty low fee and it would get notched up, the more you did for them. But every now and then you'd get something and they'd say, 'It's not a very big part, we'll give you a special low.' That meant you'd get a low fee just for the one job, then go back up the scale. Now children's television was always at a lower rate than adult drama, but for 'The Tomb of the Cybermen', they tried to knock me down to a special low of the children's rate, because I didn't have to say the lines. There wasn't the technology then to have microphones underneath the costumes, so my lines were said by a very, very fine voice actor called Peter Hawkins, who used to stand behind the camera with the microphone. My argument was that I might not have to say the lines, but I still had to learn them, because I had to open the mouth when the cue came. Luckily they accepted that.

What was the costume like to wear?
Well, the mouth was like a letterbox on a spring hinge. You opened it when the line came out and shut it after. It was a rather eerie effect. You couldn't see much, but the movements still had to be very precise to get the camera line and eye line right. As the Cyber Controller, I had a rather svelte costume and a head that pulsated. That was a damned nuisance because the batteries kept going so they had to keep stopping. They had to unscrew the helmet, change the batteries and screw it back on. It was a bit claustrophobic too, because you couldn't take it off easily. There had to be somebody standing by with a screwdriver.

That sounds very unpleasant!
I was usually in a great deal of discomfort, because there were always nuts and bolts that scraped and cut into you when you moved. But the worst bit is that people do forget that there's a human being inside the costume, because they can't see your face. I particularly remember that this Cyber Controller got his comeuppance when the Doctor wired up a door to electrocute him. This meant that I had to crash to the floor. I was meant to be dead, so there was no suggestion of putting out my hands to catch my weight. I just crashed down and, as I did that, all the studio lights went out. It was 4.15 – the electricians' tea break! Everything stopped for that. Everybody left, but I was still on the floor, all cut and bloody. So I started shouting and hollering for them to get me up. I couldn't move on my own.

Presumably going to the loo presented some 'technical' problems?
Oh yes! You had to do all that before the session started, because they wouldn't be pleased if you kept the studio waiting.

What was the first scene you filmed?
The first scene I did was pre-filming of the Cybermen coming out of the honeycomb. Strangely enough, at the time, the BBC leased Ealing film studios, and I was living in South Ealing, so it was one of the very few occasions I've been able to walk to work.

What was the atmosphere on set like?

It all seemed quite happy. Troughton was fine. In fact, it was not long after that I wrote a 90-minute radio play and he was the lead, so we met again. But he was always my favourite Doctor, because he was a very good stage actor – good voice. What I liked about him was that he was always slightly sinister. He didn't try too hard to be the loveable eccentric, because Hartnell had done that. Poor, dear William Hartnell. I actually saw him on stage and it was very sad. I forget which winter it was, but I was engaged in Colchester to play the piano for a Christmas show. The cinema in the town had theatre facilities and they had a full-scale panto starring Hartnell. I thought it would be interesting to see, so I went along. Well, the panto started as usual with a song and a dance. Then the comics came on and did a bit, and then diddly dum … diddly dum … lights go down, crash, lights go up and there's the TARDIS. The door opens and out pops the Doctor – applause. He might as well have gone home then, because the poor old bugger couldn't do anything. He made no impression at all. They were really just using his name. I suppose the BBC must have agreed to it, but it was really sad.

In 'Frontier in Space' you played an Ogron. What was that like?

Well I was the second Ogron. The first Ogron was Stephen Thorne, who was an old chum. We'd worked together years before, so we had a lot of laughs. But I never really understood the Ogrons. The thing was that we looked like gorillas and we couldn't speak very well, but we were able to fly spaceships. So we can't have been that thick! There were quite a lot of Ogrons in that story but only Stephen and I spoke. The others tended to be these pug-uglies – wrestlers and such. I do remember that we had a technical rehearsal and there were problems, so we just had to stand around. At the back of the set, there was a monitor to give us something to look at. There was a band show on, and one of the other Ogrons said, 'I've seen this in the Scrubs.' This was a bit unnerving for us sensitive actor types! Although I'm a big man myself, I'm not a scrapper. So Stephen and I rather withdrew our skirts! The other thing I remember was in rehearsals, we were in these cages and somebody came along to feed us like animals in the zoo. So, I'm in the cage and I put my plate through the bars and they put food on it. But then of course I couldn't get it back through the bars, so I turned the plate sideways and pulled it in … Well, it got a big laugh, but Pertwee wouldn't have it. Only Pertwee did jokes!

How did you find Jon Pertwee?

He was a very, very unpleasant man on that shoot. It sounds an odd thing to say, but he made me ashamed to be an actor. I was embarrassed for my profession because of the way he behaved. He made such an exhibition of himself. He was so demanding and temperamental. Little Katy Manning had obviously worked with him for quite a while and she knew how to handle him – get him a chair, a glass of water and smooth his ruffled feathers. He needed someone to make a fuss of him all the time. It was good of her to do it, because presumably he would have been a lot worse had she not. But she'd got her own job to do, her own part, her own worries. Why should she be lumbered with that? I really thought he behaved disgracefully, so I've never been much of a fan.

What about Roger Delgado?
I worked with him a lot on radio. In fact, we did this extraordinary thing together. It was a musical piece, a Prom concert at the Albert Hall [Prom 38, 29 August 1972], called *Down by the Greenwood Side*. Roger played Dr Blood, and I was Father Christmas. But Roger Delgado was just about the sweetest-natured man I've ever met. He was an absolute love. I was desperately sorry when he was killed. But unfortunately 'Frontier in Space' wasn't the happiest of experiences for me.

How come you didn't play the Cyber Controller in 'The Five Doctors'?
I was asked, but I wasn't available. I'd have liked to have done that, but I did get to reprise the role with Colin Baker [in 'Attack of the Cybermen'].

How did 'Attack of the Cybermen' compare to 'The Tomb of the Cybermen'?
It was a lot easier. I could get the head and hands of the costume on and off myself and I got to do my own lines. But the odd thing was that they'd forgotten about the earlier show, because when I mentioned it at rehearsals, there was an embarrassed silence. The designer and wardrobe people were all there and I said it was a shame they'd lost the mouth, it was so scary. But they didn't know what I was talking about. There was a bit of a fuss about one scene too. It's the one where I signal one of my Cybermen to squeeze this guy's hands because we want information from him. There was actually a close up of the blood dripping from his hands. Pretty nasty stuff. I couldn't believe this was actually going to be in the show; there were a lot of complaints.

What was it like working with Colin Baker?
He was fine, but I'm not sure he brought a lot to the role. The scripts

were so bad he didn't have a lot to work with. I had a word that became something of catchphrase throughout the recording. There I was, trying to take over the world, and my cohorts were coming to tell me it was all going wrong and I kept saying 'Excellent!' So we were all saying that to each other! 'Excellent!' Ha ha.

You added another Doctor to your collection when you played the K1 Robot with Tom Baker in 'Robot'. That looks like a difficult costume to work in.

It was a monstrous prop, and very difficult to work in, because I couldn't see. My head was in the chest and the body was so big that I couldn't see my own feet. They were these big, segmented feet, so whenever there was a slight incline I would fall over. Again, I was hacking myself to bits. There was blood everywhere. They kept covering the bolts up, but every time I fell, sure enough, I'd find another. And it was very cold. I remember we had a night shoot, at two or three in the morning, and when they took my head off to give me a cup of coffee I was shivering so much I couldn't hold the cup. I was so cold, it just went everywhere. And it's so exhausting in those costumes. You have a dresser with you, and their job is to make sure that you're available and ready when the director wants you. If you're not, they get it in the neck. So obviously they get you in the costume much sooner than is necessary, so you're in it for hours and hours.

Any memories of the recording you'd like to share?

I can remember this night shoot, having to smash in this door, and they had to keep retaking because the dogs were running the wrong way. I'm freezing inside this thing, cold, tired and cut to ribbons, and these bloody dogs wouldn't do what they were supposed to. Anyway, I was supposed to stride up to this door and smash it in. They'd cut a panel out and replaced it with something light, like balsa, and scored it through so that if you blew on it, it would go. Action – it didn't break. It just bent my pincers! Took me three goes to break it in! But that night, after the shoot, I had these nightmares about being trapped in a midget submarine, and the next morning I woke up, got out of bed and my legs collapsed under me. It was all just too much! My wife was very concerned and wanted to call a doctor, but by lunchtime I was okay, although I still had all the studio work to do. I had to get in touch with them saying I couldn't stand in the thing; it was too much. So they built a very light mock up, and I wore that for the lighting rehearsals, which was a great relief.

Elisabeth Sladen was great in that story. Did you get a chance to get to know her off set?

We did the location recording for 'Robot' at Evesham, which was the BBC's engineering facility, and I drove home with Lis Sladen because she lived close to me. Poor Lis, that was tragic; I couldn't believe it when I'd heard she'd died. She was such a nice girl and she was enchanting with the Robot. The scenes between them are so touching. But I think the director made a big mistake on that story. At the end, Tom is so exultant, going round in that open-top car, being very triumphant about killing this poor thing. I thought it should have been a more sober moment, because the Robot was a very sad creature. The director should have calmed Tom down, because he didn't know the whole set up, as they'd recorded it out of sequence.

What do you think about new *Who*?

Well, I've seen odd bits and pieces and greatly admire the effects. There's one where thousands of Daleks fly out of the spacecraft, and that looks amazing. Of course they spend so much money now. When I look at the things – the Cybermats – we had running round in 'The Tomb of the Cybermen', they were like wind-up rats. They were supposed to be dangerous, but they were just things someone had knocked up in a garage. When you compare our stories with today's effects, they look so primitive! But really I think it still works. It's all just theatre after all.

The Thal: Jane How

Date: 21st Century. Place: Spiridon. The TARDIS has made an emergency landing, and with the Doctor gravely ill, Jo Grant finds herself alone on an alien planet – where even the plant life is deadly. Throw invisible monsters and the Doctor's oldest enemy into the mix, and 'Planet of the Daleks' is classic *Who* at its irrepressible best. The impossibly glamorous Jane How was there, facing off against ten thousand Daleks …

Were you a *Doctor Who* fan before you appeared in the show?
No, because in those days it was really was a children's show and I was 21!

'Planet of the Daleks' was your first role on TV. Were you nervous?
It wasn't quite my first role. I had done a couple of things before – a show about an agony aunt called *Kate* and a children's series, *A Little Princess*. But it was early on and, in those days, the filming was done before all the studio work. So to appear at a gravel pit in Kent and have to react to a Dalek being disembowelled was quite nerve-wracking, as I hadn't met any of my fellow actors at that point!

Back in the '70s there weren't many strong female role models on TV, so it was great to have Rebec in the show. However, she does spend a lot of the serial being told what to do by the guys. Did that bother you at the time?
Not really. We were having too much fun!

Much of the filming took place at Beechfields Quarry. It seems like an uncomfortable place to work – was it?
Actually we were only there for a couple of days, so it wasn't that bad.

There are some lovely moments between you and Bernard Horsfall, who played your lover, Taron. What was he like to work with?
Bernard was divine. More like a father figure than a lover, but I adored and admired him. He was a seriously good and respected actor. No-one really remained a close friend but we all got on brilliantly and I still see Tim Preece, who played Codal, from time to time.

How did you find Jon Pertwee?
Jon was a very conscientious Doctor Who – very serious about the job –

but a great team leader and terrific fun to work with.

Who/what's worse to act with, children, animals or Daleks?
I don't think I've ever worked with animals, but I did do a series called *The Foundation* with Patsy Kensit in 1977 and she was so lovely and unspoilt. As for Daleks, they rock!

Can you share one memory of your time spent making 'Planet of the Daleks'?
Filming the ice tunnel sequences at Ealing Studios was hilarious as there was a heat-wave and we had no air con. We had to act being frozen when we were nearly expiring with the heat.

There's an urban legend, which is often told about 'Planet of the Daleks'. Apparently, during the filming, the Dalek operators were told they had to wear make-up, even though no-one could see them. In protest they appeared on set with their Daleks dressed in drag. Is that true?
Don't think so. I'm sure I would have remembered that!

You looked incredibly glamorous. Just how did you get your hair like that?
A wig!

What one thing about your time making 'Planet of the Daleks' have you never told anyone before?
Going to the loo was a nightmare as it took hours to get out of my onesie! I always thought I looked like Miss Michelin in that costume.

The Bristol Boy: Bob Baker

'... Of course, they weren't interested in the army play at all. They'd only been grooming us to see if we were right to do *Doctor Who*.'

Renegade Time Lords, down-at-heel detectives, feuding sorcerers, were-rabbits and robot dogs. During his 40-plus years in the business, Bob Baker has brought all this – and much more – to our TV screens.

I met Bob at London's Earl's Court Exhibition Centre, where Britain's biggest and brightest brand names come to strut their corporate stuff. Since Bob and his writing partner Dave Martin created K-9 back in 1977, the Time Lord's best friend has proved to be one of TV's most enduring characters and a regular guest in both *Doctor Who* and *The Sarah Jane Adventures*. The tin terrier finally got his own show in 2010, called simply *K9*. However, it's been a long road. 'My friend Paul Tams came to see me just after I'd finished the Wallace and Gromit film *Curse of the Were-Rabbit* and asked, "Why don't we revive K-9?"' That was in 2005. The good Doctor had just returned to TV after a 16-year hiatus and interest in the project was intense. 'At one time,' Bob says, 'we had interest from Disney Buena Vista, but they went down from a half hour show to quarter of an hour, to three-minute interstitials. I said, "What the hell are interstitials?" It was clear that the show just wouldn't work like that.'

Bob eventually found the backing the show needed in Australia, where the series was produced. It's now been picked up by the Syfy Channel, winning the Doctor's pet pooch a new audience in America.

Fans will know that Bob has had a long association with *Doctor Who*, having written nine stories for the show during the '70s – an era many consider to be its Golden Age. So what may be surprising is that, although the new *K9* series brought John Leeson back to voice the eponymous robot, the BBC wouldn't allow Bob to directly reference the wider Whoniverse. 'If you like,' Bob explains, 'just as the Doctor regenerates, the dog has regenerated. He's much more sophisticated now, which is lovely for John, because in the past he was monosyllabic. Now it's his show and he gets to make some nice crisp remarks.'

Creative Fire

Hit TV shows, overseas productions and promotional tours are all a far cry from Bob's early days as a stonemason in Bristol. 'I did a five-year apprenticeship with the Bristol Co-op, where I learnt to be a letter-cutter on gravestones,' he says with a wry smile, 'so I was always a writer, although it was a bit more difficult back then!'

From there, Bob went to art school, where he got the film bug. 'I did some film, some animation and bits and pieces and … I thought, "Well this is it, this is what I really want to do."' Later he met up with Dave Martin, who was also interested in writing. A successful ten-year partnership followed although, initially, work was extremely thin on the ground. 'We accumulated more and more scripts and sent them off and got more and more angry with rejection slips,' recalls Bob. 'Eventually the local TV station in Bristol, HTV, announced that they were going to do some half-hour plays by local writers, so we popped in a couple of scripts and one of them was made … It was then that we thought, "Now we're real, now we're professionals." So we pressed on.'

It was during a year and a half of 'just writing stuff, sending it off and getting rejection slips,' that Bob and Dave sent off a play addressed simply to 'the BBC, London, because we were so fed up with getting nowhere.' A year and a half later they received a telephone call about the play, called *A Man's Life*, which was based on the army experiences of mutual friend and celebrity chef Keith Floyd. The BBC loved the humour but were worried about the expense, so invited the duo to London for a meeting. 'So we went up and they got us thoroughly drunk on gin and tonics in the BBC Club. I thought they wanted to do the army film, so I was reassuring them about the cost, saying "You don't have to use tanks, you could use armoured cars," and so on. Then they suddenly said, "Do you know what we do? We do *Doctor Who*," and I said "Great … Anyway, about these tanks." And then they asked if we would like to do a *Doctor Who*, and Dave and I looked at each other and said, "Yeah, all right. Now about these tanks …" Of course, they weren't interested in the army play at all. They'd only been grooming us to see if we were right to do *Doctor Who*.'

The Bristol Boys, as the pair were affectionately dubbed by the *Doctor Who* crew, worked on the show for the next ten years, contributing stories such as 'The Claws of Axos', 'The Sontaran Experiment' and 'The Hand of Fear'. This was a period of intense activity for Bob and Dave, with work on *Who* representing just a small part of their creative output.

Daringly Different

Adults of a certain age will remember with a palpable thrill children's dramas such as *Sky, Arthur and the Britons* and *King of the Castle*, and Bob Baker and Dave Martin wrote them all. These productions were never pedestrian or predictable. *Sky*, for instance, told the story of an extraterrestrial traveller who accidentally arrives on Earth during the late 20th Century. Sky's presence quickly threatens to upset the delicate balance of nature, which becomes manifest in the form of the sinister, black-clad Goodchild. In comparison, *King of the Castle* is pure Kafka for kids.

In an era when most British children's television was about nice kids, having nice adventures in nice schools, *King of the Castle* broke the mould. The series focuses on Roland, who lives in a dilapidated council flat with his dad and step-mum. While trying to escape from local bullies, he tumbles into a fantastical, dreamlike world. In an echo of Joseph Jacob's Arthurian tale *Childe Rowland*, before he can return home, our modern-day Roland has to triumph over the dark forces opposing him.

In *Doctor Who* too, the duo's work was always daringly different. 'The Mutants' deals with racism and the abuse of power. In 'The Sontaran Experiment', we see the Doctor's companions subjected to a series of brutal experiments by the sadistic Field Major Styre. Pretty strong stuff for a Saturday afternoon family show!

Such creativity made Bob and Dave one of Britain's most prolific and successful writing partnerships, so when Dave decided that he wanted to focus on novel writing, it could have spelt disaster for the duo. Fortunately, Dave carved himself out a career as a crime writer, while Bob landed a job with the BBC as script editor and writer on a new, prime-time detective show, *Shoestring*. *Bergerac*, *Smuggler* and children's TV fantasy *Into the Labyrinth* followed. Even today these shows remain incredibly popular and, thanks to the advent of cable and satellite TV and DVD, are now enjoyed by audiences all over the world. More accolades were still to come.

It was after Bob got back from Czechoslovakia, where he was working on the science fiction film *Nexus*, that he received the call that introduced him to the wonderful world of Wallace and Gromit. 'I didn't know who Wallace and Gromit were,' Bob admits, 'so Aardman sent me a few videotapes and I thought "Interesting!" … So they put [animator and director] Nick Park and me together to see if we'd get on, and we did.' *The Wrong Trousers* was the result of the collaboration; which, Bob says modestly, 'was fairly successful.' A year later, Aardman asked Bob if he'd like to 'do another one … and then another one.'

To date, the Aardman-Park-Baker partnership has notched up awards from over 25 countries, including four BAFTAs and three Oscars. The secret to their success? 'Nick and I have the same sense of humour – very 1950s *Beano* comics,' Bob explains. Indeed, work on a new animation often begins with Nick and Bob sitting down to watch an old film. British comedies are a favourite. 'Will Hay, Norman Wisdom … that sort of thing … work well,' says Bob, 'because really Wallace and Gromit are frozen somewhere in the mid- to late-'50s. It's a period that has a kind of golden glow for me, as it was the time I was at the Co-op as a stonemason. It was a time I really enjoyed, when I met some incredible people, and I've used my experiences from that period of my life a lot in my writing.'

So what's next for Bob Baker? Does he ever plan to retire? 'No,' he says decisively. 'I can't sit around thinking maybe I'll go fishing. The only other thing I do is paint. I have a shed in the garden that has a typewriter on one side and an easel on the other side. So I often move from one to the other, but I can't stop. Writing is something I'm driven to do.' Which is good news for sci-fi and K-9 fans everywhere!

The Archer: Jeremy Bulloch

If there was ever a guy who's prepared to go that extra mile for the fans, it's Jeremy Bulloch. If you don't believe me, next time he's at a convention, hunt him out. Other celebs will be there, behind their tables and screens, with their minders in tow. Most are charming enough, although there'll always be the occasional 'star' who won't even look you in the eye. Jeremy? Jeremy's on the other side of the table with us ordinary Joes, posing for photos and shooting the breeze. Most of the time he's happy to chat about the role that made him an international star – Boba Fett in the *Star Wars* saga. But there's a lot more to the lad from Leicestershire than a jet pack and a suit of grey armour, including two appearances in two classic *Doctor Who* serials …

You seem to be really comfortable with the fans …?
I am! But what's strange is that when I was about 20, I was working in a twice-a-week soap opera called *The Newcomers* produced, oddly enough, by Verity Lambert; I played quite a well-known character, Paul Cooper, and one week a lady stopped me in the street and hit me over the head with an umbrella, saying, 'How dare you treat your wife like that!' I used to get quite embarrassed at being recognised, and I didn't think I could cope with it at all to begin with.

How long have you been in the business?
I went to drama school at 12. I'd got to that age where I was starting to think about what I was going to do after school and I'd failed every exam I'd taken. So things didn't look very good. Eventually I went to the Corona Stage Academy, and a brother and two sisters followed, although within six months they'd all decided acting wasn't for them.

What would you say was your big break?
It had to be the Cliff Richard film *Summer Holiday*. I'd been in a kid's TV show around 1960 called *The Young Jacobites*. During filming I became sort of best mates with Richard O'Sullivan. He'd been in the first Cliff Richard film but at the time of *Summer Holiday* was doing *Cleopatra* out in Rome. They were shooting, already way over budget, and looking for someone to replace Richard. Luckily I got the part.

You've appeared in *Doctor Who*, *Star Wars*, *Robin of Sherwood* … so many iconic films and TV shows. Were you ever aware that something

was going to 'be big' and, if so, how did that affect your performance?
Not really. You always have to keep a certain amount of discipline about
your work. Enjoy yourself, but be disciplined and don't worry about what
it means or how you'll come out of it.

**You made your first appearance in *Doctor Who* in 1965, as Tor in a
story called 'The Space Museum'. What do you remember about that?**
It was all a bit basic. The costume I wore was very simple: I think black
shoes, black trousers and a black top. They'd shaved off my eyebrows –
my real ones – and they stuck fake eyebrows on higher up my forehead.
But when it got hot in the studio, they started to slip down. So you'd just
pick them up and stick them back on and hope no-one noticed at home!
And really they didn't, because if the story's good, they're not going to be
looking at eyebrows. They're going to be looking at the performance and
enjoying the adventure. I also remember being warned: 'Whatever you do
Jeremy, don't lean too much to the right or too much to the left, because
part of the wall will wobble!'

How did you find William Hartnell?
A bit crotchety; a bit grumpy. I remember he asked me how long I'd been
in the business. I said around nine years, and he said, 'Well I've been in
it a long time, son, and you'll have to listen and learn from people. Don't
think you know it all, and whatever you do, when you jump on me in this
scene we're doing this afternoon, just remember that it's pretend! Don't
think you can just knock me about!' And I said, 'Oh no! Of course not,
Mr Hartnell, sir!' He was getting older and he'd had a terrific career, was a
very good actor, but I did think, 'Oh crikey, if he goes on like this all the
time I don't know what I'm going to do.' But he didn't. He laid off, and
right at the end of the serial he came up and said, 'Well done, son, you
listened, you learned. Well done!' So it was a sort of little nudge to say 'I
didn't want to appear to be too nice, but you've passed my test.'

**Nine years separate your first *Doctor Who* appearance and playing Hal
the Archer in 'The Time Warrior'. How did the two shows compare –
and which did you prefer?**
I have to say, I preferred 'The Time Warrior', because it was in colour, the
costumes were good, I got to fire a bow and arrow, and we were filming
outside. Not just in the studio but outside, in a castle. So it was very
exciting and up-tempo.

'The Time Warrior' was Elisabeth Sladen's first story as Sarah Jane Smith. How did you get on?
Oh! Yes, poor Lis Sladen; that was just very upsetting – her death. Terrible. It was so quick and she was such great fun. Funnily enough there was talk, there was the possibility, of me staying on with her as the male companion after 'The Time Warrior'. The producer, Barry Letts, asked what I was doing after we'd finished and asked me to keep myself free. I should have asked if there really was any chance. Was it going to happen? It would have been terrific, but I wasn't bold enough!

Can you actually use a bow and arrow?
Well, it's funny, the armourer was teaching me how to fire a bow and arrow, and he kept complaining. I hit the bull the first time, but despite that he said, 'No, no. You haven't got it right!' He fired, and the arrow and hit the outer ring, and I said, 'Oh I see!' So I tried it again, pulled back and hit the bull again. I just knew it was going to happen too – but I really upset the armourer!

Have you got any specific memories of your time on *Doctor Who* that you'd like to share?
I have to own up that there was an awful lot of giggling going on. Jon Pertwee was freakingly giggly. He said, 'I really don't think I can keep a straight face when you're going to be coming out dressed like that with that bow and arrow.' He reminded me of Q in the Bond films. Q would say, 'Now pay attention Bond,' and Roger Moore would collapse with laughter. Jon Pertwee was the same. He'd say his technical jargon and then pull a funny face or say something in a silly voice.

Would you have liked to have made it a hat trick and appeared a third time?
I would! In fact I suggested that, as it was nine years between the two, maybe in another nine years I could come back as another character. They thought it was a marvellous idea and said I must give them a ring about it but, of course, you don't.

What sort of character would you have liked to have been?
I think they could have done this three-headed creature. One head would be my character from 'The Space Museum', another one would be Hal and then the new person.

You have almost done three *Doctor Who*s, as you did play Chairman Skellon in the fan-produced stage play *The Trial of Davros*. How did that come about?

Yes. That was an extraordinary thing. I was asked to do it for charity and it was great fun. Bits were filmed to be dropped into the stage play, and mine were done early one weekend up in North London. When we were filming, someone was talking, and for the first time in my life, I turned round and said, 'Please can we have some quiet.' And it was the little son of the person who had brought us along. I felt terrible! It was this charity event and I was acting like the prima donna. But it was for a good cause and it was great to play another part.

You do lots of *Star Wars* conventions. Is it frustrating to be constantly thought of as Boba Fett?

Well, you know, I go to these *Star Wars* events and we do the Disney/*Star Wars* weekends, which are huge fun. But there's a bit where you get to show clips from your career on the big screen – and I show things that I did when I was 12 and then when I was 50-odd. It's lovely to be able to do that, because for the first time over the weekend I don't feel like I'm a con artist! If you just stand there as Boba Fett, with a funny helmet on, people think it's all you've done. But as an actor, there's that buzz of adrenaline that makes you want to say: 'But I've done more!'

Is it true that Boba Fett might be having a regeneration of his own?

I do go into the sarlacc pit in *Episode VI*, but you don't see me die. In fact George Lucas did say that I do get out of the pit …

You've been in Bond too – another enormous franchise …

Yes! Bond was enormous fun. I've done three of those, [*The Spy Who Loved Me, For Your Eyes Only* and *Octopussy*,] but I had so little to do in them that, again, it's become a funny thing. A bit like Boba Fett, in that people think that's all I've done.

Do you have a favourite Doctor?

I have many favourites. Jon Pertwee, because I worked with him. Tom Baker I liked; I thought he was terrific. Patrick Troughton too. I think those would be my three. I know the others and they're all excellent, but I always felt that the Doctor needs to be older. However when I see the guys playing the Doctor now, they are so very good. It's a very difficult role to take over, because people are always waiting for them to fall on their backsides.

What are you doing now?
I've actually been travelling the world with *Star Wars*. But you have to make up your mind – stay put and look for work, or go to Disney World and sit on a parade, which I've done and it's been amazing. Like being royalty! I'm not retired, but there may come a day when I wake up and I can't be bothered.

You haven't been to many *Doctor Who* conventions. Why's that?
Well, my dad always said, 'Wait to be asked,' and I have. But I'm getting on now, so perhaps it's time to stop waiting.

The Savage: Louise Jameson

**'I absolutely adore Tom Baker now – and that's a sentence
I never thought I'd say back in the day!'**

Yesterday, she was wearing nothing but a leather bikini and a knowing smile. Today, she's shuffling around on stage in a hangover haze, with last night's make up smeared across her face. Once you recover from the time-dilation effect of television, though, the real surprise is not that the woman who once played Leela is no longer 26 years old. It's that she's doing her very best to appear at her very worst.

Although she's now a familiar face on television, Louise began her career on stage, having caught the acting bug at an early age from her mother. 'Had Mum been born in a different era,' Louise says, 'I've no doubt she would have been a wonderful professional actress. She was Queen of the Am Drams, and I saw her play some fantastic roles. She was always hungry to hear about all I was learning at RADA, and we would sit until the sun came up talking about acting and lessons, scripts and directors. It's only now, in later life, I can really appreciate what a tremendous influence she was and how amazingly supportive of my choices.'

After three years at RADA and two with the Royal Shakespeare Company, Louise won one of the most coveted jobs on TV, as assistant to Tom Baker's Doctor. It was a role that put her 'firmly on the map' and, she's pleased to say, is still earning her money to this day. But did she know anything about the show when she auditioned? Was she a fan? 'Yes. My whole family loved the show. It was the only time we were allowed to take food into the living room. A real family affair, munching our tea in front of William Hartnell, never dreaming I would be part of it.'

Eliza & Henry

Being 'part of it' back in 1977 meant stepping into the shoes of Elisabeth Sladen, whose character, Sarah Jane Smith, had been one of the Doctor's longest-serving companions. Producer Philip Hinchcliffe had reportedly wanted a new companion who would be the Eliza Doolittle to the Doctor's Henry Higgins. It was in response to this that Chris Boucher came up with a character called Leela for a story entitled 'The Mentor Conspiracy'. That story was never made, but the character was resurrected for 'The Face of Evil' as a leather-clad warrior of the Sevateem. Boucher had provided the rough sketch, but now it was up to Louise to make that outline live and breathe.

'I was inspired by two sources,' Louise says. 'The little girl who lived upstairs, called Sally, who was three at the time, and my then dog Bosie. Both of them had huge intelligence but, of course, no education, and my adorable dog was part Basenji (the African dogs with the huge ears) and always knew when someone was arriving at the house, long before I did. A sixth sense, or just amazing hearing? Who knows?'

The result was a character who was intelligent, intuitive and feisty – with a natural naiveté that children could easily identify with. And, of course, dads reportedly loved that outfit! Was it easy to keep 'everything' where it should have been? 'It never crossed my mind that the costume was gratuitous,' laughs Louise, 'but I guess they made her feisty and then took her clothes off as a sort of compromise. To be honest, I had tiny breasts then, so there wasn't much to keep in place, so that wasn't a problem. Taking a pee was, though, and the cossie had to be … adjusted slightly … in order to make that a much quicker process!'

Despite her fearless on-screen persona, Louise found her first day of filming nerve-wracking. 'I was shy, nervous and under-rehearsed,' she recalls, 'but the director, the wonderful Pennant Roberts, was the perfect person to have by my side. Very supportive, very confidence-building, very astute with his direction.'

It didn't help that Tom Baker was reluctant to see his Doctor take on a new companion and was, initially, very cold towards her on set. 'I must emphasise,' Louise states, 'that I absolutely adore Tom Baker now – and that's a sentence I never thought I'd say back in the day! Yes, he was cold. He didn't want Leela in the programme, and that lapped over into not wanting me. But now we work together all the time. He has been hugely and publicly apologetic, and there the line is drawn.'

In fact, despite Tom's initial misgivings, the nine stories he and Louise shared are now ranked amongst the show's all-time classics. 'The Talons of Weng-Chiang' is a particular favourite. It's clear that the team had great fun with the Holmesian pastiche, and the scenes between Leela and the surgeon character Litefoot have a wonderful spontaneity. 'That is the brilliance of Robert Holmes' writing,' Louise says. 'It feels like an ad-lib, but the perfection is in his rhythms, his character observation, his ability to tell a cracking good yarn. Of course things developed in rehearsal – that good old-fashioned process that modern companies don't seem to appreciate – and we may have changed a line or two, or developed a theme, but by the time the cameras got to see our work, there was no ad-libbing.'

Stark Sincerity

Louise finally left *Who* in 1978 but stuck with sci-fi, playing physicist Dr Anne Reynolds in BBC Scotland's quirky drama *The Ωmega Factor*. However, it was in *Tenko* that she finally shook off the afterglow of that leather bikini. *Tenko* traced the lives of a group of disparate women, from their largely comfortable pre-War existence in Singapore to their internment in a Japanese POW camp. The series was meticulously researched and pulled no punches when it came to its portrayal of the raw horror of life and death endured by these vulnerable non-combatants. Louise played tarty cockney Blanche Simmons with a stark sincerity that won her both industry accolades and fans. 'Tenko was a series written by women for women, about women who had actually existed. The writers, Jill Hyem and Ann Valery, did an enormous amount of research on the subject, and Blanche was based in fact. In many ways, she was everything I would like to be. Feisty, honest, selfish. What you see is what you get. No hidden areas.'

Thirty years on and, on stage, Louise's ability to inhabit a character and connect with her audience is even more apparent. So much so that when her character starts talking about hot flushes, bingo wings and stress incontinence, you can see the audience squirm with embarrassed empathy. Louise couldn't appear more naked if she was actually nude. The play, called *Pulling Faces*, is about society's obsession with youth and physical perfection. In it, Louise plays television presenter Jo Taylor, about to hit 55 and under pressure to go under the knife. Louise never leaves the stage for a moment, and there are no clever prosthetics or make-up, but by the end of the play her character is completely transformed. Although not, perhaps, in the way that the audiences might expect.

Living in a world where it's increasingly hard to grow old gracefully means that many in the audience will know just how Jo Taylor feels. But how much of the character is based on Louise's own experiences? 'Really, there's too much of me in this!' she admits. 'On the other hand, vulnerability on stage is very powerful, so I hope that the sincerity of the performance shows.' Would she ever consider going under the knife herself? 'During my menopause,' she admitted, 'I lost a lot of self-esteem, and did go for a consultation to see about a facelift. I actually booked a date for the operation, then got a job, cancelled the date, got through the menopause, and never rebooked that date.'

Today she believes that decision was a 'blessed release', and it certainly hasn't affected the job offers. In fact, not only are theatre and TV roles rolling in, but she's back in the land of *Who*, albeit this time for a series of Big Finish audio adventures with Tom Baker. So how easy was it to get back into character as Leela – to inhabit that skin again? 'Easy as easy could be. The choice to say "could not" and "would not" instead of "couldn't" and "wouldn't" gave Leela's speech patterns a very distinct rhythm – and there I was, back in the skins, knife at the ready, prepared to die to save the planet!'

So has she been following new *Who*? 'Yes, and I *love* it. I do think the assistant gets a much fairer crack of the whip now, don't you? I have loved all the Doctors, for different reasons, but I think Matt has particularly grasped the "old soul in a young body" thing.' Would she be willing to come back on TV? Louise answers in a blink: 'In a nanosecond.'

It's clear that she still has great affection for Leela and the show, but Louise is equally enthusiastic about the fans. 'The intensity of the fan following,' she says, 'has surprised, moved, delighted, honoured, humbled and shocked me. Can only be good, can't it? *Doctor Who* is my pension – takes me all over the world. Thank you!'

Louise's Top Five Leela moments:
1. Nearly being eaten by a giant rat in 'The Talons of Weng-Chiang'.
2. Working with Trevor Baxter and Christopher Benjamin in 'The Talons of Weng-Chiang' – especially Trevor in the meat-eating scene.
3. Alan Lake [who played Herrick in 'Underworld'] and the BBC bar … that's not really Leela is it? But nonetheless, a very fond memory.
4. K-9 bowing his head at the same time as me in my final scene.
5. Slapping the hysterical woman in 'Horror of Fang Rock'.

The Shaman: David Garfield

'When we did the commentary for the DVD and they showed us clips, I couldn't wait to see what happened next!'

If you've ever played the Google Game, you'll know that there are quite a few David Garfields rattling around. Type the name into the search engine and press enter. There's David Garfield, the LA-based musician; David Garfield, the film editor; and J D Garfield, the Mexican-American actor. The David Garfield I'm waiting to meet is, to paraphrase the fourth Doctor, the definite article. The original, you might say.

Born in Gorseinon, South Wales, David still speaks with a quiet, lilting accent, much softened by years living amongst the Sias (English), but still pleasing on the ear. He's one of those people who seem to have a way of making you listen. Perhaps it's the way he fixes you with his deep brown eyes. Or perhaps it's just 50 years spent practising the art of keeping an audience's attention.

Oddly, though, acting wasn't David's first choice of profession. Like most teenagers, he didn't really have much of an idea what he wanted to do. 'I sort of vaguely thought I wanted to be an actor, as I have a sister who is an actress and I thought if she could do it, then so could I. But, absurdly, I never thought of going to drama school. I just thought that one day somebody would walk up to me and say, "Why don't you come and act for us!" Of course it doesn't work like that, but when you're a kid, that's what you think.'

By the time that David actually made it to the spiritual home of theatre – the Royal Shakespeare Company in Stratford-upon-Avon – he'd given up all thoughts of acting and was studying to be a sculptor. 'I was only there moving scenery around to make money to pay the bills,' he chuckles. However, the place quickly began to work its magic. The year that he spent working as a stagehand made him determined to try and break into the rarefied world he'd glimpsed from, literally, behind the scenes.

With all the unabashed confidence of youth, David decided he 'could do that' and determined to audition to join the company for their next season. There were 14 people going after just six places and David landed one of them. That was in 1959, and what a year it turned out to be! David: '1959 was *the* big season. It was the RSC's hundredth season, and that meant you got all the big, big stars turning up. We had Laurence Olivier's

Coriolanus, Charles Laughton's *King Lear*, Paul Robeson's *Othello*, Sam Wanamaker's Iago, and Dame Edith Evans' Volumnia. The directors that year were Tyrone Guthrie, Glen Byam Shaw, Tony Richardson and Peter Hall – quite a collection for a novice actor to learn from! So that's where I started. I was there for two seasons, then I left and went into TV because, really, television was a better source of income in those days. The jobs were quick and, with a family to feed, it was a good move to make.'

Having proved his mettle at the RSC, David found television offered him the chance to do lots of costume dramas, 'because anyone who could wear a costume and speak was in!' Highlights included *Elizabeth R* with Glenda Jackson, and *The Wednesday Play* about the assassination of Trotsky, in which David played Leonid Eitingon – the KGB officer chosen by Stalin to organise Trotsky's assassination in Mexico. After that, 'work just flowed'. He also has a special place in his heart for a series that he says, wistfully 'is probably unknown to most people now,' called *The Regiment*.

The Regiment was set in the Boer War and, David confesses, 'mostly was very boring. It was planned to go on forever, so it was written as a slow burn, and that didn't really work. Anyhow, I had an episode, about ten in, and it was all about me. So that was wonderful! I played a sergeant who was a right bastard to everybody, and when engaging the enemy he became convinced that his own side were trying to shoot him. I really enjoyed doing it and, unusually for me, I did get to see it, and it did look good … But the BBC wiped a few episodes by mistake, so the series will never be seen again.'

Generals and Witch Doctors

David's first foray into the world of *Doctor Who* came in 1969 with a part in the Patrick Troughton serial 'The War Games'. 'I really went up in my children's estimation when I got a part in that,' he laughs.

David played the role of the alien Captain von Weich, who is assisting a renegade Time Lord to train a human army to conquer the galaxy. As part of their 'training', soldiers from various real-life conflicts have been transported to the planet and forced to play out a series of deadly war games. Although von Weich first appears as a World War I German officer, he travels between the war zones, adopting suitable disguises for each era. How did David approach such a curious character? 'It was really a matter of casting the part in my head,' he says. For von Weich in his German disguise, David based the character on the silent-film-era actor Erich von Stroheim. When von Weich relocates to the American Civil

War Zone, he transforms into Rod Steiger!

For David's second appearance in *Who*, playing Neeva, the Shaman of the Sevateem in 'The Face of Evil', the character was a little harder to pin down. 'Neeva was off the wall,' David comments. 'He was a very strange character. He was a kind of witch doctor figure to this lost tribe, which meant that, to them, he had to appear mystical, because he wanted the power. So he was dressed in all this gear he'd found lying around in a crashed spaceship. I remember that there was a photograph, which was quite famous, of me with a glove on my head. I never worked out why the hell I had this glove on my head. Why didn't he put the glove on his hand? But it was a great story and the finale was superb. The strange thing was, though, that I hadn't seen it until quite recently. When we did the commentary for the DVD and they showed us clips, I couldn't wait to see what happened next! So when I come round the corner at the end and blast the screens away and go stark raving mad, wow, I enjoyed that. And I thought I wasn't half bad either!'

So how did the two experiences – and the two Doctors – compare? 'Well, Tom Baker was wonderful. There were various odd reports about Tom at the time, because he is as odd off-screen as he is on! So you had to be prepared to have a very offbeat actor to work against. However, he was terribly generous, very accommodating and I enjoyed every minute of it. Pat Troughton was a different kind of actor. He had a wide repertoire. Really, Tom has always been Tom, whereas Pat was a great character actor with a great range.'

David is still busy working, most recently cropping up in the hugely popular Welsh comedy-drama *Stella*. He's also starting to get to know the wider *Doctor Who* fan community with appearances at conventions. When I ask him how he's finding it all, he admits that the experience is 'fascinating. After 50 years, there's this tribe of people who still lap it up. It's incredible. The only unsettling thing is that the fans all know more about it than I do, so I can end up looking like a right idiot!' But at least he does now know exactly how 'The Face of Evil' ends!

The Faithful Pooch:
John Leeson

Fun fact of the day: at John Leeson's very first guest appearance at a *Doctor Who* convention in the USA, he realised he was 'unknown', so he disguised himself as an American *Doctor Who* fan – 'George' – from Pittsburgh. He even entered the K-9 sound-alike competition, which he lost – much to the delight of the audience when his true identity as the voice of the robot dog was revealed. These days, he's far too well known to get away with such shenanigans ... although he's still trying his very best to remain anonymous ...

How did you get into acting?
I always was an actor. I tried to escape, you know? I wasn't the happiest person at school so I joined the dramatic society and it was a wonderful hideaway. People always assume that acting is all about fame and fortune. No. If you're a proper actor, you do it because there's nothing else in the world that will light your fire, float your boat. But I'm one of those actors who likes getting behind things – make-up and costumes and whatever else. And of course a lot of voiceover work has hidden me perfectly. Nobody crosses the road to say 'You are John Leeson and I claim my five pounds.'

So, you like the anonymity?
I love the anonymity. Some other actors do as well, I think. Actors fall into two groups – the hiders and the showers – and some, like me, are poised on the cusp of both. We want to show off, we want to do the best we can, yet we don't want to be 'famous' necessarily.

You've done quite a lot of theatre and television over the years.
Yes, early on I got a good deal of work in repertory theatres and London 'fringe' productions, and then my first West End role of any note was in a play called *Plaza Suite* by Neil Simon. I was playing two parts, one of which was a bridegroom; and that year, '69, I actually got married. Unfortunately my understudy was six foot two. Even on my better days I'm only five foot six, so he would never have got into the costume. So on my wedding day I got married three times. For real in the morning, then I had to absent myself from the reception to play at the matinee performance, and then a group of wedding guests came to see the evening show!

Telly kicked in the '70s. I did sitcoms like *Dad's Army*, *My Wife Next Door*, *Take Three Girls*, *Comedy Playhouse* and a series called *Sorry* with Ronnie Corbett. I did lots of TV commercials both here in the UK and abroad as well, which is quite fun. English actors are considered relatively cheap to hire when it comes to working in commercials on the continent, you see!

Did you advertise anything embarrassing?
Not exactly, but I did do one thing … It was for German television, advertising Lifebuoy soap. The opening shot is of me in a bath, taken at bath-rim level. You see the soap first, then my hand coming out for it, then me soaping away. The camera pulls out a little bit, and from the other end of the bath, up comes my 'wife', and we start soaping each other! But the client was rather worried that my wife wasn't sufficiently 'Germanic'. My goodness me, they tried applying camera tape strategically to this girl's body to … ahem … enhance her natural assets … and she had very delicate skin and was in agony. So they had to recast. Within an hour, in came a new 'wife' who didn't need any camera tape at all! It was a very memorable commercial.

What's been your strangest job?
I was the original Bungle Bear in the children's show *Rainbow* for a year. It was an extremely hot job, because the studios out in Teddington were very brightly-lit, and very, very hot. Running around in that bear suit, I had to be issued with salt tablets to keep going. Roy Skelton was voicing Zippy, and Peter Hawkins, who was the king of voiceovers, was George. Peter was wonderful – heroically classic. But, by the end of a year, I was shrinking so fast that I was turning into a Giacometti sculpture. As my contract had come to a natural close, I felt there'd be nothing left of me if I took another one on. I think the next actor they got in was Stanley Bates. He was even smaller than me, so he came pre-shrunk as it were!

How did you come to be offered the role of K-9?
The part arrived entirely by accident really. A director I had worked with in Nottingham rep knew that I had played Bungle Bear, and he suspected I might be up for doing silly things, and he said there might be something for me to play in *Doctor Who* – but he didn't say what it was. Eventually the BBC rang up and asked if I'd like to do the voices both for a huge prawn-like 'virus', and a metal robot dog. K-9 was only planned for one story ['The Invisible Enemy', 1977], so both my agent and I thought I had

nothing to lose. But, of course, that one story led to an entire season …
and a place as one the Doctor's most faithful companions.

Is it true that when you were on set, you actually used to go down on all fours during rehearsals?
I did, because the physical module that was K-9 wasn't built until the very last moment. I was offered sight of the blueprints when I first met the producer, and he asked if I could come up with a voice that would be suitable. I said, 'I see it's got a tartan collar on, perhaps you want it Scottish?' They very quickly said, 'No, no, no. No thank you!' So we arrived at a voice that sounded as if it came out of a cheap, tin-pot transistor radio.

You actually appeared – in the flesh – as Dugeen in 'The Power of Kroll'. How did that come about?
K-9 hadn't been under-sealed or something, so he was confined to barracks. My understanding was that they were going to have someone like Martin Jarvis to play the part, but apparently, as a busy and much sought-after actor, he was unavailable at the time. Besides, I dare say that as I was already 'in the building' and contracted on a running fee, I was probably cheaper!

Was it fun to be actually standing next to Tom, rather than biting at his heels?
Yes. You got to meet the actors eye-to-eye, rather than eye-to-knee. Of course, in the studio recordings of the classic *Doctor Who*, I was always right around back of the set somewhere with a pair of headphones and a monitor, feeding the voice in live. The fact that I was still sharing the same studio floor with Tom, though well out of sight, meant that we could spin off each other. The dynamic of the performance we had achieved in rehearsals when I was running around as K-9 could actually be carried through. Nowadays, when voicing K-9, I am called to add K-9's voice to the film or recording afterwards. So sadly that 'live' dynamic has gone.

Interesting that you say that. It always seemed that the banter between K-9 and the Doctor was very spontaneous.
Well, a lot of it was. In 'The Sun Makers', for instance, there's a scene where the Doctor and K-9 are playing chess and, if you look at it again, the speed of the dialogue couldn't really be achieved any other way than Tom being there and me being there and trampolining off one another.

So you prefer the old way of doing things?

You bet! I always prefer working with other actors. It's a live event. Actors aren't just actors – they're reactors. You can't react in the same way to film or videotape.

I have a disturbing memory of an outtakes video, which was doing the rounds at school in the '80s. There's Tom in his dressing gown, and Mary Tamm in curlers, and the Doctor's asking K-9 if he can help. K-9 says 'Negative, Master' and Tom launches into this tirade. It was very alarming to hear the Doctor swear! Was it all just a horrible nightmare?

No, that happened! You'll probably find it on YouTube. A lot of silliness like that happened. One Christmas, I wrote a little sketch that went: 'What do you want for Christmas, K-9?' So I start singing, Mary answers, then we ask Tom what he wants for Christmas and Tom looks lasciviously at Mary. Cut!

Do you have a favourite story?

'The Sun Makers'. It's a lovely story. Robert Holmes did a brilliant job with the script. The other one I remember quite well is 'The Stones of Blood', which was filmed out at the Rollright Stones in Oxford, with the lovely Beatrix Lehmann playing the elderly professor. Well, in another part of my life, I had taken photos of actors, and I took some of her just on spec, and she came in during rehearsals with a paper bag. I thought she'd been to the greengrocers or something, but she says, 'That's for you, dear. I want you to have it.' Inside was a 1936, 35mm Leica camera that she had been given as a present when she was young by a famous actor. I protested, but she said, 'It's for you. I shan't need it anymore.' And of course a few weeks after the filming, Beatrix departed.

Did she know … was she ill?

No. But now my son has custody of it. I'll not say that it's his, but he's a very fine photographer and director, so he can have custody of it for now.

It sounds like you were having fun. Why did you leave?

Career pragmatism, really. Much as I loved having created the character of K-9, it's bad to be out of view for a long time as an actor. Besides which, you couldn't progress K-9's character very much more. K-9 is a bit WYSIWYG – what you see is what you get. No emotional development, no sex life that I know of! So I left in '79, but came back in 1980 because K-9 was going to be written out over five stories.

Apparently in one of K-9's final serials – 'Meglos' – Bill Fraser, who played General Grugger, only appeared so he could give K-9 'a damn good kicking'. Is that true?

Groan! Probably. K-9 got very badly treated from time to time. I used to do the kind of noises you'd get from running a quarter-inch recording tape backwards whenever my head was kicked. There, that dates me as having been born well before the digital age! Just to put it in the frame, producer John Nathan-Turner was not a fan. He had decided to run K-9 out of the storylines and he asked me back for those last few stories, which was nice because I quite liked the character I'd created and wanted to see him out properly. It was during that run of stories that K-9 got really bashed about. I don't know if John Nathan-Turner was laughing under his sleeve or not at the time!

K-9 came back in new *Who*, in *The Sarah Jane Adventures* and in his own series. Can you tell us a little about that?

I was taken rather by surprise, because I knew very little about it before it all happened. But sadly, with the Australian *K9* series, instead of getting to go out to Australia, I only went as far as a little dubbing theatre in Soho.

So, you felt that you had something new to bring to the character?

Well, in the *K9* series they wanted it to be K-9 but 'different'. Did they know what they meant? Probably not. So we tried various things and, at the end of the day, I can't say if it worked or not, but he's younger and snappier. In the Australian series he even flies. So he's a sort of all-singing, all-dancing version, which the K-9 as I knew him certainly wasn't.

It's really not the same now that K-9 can fly … How's he ever going to get stuck in the mud?

I know! With the original K-9, if he was on a flat studio floor and someone put a match down, he'd come to a grinding halt, because the original model was dreadfully underpowered, dreadfully noisy and they'd always have to stop and pick him up to carry out running repairs. They spent a lot of studio time doing that – and time is money – so I never conceived that the original K-9 would last as long as it did.

What do you think of the new *Doctor Who*?

It's fantastic. What the new actors have brought to it is absolutely wonderful. Not only youth and energy, but real involvement. I wasn't quite sure how I would take to Christopher Eccleston, who is a superb actor yet a bit serious – as though he shouldn't really be playing the Doctor. But it's been fabulous.

So how many Doctors has K-9 known now?
Really just Tom Baker and David Tennant, and of course a number of very talented companions including Lis Sladen and the lovely Mary Tamm. So sad that neither of them are still here with us. It doesn't do to lose mistresses.

It was sad. Would you like to share any memories of Mary or Lis?
Mary was lovely and had the driest sense of humour imaginable. She was great. Really dry. A cool patrician beauty and a complete contrast of casting to the intuitive savage Leela, played by the incomparable Louise Jameson. Lis Sladen used to live about half a mile from where I live and we used to meet in the village street. She was very protective of her little team of children in *The Sarah Jane Adventures*. She was very concerned that everything was right. She never seemed sure that she'd got the measure of things and was always asking for advice.

But she was such a staggeringly fine actress.
She was. Indeed she was. And did she look her age? No, she did not. As K-9 might say: 'Edible, Mistress.' Oops. Bad dog. Bad K-9! [Laughs]

What has been your favourite role to date?
The role that one's playing at the moment tends to be one's favourite. That's a terrible cop out, I know. I seem to have played so many. It hasn't been K-9 really, although I've had a great deal of fun playing him. I sometimes tell people, and they're horrified, but I'm not actually a *Doctor Who* fan. I'm an actor doing a lovely job in what happens to be a very successful sci-fi series.

What role would you like to play?
There's a play called *Hadrian the Seventh* by a playwright called Peter Luke about a renegade pope. It's a fantasy about this extraordinary pope who is completely off the wall. It's a real gift for any actor to play.

What are you doing now?
Talking to you! What I'm about to be doing is more Big Finish audio

dramas. There are some that Tom Baker and Louise Jameson and I will be involved in. Other than that, I'm wearing my other professional hat as an accredited wine educator. I'm giving one-off lectures and teaching courses here in London. Not much money in it, but it keeps you off the street. I have also just launched an updated and expanded version of my autobiography, as the original is no longer available in print. Published by Fantom Films, it is called *Tweaking the Tail*.

So, are you a wine fan?
Ah yes! It's nice to be asked about my parallel profession as a wine educator! I'm a devotee of the Old World, Italian wine particularly. The thing with some New World wine styles is that they – again – can seem a bit WYSIWYG. They don't give you as much to find as those from cooler places in the Old World. They can also come to maturity that much quicker than some of their European counterparts. I prefer the Old World style, but then I'm possibly an old-world person.

Presumably you must like cooking as well?
I do! I've even won an award for cooking. The *Radio Times* magazine ran a competition many years ago called *The Taste of Italy* and my wife, because I'm the household cook, made me go in for it. About six months later I got a letter from the BBC saying I'd won. It was fantastic. I didn't have to cook anything, just submit a recipe! I had a long weekend with my wife and a couple of other folks in the Cipriani Hotel in Venice, culminating in a seven-course Venetian banquet cooked by Antonio Carluccio. If you're interested in the cooking side of my life then Fantom Films are also publishing my lifetime's collection of favourite recipes, brought together under the title *Dog's Dinners* ... Sorry... but what else could I call it!

What's your signature dish?
Probably zewelwaiea. It's Alsace onion tart – you'll even find it in the book! In fact, I must run. I have a casserole in the oven right now!

The Grifter: Nigel Plaskitt

' ... Tom strode into the room, threw the script across the table
and demanded "Who wrote this horse shit!"'

*Pipkins, Doctor Who, Sesame Street, Spitting Image, The New Captain
Scarlet* ... Nigel Plaskitt is one of those talented men whose CV seems to
include almost every memorable kids' television show of the last 40 years.
It was Nigel who provided the voice of the inimitable Hartley Hare –
Pipkins' irascible host – as well as co-writing the show. Remember the ITV
digital monkey? The "Course you can Malcolm' Vicks Sinex commercial
that created a schoolyard catchphrase? Have you ever been to see *Avenue
Q* or a live Gorillaz gig? All Nigel's work.

With the exception of the six Vicks commercials he did between 1972
and 1981, and the follow-up ad in 1993, for most of his career Nigel has
been in that curious position of being famous without being well-known.
Having started out as an actor, he got his first 'real break' as a puppeteer
for the much-loved *Pipkins*. Adults of a certain age will fondly remember
the show and the manic, moth-eaten Hartley Hare.

Hartley was a sublime creation. A vain and frenetic puppet who, after
the death of Inigo Pipkin (played by George Woodbridge), came to rule
the roost. 'I started as an actor and very early on in my career – within the
second year – I was asked to do *Pipkins*,' Nigel recalls. 'I'd worked as a child
in the Little Angel Theatre in Islington, and a friend from there knew I
could do character voices. So I didn't even have to audition. Hartley came
out of that, along with around ten other characters.'

When *Pipkins* finished after a nine-year run, Nigel 'stopped
everything', having had 'enough' of the showbiz world. 'I'd had done a very
high-profile TV commercial so I'd been famous and stopped in the street
and got all that out of my system and I thought "Is this really what I want
to do?" For me, there are always these crossroads. They seem to go in ten
year cycles – so I decided to try and get into TV production.'

Nigel produced a children's TV series for Yorkshire Television called
Heggerty Haggerty. The series was a success, but when faced with the
opportunity of working full-time for Yorkshire TV, he decided it wasn't
for him. 'I've never really been attracted to the struggles that come with
working full-time for a company,' he says, 'so I decided to walk away. Just
as that happened, *Spitting Image* came along and that dovetailed nicely.'

Spitting Bile

You probably need to have grown up in the '80s to appreciate the impact that *Spitting Image* had at the time. In Britain, unemployment stood at three million, urban centres were becoming ghost towns, youth suicide rates were at an all time high. The only thing any sane person could do was laugh, and *Spitting Image* delivered a weekly vein-full of visceral political satire to soothe the nation's battered psyche.

'I played hundreds of characters over the years,' says Nigel. 'It's difficult to remember them all, but I was definitely John Major when he turned grey. Physically, we were never involved in how the puppets looked, but there was quite a lot you could do with the body language. We did a series of sketches with Norma and John Major eating peas. The writers were nervous of letting us perform without dialogue, but those sketches really stood out.'

At the time, many people considered *Spitting Image* to be the one shining light of sanity in '80s Britain. Was he aware that the show was an important 'voice of dissent'? 'We were aware,' Nigel confirms. 'We were usually filming on Sunday evening for the following week so we rarely got out to see the impact at the time, but we would hear people talking about the show. Viewing figures were huge – six million for Sunday night, where previously they'd had two million. At its height, it was pulling in 15 million, so it definitely had an impact. David Steel [Leader of the Liberal Democrat Party at the time] still claims that it was the ruin of his career. I think it made people aware of what was going on and possibly we made some people more politically aware too.'

The Sting

Spitting Image ran from 1984 to 1996. So, we have to jump into the TARDIS and head back to 1978 to catch the 28-year-old Nigel as he joined the cast of *Doctor Who*.

Director George Spenton Foster had seen the Vicks commercials, liked them, and asked Nigel if he wanted to be in a new *Doctor Who* story he was casting, called 'The Ribos Operation'. This was to be the first serial in what would be a season-long quest for the Key to Time.

'I'd been watching *Doctor Who* since I was a kid,' says Nigel. 'I'm not going to say it was a dream come true – that's a bit melodramatic – but it was a really great experience. It was a great cast and a great time to be working on the show with Tom Baker as the Doctor, and as eccentric in real life as you can believe.' A lasting memory on the first day of rehearsals was doing a read-through when Tom strode into the room, threw the script across the table and demanded 'Who wrote this horse shit!'

Despite Tom's comments, 'The Ribos Operation' was a highlight of the season, with Iain Cuthbertson and Nigel playing the intergalactic conmen Garron and Unstoffe, looking to sell a small, medieval 'Class 3 planet' to the despotic and ever-so-slightly unhinged Graff Vynda-K (Paul Seed). The con relies on convincing the Graff that the planet has an abundance of jethrik, which just happens to be the rarest and most valuable mineral in the galaxy. The rest of the story is a romp, with the Doctor and his new assistant Romana (Mary Tamm) playing very much second fiddle to the big 'sting'.

Nigel thought that it was a great script too: 'We all did. It was beautifully written and quite unusual for *Doctor Who*, because there was very little action in it. One of the things I do remember was that I hadn't done any really meaty roles on TV before, apart from *Pipkins*, which really fitted me like a glove. When it came to the first meeting for "The Ribos Operation", most people already had their scripts down. I hadn't given it much thought, just read it through a few times. But the remarkable thing was that I did seem to know it. Not without the odd prompt or two, but the writing was so good that it seemed to flow naturally.'

Working with Iain Cuthbertson was, Nigel says, 'just so easy,' and the two made a memorable double act. The scenes the actors have together are played with such relish that it's impossible not to be swept along by the magnificent silliness of it all.

A Shaggy Dog Story
Nigel also has nothing but praise for the serial's set and costume design: 'The whole thing was so well done. I know *Doctor Who* sets could be a little ropey, but we had a fantastic designer on that story and you just couldn't help but feel like you were there. Of course outside it was the middle of summer, and we were supposed to be on this icebound planet, but she got some wonderful costumes for us and it was very easy to enter into the spirit of the whole thing.'

Does he have any other lasting memories that he'd like to share? 'Well, I can tell you the dog story, which you've probably heard before, but Tom tells this in a completely different way. My version is the truth. But then I would say that, wouldn't I? Anyway Paul Seed, who played the Graff, brought his dog in every day to rehearsals and left him in the car, obviously in the shade, with the windows open and all that. At lunch, though, he would let him out and bring him to the pub next door to the rehearsal room. On this one occasion we were sitting having lunch, with the dog beside Paul, and in comes Tom. Paul says, "Whatever you do, don't say hello to the dog." Of course, Tom says "Hello," and the dog growls. And Paul says, "Tom, don't!" So he gets a bit closer and goes "Hello," and – now this is the truth – on the third "Hello," the dog jumped forward and bit a chunk out of his lip. So now Tom's standing there, looking rather shocked, bleeding profusely. I took him to the nearby Middlesex Hospital, and there he was, standing in casualty, looking for all the world like Doctor Who, because he dressed like that in everyday life! It was very bizarre. But now Tom had this chunk out of his lip, which meant that they had to shoot him with his lip away from the camera, which wasn't always possible. They tried to cover it with make-up and it got infected and was a real mess. But Paul was very, very clear!'

Since *Who*, life has remained busy for Nigel. He returned to puppetry with credits on films such as *Labyrinth*, *Little Shop of Horrors*, *The Muppet Christmas Carol*, *Muppet Treasure Island*, *Lost in Space*, *The Hitchhiker's Guide to the Galaxy* and a new Muppet movie, which is out in Easter 2014. He admits that performing isn't his 'life blood. I enjoy it but I'm happy doing something else as well.' That something else includes everything from television ads to stage plays. Does he ever hanker to return to the world of *Who*? 'I'd love to do Unstoffe again,' he says enthusiastically. 'It's a great character. I know that Iain's no longer with us, but it would be nice to work out a double act again.' Now there's a wonderful thought.

The Mentiad: David Warwick

From dating Louise Jameson – twice – to working with ex-RADA chum Mary Tamm on 'The Pirate Planet', David Warwick's links to *Doctor Who* are like the veins in a blue cheese. On the surface you see very little, but inside is a labyrinth of connections running through his life …

Is it true that you're named after the famous actor David Niven?
I was born on 15 January 1948, which was the same day that David Niven married his wife. So, yes, my mother was a huge, huge fan and she named me after him. Although there's no history of theatre or performing in the family, I think it was her love of film and acting that really sparked my interest. In fact apart from my dad and my uncle, who left Crewe to go to war, I was the only person in my family who, at that point, had ever left my hometown. And the reason I'd left was to go to RADA.

Tell us a little about that …
When I left school, I went to teacher training college and was doing French and English. I didn't enjoy the French at all so I changed to Drama to supplement the English. I quite enjoyed lighting design and stage management, so that's what I did. Halfway through my second year, though, I realised I was not fit to be a teacher. I lacked the patience and I was probably a bit scared. It takes a saint to become a teacher – and I wasn't destined for sainthood! So I left and I joined the local repertory theatre in Crewe as what they call a technical assistant. It was the lowest of the low – below the person who makes the tea. It's the person who gets kicked by the person who makes the tea! Over the next year and a half, I worked my way up to become an acting assistant stage manager. Although my mother's interest steered me towards film and acting, it was only being in the middle of an acting fraternity in Crewe that made me realise what an exotic fraternity they were – compared with people who lived in Crewe! By then, I was doing some small acting parts and I liked it so much that I applied for drama school and got into RADA. Mary Tamm and Louise Jameson were in the same year as me.

What happened after RADA?
After graduating, having left Crewe, I went back to the same theatre I started at three years previously, but as a full member of the company. There I was spotted by a lady called Margaret Crawford, who was the casting director for Granada Television, and she asked me to go up for a part. It was in a play

called *Passengers* by Susan Pleat. I got that, then another one, which was amazing, because I didn't even have an agent at the time. After that, the ball really started rolling. I did a sitcom at the BBC with Ronnie Corbett called *The Prince of Denmark*. That got me *The Fall and Rise of Reginald Perrin* in '76. In the same year, I got my first West End play with Ian Marter, who of course had been in *Doctor Who*. I caught up with Ian again in 1981 when I got married in New Zealand. Ian was over there doing some work, so he was the only other Englishman at my wedding party.

Were you a fan of *Doctor Who* before you appeared in it?
I was a fan right from the early episodes, although I go back to a pre-*Doctor Who* era. Back in my day it was *Quatermass* that we watched from behind the sofa!

How did you come to be offered the part of Kimus in 'The Pirate Planet'?
My agent Carol James was friends with the director, Pennant Roberts – there's another *Doctor Who* link – and I got the job because he respected her opinion. There was a meeting, but it wasn't so much an audition as 'Would David like to do it?' But there was an awful lot of work around at the BBC then. They had rehearsal rooms out in Acton. There were, I think, seven floors. At the top was the restaurant, the ground floor was offices and in between were rehearsal rooms – three on each floor. At any one time there were 15 productions on the go. You could go to the restaurant at lunchtime and meet half of Equity [the actors' union]. They were great days and you could literally get work because you'd been talking to someone in the restaurant.

How involved was the writer, Douglas Adams, in the filming?
He was around but I didn't have much to do with him. Our producer, though, was a guy called Graham Williams, and I knew him because he was the elder brother of somebody else I was at RADA with – Nigel Williams. So, once again, wheels within wheels.

Was it an enjoyable experience?
Very much so. We went off to do the pre-filming in South Wales out in the Cathedral Caves. We were staying in a very nice hotel in Monmouth and commuting in everyday. We were having a ball and, of course, never having worked on *Doctor Who* before, it was very odd to see John Leeson, who played K-9, on all fours in the studio. He didn't have to do it, but it gave everyone an eye line. John was such fun and work was really play.

Tom Baker had a reputation for being tough on people who didn't take the show seriously …?
He only ever had the interests of the programme at heart. He could be very funny on set though – and a bit naughty – but only if he knew they were going to cut a scene anyway. He was always very professional about everything. One thing that really sticks in my mind though was that nobody was quite sure where he was living back then. He had two silk shirts and he'd come in and hand the dirty one to the assistant floor manager, whose job it was to wash it. He carried a toothbrush and a comb in his top pocket, and who knows where he spent each evening?

Anything else you remember?
There's one anecdote I always tell. While we were filming, Tom got to know this charming little boy who was on holiday. He discovered that the boy was being bullied at school, so he found out the name of the school, and one afternoon, when he was free, he got the unit driver on standby, put on his costume, and they drove to the school. He sat outside waiting for the kids to come out for their break. When they did, he saw this boy and the bully was with him. So he strode into the playground in full *Doctor Who* regalia and said, 'Who's Bully Forbes?' This startled seven-year-old put his hand up and Tom said, 'You're not to bully again!', then swept out. It's wonderfully heart-warming, but you do wonder how that boy took it. Probably left him traumatised for life!

Did you get to see much of Bruce Purchase and his famous mechanical parrot?
No, I didn't see those bits. In fact, I didn't see the episode at all until I went to a convention in 2005 in LA. Louise and I were an item at that point and we were staying at the Marriot Hotel overlooking LA Airport. That was great for me, as I'm a plane freak. They were showing 'The Pirate Planet' episodes on a loop and that was the first time I'd seen it.

What did you think? Was there anything you would have changed?
No. There's no point worrying about the nuances of a performance after 30 years!

You returned to *Doctor Who* to play the Police Commissioner in 'Army of Ghosts'. What was that like?
Completely different. When I filmed my excerpt, I ended up in a lock-

up warehouse on the outskirts of Cardiff. I'd travelled down by train, they put me up in a nice hotel, picked me up by car, put me in the Police Commissioner's uniform and then I sat around all day waiting for people to arrive. Around about seven o'clock in the evening, this body of people finally turned up and that was it. No rehearsing. No meeting. Just shoot and go. It's changed completely.

Do you enjoy going to *Doctor Who* conventions?
They're fun. My first convention was in Barking. I went with Louise because we were back together then. We've had two bites of that cherry! I've known her since she was 17 and she's a very, very good friend, and I went along on her coattails the first time. The second time was in LA, where she and I did some clips of a little play we do together called *Sex Wars*. At the end, I said 'One of the bonuses of this is I get to spend four nights in a very nice hotel with Leela. Who could ask for more!' I'm sure every man in the room was envious of me – and rightly so!

Do you enjoy the fan attention?
It's nice, but I never get the really interesting encounters. For instance, I did a tour of *Dad's Army*. I was doing my Sergeant Wilson and Leslie Grantham, who has appeared in *Doctor Who* too, played Private Walker. We were in Sheffield, sitting in the sunshine, waiting to go into the theatre. This lady came up and asked for an autograph and Leslie asked what she wanted him to sign and she revealed her upper halves! She was not a small lady and she was well able to take the full signature on each. Sadly that sort of thing doesn't happen to me!

What are you up to at the moment?
I direct more than I act nowadays. Early this year, I was in Kuala Lumpur and Singapore. I get friends together and we do Ray Cooney farces. We have a few days rehearsing in London, then fly out, stay in the Raffles Hotel and put on these plays. Then we drive North and end up at the Kuala Lumpur Hilton and we perform on a stage specially built for us. It's very much dinner theatre with lots of ex-pats and local dignitaries in attendance. It's a very, very nice job.

What would you say the lasting legacy of working on *Doctor Who* has been?
The enjoyment. If only I could enjoy all my work as much as *Doctor Who*. Everyone who works on it loves it – and it shows.

The Ones We've Left Behind:
Mary Tamm

**'I think,' she said, 'that perhaps [the fans]
all prefer the other Romana.'**

She may have been a brunette but, on screen, she always had the icy allure of a Hitchcock blonde. In real life, that chill melted away the moment Mary Tamm spoke.

Despite the cut-glass accent, Mary was born in Dewsbury, Yorkshire, to *émigré* parents and didn't learn English until she went to primary school. It was there that she caught the acting bug.

After school she studied at RADA before embarking on a successful theatre career, appearing with luminaries such as Derek Jacobi in Harold Pinter's *The Lover*. However, it was on screen that she really started to make a name for herself. Roles in films like *The Odessa File* (1974) and the big screen spin-off of *The Likely Lads* (1976) were followed by high-profile TV dramas *A Raging Calm* (1974) and *The Girls of Slender Means* (1975).

When the call came to audition for *Doctor Who*, Mary had little interest in playing what she felt would be just another damsel in distress. But when presented with the part of Romanadvoratrelundar, Romana for short, she was taken by the possibilities the character offered. It also helped that Louise Jameson was an old pal from drama school and could chat to her about what the experience was like.

Louise was totally frank about the plusses and minuses of being the Doctor's side-kick. Mary told me later, and with typical dry humour, 'Louise told me everything – I underline everything – in the strictest confidence. So, of course, I went out and told everybody I knew what she'd just said!'

At this point, it should be recalled that Louise hadn't had the best time working with Tom Baker. So it was with a deep intake of breath that Mary accepted the role, having been reassured that the character would be 'far removed' from anything that had gone before.

Romana would be the first 'Time Lady' the show had seen – and every inch the Doctor's equal. From her elegant gowns that she helped design – the purple one from 'The Androids of Tara' was her favourite – to her haughty demeanour, Romana was a showstopper. Yet what made her character so appealing was that beneath that confident, almost arrogant exterior, Romana was a real babe in the woods. A wide-eyed innocent, who gradually comes to appreciate the Doctor's experience and eccentric ways. There have always been smart, independent women in the TARDIS but, decades before River Song came along, Romana was the first to tell the Doctor he was flying it wrong.

Although Mary played the role for only a year (1978-1979) during the Key to Time story arc, she managed to create a character that fans came to love. Compare the Romana we see in her first story, 'The Ribos Operation', who falls so charmingly for conman Unstoffe's 'honest face', with the much more worldly-wise figure in the wonderful *The Prisoner of Zenda* homage 'The Androids of Tara'. The subtly of her performance, infused with wit and charm, made her a firm favourite.

Mary left the show at the end of that season, feeling that she had gone as far as she could with the character. It was a testament to the popularity of her creation, though, that the Beeb chose to have Romana regenerate rather than leave for good.

After *Doctor Who*, Mary was busier than ever, working on both stage and screen, with roles in soaps such as *Brookside* and *EastEnders* as well as guest appearances in *Wire in the Blood*, *Poirot* and *Jonathan Creek*. On stage, she won rave reviews with a blistering Beverly in *Abigail's Party* at the Chichester Festival.

I met Mary Tamm just once and was blown away by her frank, funny and self-effacing nature. That was back in 2004 and I remember her confiding that she was rather put out not to have been invited back to play Romana by Big Finish. 'I think,' she said 'that perhaps [the fans] all prefer the other Romana.' Just a year later, Big Finish did indeed invite her back, proving her apprehensions spectacularly wrong.

Back then Mary was, oddly enough, dressed in Romana's signature colour – white – with a plain jacket and a silk crossover blouse, complementing a pair of comfy slacks. Her hair was down and she was wearing glasses, which made her look slightly mumsy. Or at least how your mum would look if she were Lauren Bacall crossed with Grace Kelly.

Unlike many actors, Mary Tamm seemed to have no worries about how she looked on camera. When, after the interview, I stumblingly asked for a photo, she immediately put me at my ease. Suddenly, I wasn't a journalist wanting a slice of the pie anymore. I was a fan. 'Come on then, chuck,' she said in perfect imitation of my flat Northern vowels. She wouldn't hear of having time out to comb her hair, arrange her lipstick, take off her glasses, or any one of the million things most of us women do when confronted with a photographer. She just threw her arm around me and smiled the most radiant smile. Not that she was confident about her looks. Quite the opposite. 'You'll have to wait all day for me to make myself beautiful,' she said.

Warm, witty and wonderfully free of showbiz froth, the actress who will forever be remembered as Romana to Tom Baker's fourth Doctor, lost her battle against cancer in 2012. Her death left friends and family devastated and, coming fast on the heels of the deaths of Nicholas Courtney, Elisabeth Sladen and Caroline John, left the Whoniverse a bleaker place.

Back in 1987, I remember sitting in a bar in the Adelphi Hotel in Liverpool where a group of us used to meet every few weeks to rewatch favourite shows and chat to like-minded souls. This particular weekend, the revels were brought to an abrupt halt by the news that Patrick Troughton had just passed away. As we digested the news a drunk, who'd been taking the piss all evening, leant over and slurred, 'Who's that then? Another of those sci-fi tossers?' My friend started explaining, then stopped. 'Just a mate', she said, and that's how it felt. It felt the same when Mary Tamm died.

Mary, Nick, Elisabeth and Caroline. William Hartnell, Patrick Troughton, Jon Pertwee, Roger Delgado, Anthony Ainley, Michael Craze, Jacqueline Hill, Ian Marter … The list of those no longer with us is too long but, in a little corner of the space-time continuum, Sarah Jane will always be wearing that Andy Pandy suit; the Master will always be demanding that we obey him; the Brigadier will always be ordering 'five rounds rapid'; and Mary Tamm will always be the noblest Romana of them all.

The Meglos Survivor:
Crawford Logan

Crawford Logan has been counting steps. When we meet in his dressing room at the Fortune Theatre, near London's Covent Garden, he's just about to go on stage for the mid-week matinee. Crawford is playing Arthur Kipps in the hit play *The Woman in Black*. By the end of the day, the stair count will be 628, so it's clearly a job that's going to keep him fit! Later, as we say our goodbyes – and he takes to the stairs one more time – I ask him if he could sign my notebook. He signs '... Crawford Logan ... "Meglos" Survivor ...'

What inspired you to act?
Probably because I couldn't do anything else – and I probably can't even do that! (Laughs) My family have nothing at all to with the theatre. They're quite military and establishment, but there's a strong tradition of mimicry and storytelling. So I grew up with that. I'd done some acting at school, and when I went to university I got involved in drama. Then I got the chance to go and work in the summer-stock theatre in Vermont, USA, which was great, because you got away from the university thing where you do shows and your friends say, 'That's terrific.' I didn't know anyone, so if someone gave praise, it really meant something. Once I'd started out, I thought I'd give it seven years and if I was successful, great. If not, I'd go and be an accountant or whatever. After seven years, I was neither massively successful nor particularly dreadful, so I stuck with it!

Are you driven to do it?
Yes, absolutely. People often say 'How can you do this – the same play – week in, week out?' but today is Tuesday, I've had two days off, and I'm starting to miss it!

You've appeared in the radio soap *The Archers* twice ...
Radio is one of the things I couldn't be without. The only place in life where I feel 95 percent confident is sitting in front of a microphone, because I feel I know what I'm doing. So yes, I've done lots of radio, including *The Archers*. I played a Captain Fraser, who was a rather mysterious figure, possibly an ex-member of the SAS, who had an affair with Caroline Bone – like everyone else! Then I reappeared after six years as Dr Matthew

Thorogood. My theory always was that he was really Captain Fraser again. He'd come back to Ambridge, after having been to some shady South American republic, with a bogus degree in medicine and a new name!

You're also the voice of amateur 1930s detective Paul Temple …
I am indeed Paul Temple! It's a fab show. We meet all number of dead bodies without ever having to go to any kind of inquest or get our clothes tested for DNA. And we jump straight from a body falling out of a cupboard to 'Pass the marmalade, darling!' I love it. For people who enjoy it, that's the charm. It's completely off the spectrum of being believable. I've got another one coming out soon, a ten-parter, and it's just as daft as all the rest. Eventually people are going to twig that all the plots are exactly the same!

Paul Temple is very popular with the ladies. Do you get fan mail?
Not much. I get more for *Doctor Who*.

The Archers, Paul Temple, Doctor Who … **You seem to be collecting these iconic shows.**
I suppose so! I've done very little telly but what I have done is *Doctor Who*, *EastEnders* and *Secret Army*, which is another iconic show.

Of the work you've done so far what's been (a) the most fun, (b) the most demanding and (c) the most surprising?
This play [*The Woman in Black*] is fun because it's just the two of you and the ghost, and provided we I get on, which we do, we can throw anything at each other. It's different every time, because the audience is different every time. Almost everything on radio is fun too. I love the imaginative thing about radio. Not everything is as it seems and very often with live sound effects – which they don't do very much anymore – the real thing doesn't necessarily sound like the real thing. I love the idea that walking through snow is twisting a piece of polystyrene. Demanding … Musicals are quite demanding. In 2010 my wife and I were in the Lake District and we'd stopped at a service station because the phone had been ringing like crazy. It was the theatre in Pitlochry asking if I could do the evening show of *Kiss Me Kate* because a cast member had been taken ill. That was 12.30. We turned round, I got up there by about five o'clock, was shown a video of the dress rehearsal, given the script, and at eight I was in the show. That was a bit like standing in front of a speeding train. Surprising … Well, radio again I suppose. I played a talking radiator once. But that's the joy

of radio. You can play God or Hitler!

You played Deedrix in the *Doctor Who* serial 'Meglos'. Tell us a little about the character?
Well, usually when you say you've been in *Doctor Who*, the expectation is that you've worn a mask and been completely invisible, but I was a fairly normal character. I wore some funny clothes, had a peculiar haircut and was probably a bit of a gay icon! I know that my girlfriend at the time – she's now my wife – quite liked the satin trousers.

Did you keep them?
No! But I did find the top half of the costume online. I can't remember now how I even found it, but it was listed as 'worn by Crawford Logan'! But Deedrix was quite an earnest young man.

Were you an earnest young man?
I'm afraid I was. Probably still am – though I'm not very young any more!

You have a bit of a pub quiz fact to reveal about 'Meglos' …
Yes, a little known fact – and a very good pub quiz question – is that as well as playing this rather peculiar scientist, I was also the voice of the cactus. I don't think people know that because there's no credit. So I sat in the box with John Leeson and we did the voices together – great fun. I loved K-9. On recording evenings, we'd start at seven, and they'd have parties of kids in during the afternoon, and always the last prop they put out was K-9, so that all the kids could pet him before they left.

You realise that now you'll be inundated by people turning up with pictures of cacti for you to sign?
It has been done once, which was great! The cactus was, of course, quite a big deal at the time, because it was pre-CGI, so every bloomin' needle had to be stuck on individually. Tom didn't like it very much at all. He didn't have much patience with that sort of thing, but I probably shouldn't be saying that!

What was it like on set?
It was a bit manic because there were all these roots and pneumatic plants trailing off through the jungle and the effects didn't work terribly well. Tom got rather cross. Well, more than cross! The other thing was this very, very peculiar dodecahedron, which was a sort of pulsing crystal

worshipped by the fanatical Deons, who were as camp as many rows of tents! They were hysterical. Very funny to work with. But the best thing about it was Tom Baker walking round pronouncing 'Meglos' in those deep tones of his … 'Meglos'. He loved saying it!

'Meglos' is noted for its use of a camera-linking system called Scene-Sync, which allowed actors to be superimposed onto a miniature set. Did you have any experience of that?
Yes, and it was fascinating to see the models. You had to be very precisely positioned against the blue screen so that you could be 'placed' in these tiny models of spaceships. I'd never seen anything like it before.

Lalla Ward said that Tom Baker playing Meglos was only slightly more demonic than usual … is that about right?
Yes, that seems like a fair comment. Only he was a little more spiky!

Did you get a chance to get to get to know Jacqueline Hill, who'd returned to *Doctor Who* to play Lexa?
Sadly, not really. But she brought a touch of calm and elegance to the proceedings in amongst the various furies.

You mentioned that you attended a *Doctor Who* convention recently. How have you found the fans?
Generally very nice. There are usually a few who turn up to each show. In fact I had two guys come up to me in Glasgow last year. We got talking and it turned out that one of them was the man who pours the mixture for Tunnock's Tea Cakes. Good man! But I guess z-listers like me have the same sort of experiences. Tom must have full-time employees to deal with his fans.

You're in *The Woman in Black* until January. What would you like to do next?
Really, I would just like to carry on doing what I like to do. I did a one-man show about Sir Walter Scott [entitled *The Ragged Lion*] at Scott's home in Abbortsford, so perhaps I'll dust that off again. But the thing with acting is that you're always moving on. I remember being in Southampton after six months of being in a show and walking out on a winter's night with a bag on my shoulder, having been in digs somewhere, and I didn't know what I was doing next.

Chapter Three: The '80s

'Ahhh … a noble brow. Clear gaze. At least it will be, given a few hours sleep. A firm mouth. A face beaming with a vast intelligence … It's the most extraordinary improvement … My last incarnation… oh, I was never happy with that one. It had a sort of feckless "charm", which simply wasn't me.'
(The Doctor, 'The Twin Dilemma')

The '80s are often condemned as an era of mediocrity and greed, when PR and marketing took the place of creativity and passion. It certainly wasn't the most cheerful of decades. In fact if you lived in the UK, the '80s meant rampant inflation, record unemployment and the Falklands War. On a global scale, there was the Chernobyl nuclear disaster, Mount Etna erupted, and a new plague was officially identified and given the label AIDS. It's no wonder that Frankie Goes to Hollywood spent 48 weeks in the UK charts telling us all to 'Relax'.

However, the 1980s did have some saving graces. This was, after all, the era that gave us Live Aid and liquid soap, Pac-man and Prozac, Breville toasters and Bill & Ted. It was a time when Daisy Duke had all the best outfits, Hannibal Smith had the best plans and Skeletor had the best one-liners. The '80s may have been bleak, but they certainly weren't boring.

In the world of *Doctor Who*, things were being shaken up too. On 21 March 1981, in the final episode of 'Logopolis', Peter Davison was revealed as the newest face of the Doctor. It's hard to believe now, but at the time, Davison was a controversial choice. Many considered that, at 29, he was far too young for a role that required an actor who could bring experience and gravitas. Ultimately, though, the decision turned out to be inspired. As a younger Doctor, Davison was able to bring a vulnerability and uncertainly to a character that had, for so long, seemed indomitable. This new Doctor was more willing to admit his doubts and deliberations. He was more willing to be led rather than lead.

However, if Doctor five was plagued by doubt and bowed down by the weight of the universe, then six was egotistical, cocksure and abrasive. Colin Baker's Doctor was an intriguing creation. If Peter Davison's performance foreshadowed the more caring-sharing Doctors of recent times then Colin Baker's harked back to the show's origins. His Time Lord was an altogether more dangerous and alien character.

Sadly Colin Baker barely had the chance to establish himself in the role. His tenure (1984-1986) was plagued by political manoeuvring at the BBC, who were widely believed to want shot of the show. In fact *Doctor Who* was put on hold for 18 months between Season 22 and Season 23, eventually returning with the ominously-named 'The Trial of a Time Lord'. The sixth Doctor was indeed on trial, and at the end of that run, he received a very definite thumbs down from the BBC hierarchy. Colin Baker was asked to leave, and for the first time in the show's history, a regeneration sequence was recorded without the outgoing actor being present.

Colin's Doctor had been Hartnell-esque but Sylvester McCoy's was perhaps more Troughton-esque. There was the same clownish nature. The same tendency to distraction and buffoonery. But he was also a dark Doctor – secretive and manipulative. Seven is the player of games and, as his companion Ace remarks, 'well devious.'

With such a diversity of Doctors, the '80s should have been a decade of delight for *Who* fandom. Instead it was very much the beginning of the end. After the last episode of 'Survival' aired on 6 December 1989, the BBC decided that the show was to be put on indefinite hiatus. No-one really wanted to believe that *Doctor Who* had gone for good. We just waited and hoped to see what the next decade would bring.

The Megalomaniac:
Terry Molloy

**'... if *Doctor Who* fans are considered as anoraks,
The Archers fans are definitely Barbours!'**

Terry Molloy's a funny guy. When I e-mail him about doing an interview, he suggests I give him call. He's just about to jump in the car and head up to Birmingham and he figures he can kill two birds with one stone by doing the interview *en route* using the mobile on hands-free. I have this sudden image of Terry in the fast lane, in charge of several tons of metal, being distracted by my questions. I can almost see the headlines in the *Sun* now: 'Beloved actor maimed by jabbering journo. Fans say "Hanging's too good for her". I express my concerns and he promptly e-mails back: 'TONS of metal?? On a pushbike? With a rolled up map as a SatNav and a megaphone for hands-free ...?' He attaches a photo to prove his point.

When we finally do get to chat, it's like talking to a dozen different people at once. One moment he's Davros, the next he's *The Scarifyers'* Professor Dunning, then, in a blink, he's Mike Tucker from *The Archers*. With such a natural affinity for creating characters it's no wonder that he took to the stage. But acting is just one of many strings to his bow. He's also a musician, writer, director, producer and, he says chuckling, 'all round big head.'

So what came first? 'Well, I think acting has always been there, because it was in my family. My mother was on the stage until she married my father. I actually wanted to be a vet but my O Level results came out with not one single science subject. It took me three goes to get Maths, which put the nail in that coffin. But I'd always been interested in music and was very proficient on the clarinet. I thought about going to drama school but my father had just died and I would have needed to get a scholarship to go.'

Eventually Terry decided to study Music and Drama in Liverpool. Music was such an important part of his life that, after graduating, he seriously considered turning pro. 'The thing is,' he says, 'I'm a lazy swine and I knew I'd have to work really hard to be as good a musician as I wanted to be, but acting's dead easy and there are more days off!'

His first acting gigs were far from easy. Terry joined the Theatre Centre, who specialised in bringing drama to the classroom. It was a fabulous learning experience 'because there's no way you can fool children. Not when you're that close. If they sense any falseness, they'll just tell you.' Later Terry moved into repertory, starting at the Victoria Theatre in Stoke-on-Trent.

Soaps and Social Realism

The '60s was a thrilling time to be involved in theatre, with directors such as Joan Littlewood and Peter Cheeseman at the forefront of social-realist drama. The Victoria Theatre's speciality were plays that 'spoke' to the local community, such as *The Fight for Shelton Bar*, about the closure of a nearby steelworks. It was the sort of drama that had a special resonance for Terry: 'My family were originally from Tyneside, from the backstreets in North Shields. But I'd been fairly privileged growing up, because my father was in the Royal Air Force and I spent most of my time in preparatory schools and private boarding schools. So I was actually interacting with the people I didn't grow up with, but should have.'

After kicking about in rep for a few years, he was invited to work on the BBC's longest-running radio soap, *The Archers*, and radio remains his 'first love'. For an actor, the appeal is easy to appreciate. 'Radio gives you the most control over the finished product,' he says. 'That's because it is just you and the microphone and the listener at the other end. We always say that the pictures are so much better on radio but it's true, because your imagination is so much more vivid than any effect someone can conjure up. Also, as an actor, it doesn't matter what the hell you look like. I'm a fairly dumpy 66-year-old yet I can still play 30-, 40-year-olds, or different physical types, because it doesn't matter what you look like as long as you can do it vocally.'

Eventually Terry landed his first major first job in television, working on *Carrot del Sol*, an improvisational-style comedy show featuring one of the '70s' most popular comedians, Jasper Carrott. This led to a regular role in the hidden-camera show *Beadle's About* – and all without Terry bothering to find himself an agent!

Then, in 1984, Terry landed the role that assured him a place in the *Doctor Who* dictionary – Davros, the creator of the Daleks. 'I was invited to do a 26-part TV series set in a radio studio where I play a twit of a disc jockey who's like a cross between Tony Blackburn and Mike Reid – all a bit Smashy and Nicey! One of the directors on that was Matthew Robinson, and a month or so after we finished, he rang me up and said he'd been asked at short notice to take over a *Doctor Who* serial, and did

I know anything about the Daleks? I'd watched them in the days of Pat Troughton and William Hartnell – those were my Doctors – but I didn't know anything about Davros. So I went down to the BBC and watched Michael Wisher's performance in "Genesis of the Daleks". Matthew said that Michael wasn't available so they were looking for someone who could get as close as possible to his performance but bring something fresh to it. I thought it was really intriguing. It was like doing radio on television, because the mask is almost immobile – or it was in those days – so I'd have to do everything with my voice.'

I, Davros

Terry initially thought that the role would be a one-off – just five weeks' work. Thirty years later, he's still playing Davros on audio, and has seen the character evolve from 'a sort of intergalactic Hitler' to something 'much subtler'. Terry has played Davros on screen three times, in 'Resurrection of the Daleks', 'Revelation of the Daleks' and 'Remembrance of the Daleks', but it was only when the Big Finish audios arrived that he really began to explore who Davros was and where he came from. And it's clear that he's enjoying getting under the skin of such a complex character.

'Nobody is born evil,' Terry says, 'not even Davros. It was Gary Russell, who was then producing and directing for Big Finish, who came to me with the idea of doing a four-part mini-series called I, Davros with distinct echoes of I, Claudius. What we were going to do was explore his development from a 15-year old boy up to the point when the very first Dalek is actually brought to life. Through that we were able to explore the effect of nurture as well as his nature. It was too easy to say that he's just a bit bonkers. I started from the basis that he might have some form of autism. He has this savant mind. He's a brilliant scientist, a brilliant mathematician, can see and conceive phenomenal ways of dealing with problems, but in a totally focused way. He only sees the problem and focuses all his energy on finding a solution. But he tramples over anyone who gets between him and that solution. If we go back to "Revelation of the Daleks" you see the germ of that idea. Davros is in the middle of this necropolis, where all the dead people are kept until there's a cure for them. But he's turning them into food to feed the starving galaxy. From his point of view, he's doing good: he's the Great Healer. He doesn't see the moral dilemma. He can't see the problem from anyone else's perspective. The interesting part of the meetings between Davros and the Doctor is the intellectual chess games they play with each other in order for each of them to achieve what they want. There's this ongoing relationship between the two. They are on an intellectual par and they recognise that they have the same intellectual strengths. That, for me, was the fascinating thing about being able to carry on doing Davros and expanding the TV character out into the audio world.'

Davros is, Terry says, a character he has begun to wear 'like a comfy coat. The character I play in *The Archers* is like a pair of old slippers that I pop on every month, and Davros is the same. I'm not a method actor; I'm intuitive. Whatever jumps off the page and bites me on the bottom when I read a script is what I go with. I slip into him so easily now because I know where he's come from. That has come through doing a lot of scripts – audios especially – and talking about him. In fact, I probably know far too much about Davros. I'm probably more geeky than the geekiest geek I could find on the topic!'

Under the Mask

Terry may be comfy in the role, but in the chair, under the mask, it's a whole different ball game. 'It's horrendous,' he says. 'Probably one of the hardest things I've ever had to do.' The 'chair' itself is a pretty hefty item built 'of 4x2 timber with two 12-volt car batteries in the back,' which the actor has to drag along using his toes. 'Plus,' Terry says, with an audible shudder, 'you're bolted in so you can't get out to have a pee unless they de-rig you, and that takes 25 minutes.'

The mask itself is a claustrophobe's nightmare. 'You can see through the eye slits but only in one direction. You've got no peripheral vision at all and, because you're bolted into the thing, you can't move your head. You have to really feel your way around, which is why, in the early stories, we had these great long extenders on the switches, because I couldn't see where they were. I had to feel for them with my hand.'

For Terry's first outing as Davros in 'Resurrection of the Daleks', the prop department made Terry a new mask by doing a complete head mould. 'Actually,' he laughs, 'the older I get, the more I'm beginning to look like the mask! Soon I won't need one.'

It fitted like a glove but it was still very uncomfortable. Not only was Terry screwed into the chair, but his mouth, teeth and tongue had to be blacked out by gargling with black food dye. 'It was not a pleasant process!' he says with heartfelt sincerity. Worse was to come.

Fortunately, despite the heavy make-up, his young sons watching at home were completely unfazed by Dad's horrifying transformation.

'The first appearance of Davros, I remember, was in "Resurrection of the Daleks". I'm sitting behind a giant Perspex screen while dry ice is pumped in all around me. That's probably the coolest I've ever been as Davros, because I had to sit there for quite a while in order to get this mist to swirl out from under the door when they finally released me from cryogenic slumber. Some years later, my two sons, who were about five and seven, had got up very early in the morning and had "Resurrection" on the telly. I came downstairs just as Davros made his very first appearance and I thought, "Oh they're going to be terrified." But all I heard was my very youngest son Philip go, "Ooh look, it's my dear lovely daddy!" I thought, "Do I really come across like that!"'

For King and Country

On television, the discomfort of playing Davros was at least broken up by regular breaks, but when Terry appeared in the fan-produced stage play *The Trial of Davros* for the Children in Need charity, he was on stage for two-and-a-half hours non-stop. There were a number of occasions when he says that he could 'sense myself drifting off'. When, at the end, he stepped out of the chair, the whole interior was white with salt crystals generated by the heat and sweat. If it hadn't been for an on-stage technician feeding him water he believes he might have 'just gone completely'.

These days, as well as continuing to explore the 'loopy' world of Davros, Terry is also winning himself new fans playing Professor Dunning in the brilliantly-conceived and magnificently-performed *Scarifyers* audio series. This is produced by Bafflegab Productions and based on stories written by Simon Barnard and Paul Morris. The team behind it are *Doctor Who* fans, and Terry was paired up with Nicholas Courtney, who played DCI Lionheart – an outrageously rambunctious copper who suffers fools with no gladness at all. The series is set in the 1930s and blends real-life events with supernatural happenings, investigated by Lionheart and Dunning, for King, country and MI13. It's all terribly British and wonderfully daffy.

'What I like about it,' Terry says, 'is that it's from that period when you had proper goodies and baddies and they fought with lantern jaws and a pipe clenched between gritted teeth. We occasionally refer, in a fond and kindly sort of way, to lines or ideas from old film scripts, as an homage to the original. *The Devil of Denge Marsh* for instance leans on *The Wicker Man* – except we have a wicker fish!'

Nicholas Courtney's death in February 2011 meant that the duo's last story together was *The Magic Circle*, and for Nick's friends and fans, that story had something of an emotional ending. 'We had to think really hard about whether or not we should carry on. We had a story on the stocks ready to go, but Nick became more and more ill during that year and wasn't able to it. So eventually Simon approached David Warner, who very readily took on the role of Harry "Thumper" Crow, and we did the same story we would have done with Nick, except Lionheart is dead, but we don't know it.'

In the story, Stephen Thorne – another *Doctor Who* alumni – plays a music hall comic who gets killed and then, at the end, is revealed to have been taken over by the ghost of Lionheart. 'Stephen and Nick,' Terry continues, 'were the closest of friends in real life, and Stephen has this amazing ability to impersonate Nick's voice, so when he reveals himself at the end as being Lionheart, it felt like Nick was in the studio with us. I remember getting the CD and listening to it on the A1, *en route* to visit family in Tyneside, and I had to pull over. I was just in floods of tears.'

Though no-one could ever quite fill Nick Courtney's shoes, David Warner has now played Harry 'Thumper' Crow in three stories, and fans are eagerly awaiting the next instalment of a series that could run and run. Terry's also back as Davros in another seventh Doctor audio story, 'Daleks Among Us', for Big Finish. And he remains very active on the fan circuit. So has he noticed any difference between *Doctor Who* fans and *The Archers* fans? 'Well, if *Doctor Who* fans are considered as anoraks, *The Archers* fans are definitely Barbours! But really I'd say the difference is that most *The Archers* fans listen to the programme with their tongues placed firmly in their cheeks. They take it all with a very large pinch of salt, whereas there are quite a few *Doctor Who* fans for whom it is terribly, terribly real. I'm not denigrating that at all, but at times you need a bit of perspective. I'm not Davros. In fact I'm really a nice guy.' And that's true. He is.

The Aristocrat: Sarah Sutton

When Sarah Sutton joined the TARDIS in 1981, the actress, who was nicknamed 'Basingstoke' by Tom Baker, added an unmistakable touch of class to the proceedings. Sarah played the young aristocrat Nyssa of Traken who, over the next two years, grew into a confident and compassionate young woman, eventually leaving the Doctor to tend the infected Lazars onboard the derelict space station *Terminus*. She also proved to be a great role model for brainy geek girls everywhere …

You were a child actor … ?
Yes, I started acting when I was very young. I went to ballet school when I was about seven, and while I was at the school, an agent came in to see the end-of-term shows and she spotted me. She was looking for someone for the part of Baby Roo in a West End production of *Winnie the Pooh* and thought that I'd be perfect for it. Initially the director wouldn't see me, because he wanted a boy to play Baby Roo, but she nagged and nagged and nagged until eventually he said, 'For goodness sake, I'll see her!' So I went to the audition in London. There were 99 little boys and me and I got the part! And I thought 'Yeees!' I did that for three Christmas seasons, and then I got my first television when I was 11.

You were already a bit of a seasoned pro by the time that *Doctor Who* came along. Were there any roles that you particularly enjoyed?
I worked a lot when I was younger but I think the BBC serial *The Moon Stallion* was my favourite. I played a young blind girl and the part took quite a deal of preparation and thought.

Did you know when you auditioned for the role of Nyssa in 'The Keeper of Traken' that you'd be joining the TARDIS crew?
No. When I initially met the director, John Black, there was no suggestion of me staying on.

I have to ask about the clothes, because it was the '80s …
Yes! The clothes. The hair – that '80s hair! Makes me shudder!

Did you have any say in what you wore?
No, not really. I was very lucky in that my purple trouser suit was very practical, and Janet [Fielding]'s outfit, with that tight skirt and heels,

wasn't. As an actor, you're always very pleased if you do have something that is vaguely practical, because with outdoor filming, it's a necessity.

It looks very hot. Was it?
It was quite hot actually. 'The Keeper of Traken' outfit had two layers, with real fur – not very PC now – but it was my favourite outfit. That and my very last outfit were my favourites. I also liked the stripy one from 'Snakedance', but Peter [Davison] didn't like that at all, so it didn't stay very long.

Is it true that in your last story, 'Terminus', you specifically asked to wear something sexy?
I don't remember saying that! I might have done, but I don't remember it! I was only 19 when I started *Doctor Who* and the character had matured quite a bit over my two years. I probably thought it would be nice to have something more grown-up for that last episode. I thought that Janet used to get all the sexy kit while I was up to my neck in fur.

Did you have any favourite episodes?
Peter didn't like this story, but I liked 'Black Orchid' because I got to wear some different clothes and got to be someone else! 'Earthshock' I quite enjoyed, and I enjoyed my last story funnily enough, although it was sad for me because I knew I was leaving. In fact, I found it all a bit too much – a bit emotional – but it was quite a good story.

What was it like working with Nicholas Courtney in 'Mawdryn Undead'?
It was lovely. He was such a nice man and such a big part of *Doctor Who* history. It felt right to have him in.

You were there when Tom Baker regenerated into Peter Davison. How did the two actors compare?
To be honest, at the time, Tom absolutely terrified me! He was always very nice but just so imposing. Peter was lovely and I think we [with Janet and Mark Strickson] did make a good team. We did have a laugh actually and I have very fond memories of being in *Doctor Who*. It was a very happy time.

Was it your decision to leave?
No, it wasn't my choice. I think producer John Nathan-Turner had decided

that Nyssa should go. It's a shame [that] when I was in *Doctor Who* it was a very crowded TARDIS. There were a lot of assistants and it was a shame because no-one ever really got a decent story. For example, in 'Kinda', in order for Janet to have a good story someone had to go and have a headache and go and lie down for three episodes – and that was me! So I think it was a shame in a way, but it's been very nice doing some of the Big Finish audios. Finally Nyssa's got the chance to actually work with the Doctor on a one-to-one basis, and I think that relationship works really well.

Were you given much warning about leaving?
I think when the contracts were signed for the next season, they said 'That's going to be your last. That's it.' It's all very brutal! It's tough, but you get used to it. There are not very many jobs in the acting business where you get to work for such long periods of time. Normally it's a few months. Then you stop and go on to something else. But to be in a long-running series is great, and I think it must be very tough for the big soap stars. It must be a big shock getting written out after having had regular work for years at a time.

Making that transition from a child actor to an adult actor is notoriously hard. How did you find it?
It was very, very difficult. In fact, after I left *Doctor Who* I didn't do much work. I don't know if it was *Doctor Who* that finished my career or circumstances, but it was very difficult. When you're a child actor, you're a big fish in a small pond, and then suddenly, when you get older, you realise that actually there are a lot of people in the business. It is very difficult.

What happened after *Doctor Who*? Can you give us a quick run-down?
It'll be a very quick run-down! I did an episode of *Casualty*; I did a play that toured, called *Policy For Murder*; and that was pretty much it really. I got married and had a daughter and I don't live in London anymore. I live in the country.

Have you left acting for good?
Well, actually, for the first time in a long time, I've thought, now that my daughter's grown up, I might have time to think about myself again. But it's been so long and the business has changed so much. It all looks very scary now! I don't know. I might give it another go, because I don't

really have anything to lose. When you get older, I think perhaps you don't worry quite so much.

It's a good time to do it now that *Doctor Who* is so hot again …
That's a very good point! I think you're right. Perhaps now is the time for me to give it another whack!

What would you like to do?
I love things like *The Inspector Lynley Mysteries*. I love detectivey type things. *Dalziel and Pascoe* and all that. That's the sort of thing I watch on television, so I'd love to be in something like that. In fact, I'd love to be in something with Peter again, actually, but he's so busy. He's always doing something.

You mentioned that you've returned to the role of Nyssa with Big Finish. How does voice work compare to 'straight' acting?
Oh, I love it. I love it because I'd done quite a lot of radio plays when I was younger with the BBC, so I enjoy that medium a lot. It's great fun. It's great not to have to worry about what you look like! You can just use your voice – and hearing yourself back on cans, I find fascinating. I absolutely adore doing the Big Finishes.

What's the fan reaction been like to the audios?
Very good. I haven't listened to them, as I don't like listening to myself, but people will say to me 'I really like "Spare Parts"' or whatever, so I'm really pleased. The reaction's been excellent.

So presumably you don't like to watch yourself either?
No. I don't like to. Sometimes, when they call me in to do the commentaries for the DVDs, I think, 'I need to watch this,' so they send a copy and I sit and watch and think, 'Oh my God!' But it sparks some memories of things to talk about.

What do you think of the new series?
I haven't watched a lot of it but I'm very, very jealous! It's fantastic. Wonderful special effects, and things are very different. The assistants have much bigger roles. Sadly they've done the trick of bringing back an old assistant – Lis Sladen – so they're not going to be doing that again. Which is a shame, because I would love to be in it now!

The Space Pirate: Liza Goddard

'Can you believe that was my own hair! It was back-combed with blue spray, which, typically, came out green'

Liza Goddard talks 20 to the dozen. Despite being in her sixties, she still has all the frothy enthusiasm of a teenager about to go on a first date. Her sentences all seem to end in exclamation marks. I like her a lot.

Since finding fame playing Clarissa 'Clancy' Merrick in *Skippy the Bush Kangaroo*, the Smethwick-born actress has worked steadily, notching up credits in TV series such as *Take Three Girls*, *The Brothers*, *Bergerac* and *Woof!*

Having a dad in the business meant that acting was always on the radar. 'My father was a producer and director at the BBC,' she says, ' so I grew up surrounded by theatrical people. When I was six I was used as an extra in [the 1956 BBC series] *Jesus of Nazareth* with Tom Fleming – you know, "Suffer the little children" and all that. I was suddenly on live television and I thought it was marvellous. I think that got it all started, really. From then on, all I wanted was to be a child actress like Hayley Mills, but my father wouldn't let me!'

A move to Australia in '65, when Dad was appointed Head of Drama at the Australian Broadcasting Corporation, changed all that. It was while down under that Liza finally got the chance to scratch that acting itch, with appearances in Australian shows like *Adventures of the Seaspray* and *Homicide*. Despite a burgeoning career, though, she still managed to have 'a completely ordinary childhood. Nobody takes showbusiness seriously in Australia!' she laughs. 'They're all very down-to-earth.'

Children and Animals
W C Fields is credited with the much-used line, 'Never work with children or animals.' Presumably not only because they're unpredictable, but because no actor wants to be upstaged by a cute marsupial. 'The trouble with them – there were lots of Skippies – was that they were completely untrained,' Liza reveals. 'Usually in shots, they organised it so that there was a prop man hanging onto Skippy's tail, so it wouldn't run off. So you'd film as much as you could before the kangaroo ran off and then you'd wait around for someone to catch it and bring it back. There was a prize at the end of the week for the crew member who caught the most Skippies! But the wonderful thing that you learn working with children and animals is

that you must always get it right, because the take where the animal gets it right is the one they use. If you get it wrong, you'll look an idiot! So the one good lesson I've learnt from working with children and animals could really be a good lesson for life: "Get it right!"'

Fortunately *Skippy the Bush Kangaroo* proved to be less of a hindrance and more a passport to success for Liza. 'I did a lot of theatre and television over in Australia. I was in *Skippy* for two seasons and all I thought at the time was that two years is a good job. I've just recently done a couple of days' filming for *Grandpa in My Pocket*, and it's reminded me how spoilt you are as a child actor. I was a teenager in this world of adults, and your every need is taken care of. You're picked up in the morning. You're provided with breakfast and lunch. It was just a wonderful time. But what was quite extraordinary was that it was only when I moved away from Australia that I realised how huge the show was. It was an international success. Amazing!'

More success was to follow. Returning to the UK, Liza landed a role in a new series called *Take Three Girls*, which featured the lives and loves of three single women in swinging London. It was radical stuff for the time. 'It was the first programme to star young women, the first programme to have a pop song as its theme, and it was the BBC's first colour drama. It was enormously successful, and again we had no idea. It was a jolly good job and had wonderful scripts. We were just blessed with our writers!'

Liza has always been attracted to 'strong woman' roles, and when we spoke she was just about to go on tour with *Go Back for Murder*, based on Agatha Christie's Hercule Poirot novel *Five Little Pigs*. Liza plays a 'sensible-shoe'd governess … Agatha Christie always wrote at least one blue-stockinged women's libber in these plays and Miss Williams is just that,' she says with evident relish.

Mrs Jessop in *Woof!*, Philippa Vale in *Bergerac* and Kiri in *Doctor Who*'s 'Terminus' also feature on her list of most memorable roles. They too are strong, independent woman, which she found 'great fun to play.' And you have to agree. What would you rather be, a damsel in distress or a fearsome space pirate?

Monsters and Zombies

'Terminus', as a production, was fraught with technical difficulties, which meant that recording overran and scenes had to be rushed – much to the frustration of the regular cast. The one thing that even the severest critic would agree with though, is that the sets and costumes looked great, especially Kiri's wonderfully retro outfit that looks like something straight out of a '50s B-movie ... although Liza wasn't entirely convinced.

'"Terminus" was brilliant fun because Peter Davison is just lovely. We had the lot ... spaceships, a monster, zombies, laser beams ... but the costume ... Can you believe that was my own hair! It was back-combed with blue spray, which, typically, came out green. The helmet kept on steaming up, so you'd have to keep taking it off and wiping it dry, and my gun was useless. Every time I drew it, the end fell off, which caused great hilarity of course. But the worst thing was that the Garm, played by R J Bell, got so hot inside his rubber suit that he would sweat and sweat and then black out. They'd have to keep taking his head off and taking him outside to cool off. Poor man!'

Despite the problems, Liza had a ball. 'Dominic Guard played my sidekick, Olvir, and we had a wonderful time doing it. I will always remember going to lunch with all these lepers. There would be Bruce Forsyth and all these other BBC stars and then us and all these zombies walking into the canteen. Hilarious.'

Liza also enjoyed catching up with the director, Mary Ridge, whom she had met working on *The Brothers*. 'Of course you just took it for granted that women directed,' Liza says, 'but really they were pioneers.'

Although Liza's appeared in *Doctor Who* only once, she was married to a Doctor – Colin Baker – whom she met while working on *The Brothers*. A rumour has been doing the rounds on the internet for years, effectively blaming Liza for Colin's dismissal from the show. According to former *Doctor Who* production manager Gary Downie, writing in *Doctor Who Magazine* (Issue 338) in January 2004: 'There's a history between Michael Grade [BBC1's Controller at the time] and Colin. Liza Goddard was Colin's wife. And she was Michael Grade's best friend. The divorce was acrimonious and she moved into Michael Grade's house while she was getting over the divorce. And I'll say no more. Michael Grade was determined. He did not want Colin working for the BBC.'

When I ask her if the story is true, Liza is clearly horrified. 'It's such a load of nonsense. He was my boss at London Weekend Television – a good boss – but we were never even close friends. I certainly didn't go to his house to get over my marriage. Why would anyone say that?' Scurrilous stories that are published as 'fact' are nothing new, but Liza is keen to put the record straight. 'No, it's not true at all. Colin was married to his present wife at the time. It's amazing how these stories get about, but then there's a lot of fiction about people on the web!'

As she talks, Liza's conversation is peppered with laughter. As well as acting, she's a devoted mother, grandmother and animal lover. An ideal day would, she says, be spent out and about on the beach with her four rescue dogs or her pony, Tufty. She's clearly a woman who loves life and lives it to the full, especially since a cancer scare in the late 1990s. 'Well, I think it's true what they say. With something like cancer, you're suddenly faced with your own mortality. You blunder along in life, thinking you're never going to die, and one day it hits you that you might, and you'd better pull yourself together to enjoy it to the full. Now I treat each day with joy. I wake up and think "I'm alive. Hurrah!"'

The Sixth Doctor: Colin Baker

When he burst onto our screens as the sixth Doctor in March 1984, Colin Baker stepped into *Who* history – and controversy. On the surface, Colin's Doctor was an unstable personality: egotistical, bombastic and irascible. Unpeel the layers, and the sixth Doctor emerges as a much more sympathetic character, with all of his predecessors' tenacity, wit and compassion. Originally unfairly blamed by some for the show's hiatus, these days Colin Baker enjoys his place as one of classic *Who's* most popular Doctors …

Was there anyone in particular who inspired you to act?
I was brought up in Manchester and a lot of plays tried out up there. I saw people like Paul Scofield, who was wonderful, but it was the whole experience – the theatre – that I thought was magical. Then one day, I was sitting watching a production of *The King and I* at the Palace Theatre with my mother and I said 'I'd love to do that.' The man sitting in front turned round and said, 'I'm the Chairman of the North Manchester Amateur Operatic Society. Come along next Friday and audition.' And I did. That's where it all started.

So you sing?
No! I did the plays, although I did do a Gilbert and Sullivan opera – *HMS Pinafore* –for a year. I played Sir Joseph Porter and people seemed to think I was all right.

But didn't you train to be a solicitor?
Yes, but I never wanted to be one! I wanted to be an actor, but when I was 18 my father told me what I was going to do – and 18 year-olds back then did as they were told. Then five years later I thought, in the words of the song, 'It's my life,' and I jumped ship and went to the London Academy of Music and Dramatic Arts (LAMDA). So I was 26 when I started acting.

What was your big break?
There were three, I suppose. The first was in 1972. I did *War and Peace* with Anthony Hopkins. He played Pierre and I was Anatole. That got me a level of recognition. Then, two years after that, I joined a series called *The Brothers*, which was hugely popular in the '70s, and I became the most hated man in Britain. So I went from being the most hated man to being the most loved man in 1983 when I joined *Doctor Who*.

Which did you prefer out of *War and Peace* and *The Brothers*?
They were both great. No preference! Villains are always good to play.

Actors always seem to say that. What's the appeal of playing the villain?
Well, you've got plenty to get your teeth into, and at the end of the day you've been horrible to everybody, so you get it all out of your system. You can go home and be nice to people. When you've been nice all day, it can be a bit trying!

When you got *Doctor Who*, did you base your performance on any of the pervious Doctors?
No. I was a fan of the show and I used to watch it. I probably would have never gone to a convention, or anything like that, but I enjoyed it and liked it. I'd watched all the previous Doctors so I had an idea of what the programme was about and I just did my own thing really. Drew little bits from each of them.

I remember watching your first episode and it was so exciting. Peter Davison was good, but he was never an exciting Doctor to watch. How much was you, how much was the script?
No, he wasn't exciting, was he? Not like me! (Laughs) The fact that the Doctor was manic was the script, but the script was probably like that because they thought I was like that in real life. As with any performance, it was a combination. You need the script in the first place, but the personality of the Doctor was certainly my invention.

Everyone must ask you about the costume. How much of a say did you have in the final look?
I never cared for it, but it was a reflection of the era in which it was made. The '80s were the time of glam rock and all that. Looking back on it now it's a bit OTT, but luckily I was on the inside looking out.

Did you have any say in choosing assistants?
No. Lovely Nicola was there when I came. When she went, along came Bonnie Langford, and they were both charming and delightful. But I had no say.

Do you have a favourite story?
I suppose 'The Two Doctors', because I got to work with Patrick Troughton who was, for me, the best Doctor, because he did the hard job. He did the

first regeneration and, without him, I wouldn't be talking to you now.

What was he like?
Charming and disarming and friendly. He wasn't actory. He was just a nice bloke.

What do you think of the new series?
I am very impressed. I think Russell T Davies is a genius. What he's done is he's retained the heart of *Doctor Who*, the essence of *Doctor Who*, but he's given it a 21st Century twist. They've all been superb Doctors but I really envy Christopher Eccleston his costume. That's the one I wanted. Long black coat like in *The Matrix*, you know? That would have been fab.

Do you find that, even when you're appearing in a play, there are lots of *Who* fans in the audience – and does it bother you that they've come not to see Colin Baker the actor, but Colin Baker the Doctor?
No. Why should it bother me? If my name and the association with *Doctor Who* get people into theatres who might not otherwise go, then great. I often meet *Doctor Who* fans outside the stage door, and one or two have never been to the theatre before but came because I was in the play. It turns them on to theatre, which is lovely.

What's been the most satisfying moment of your career so far?
I suppose the whole thing really. I can't separate it out because every job brings new challenges. *Doctor Who* is the obvious one to say, but in fact everything I do, I wouldn't do if it wasn't interesting and usually satisfying.

Is there anything you'd like to do that you haven't had the chance to do, yet?
Just more, more, more, more! I'd like to have a series on TV. I'm too old to be a policeman now, but a detective show would be fun. That's what I'd love to do.

Do you have an autobiography in the pipeline?
No, but there ought to be. I do have a tale to tell! But I'm far too young.

Lots of people would read it.
Promise you'll read it?

Absolutely.
Then I'll write it!

The Other Side of the Table: Sylvester McCoy and Lalla Ward

'I was inclined to let her jump, but my wife's much nicer than me and persuaded me to go and talk to her. So I signed an autograph and saved her life!'

I often think how much fun it would be if life were like a computer game. You'd get to erase all those embarrassing bits, and replay all your favourites. If it were, then conventions would definitely be at the top of my most replayed moments. This got me wondering what perspective the show's stars might have on the whole convention phenomenon. What, I wondered, is it like to be on the other side of the signing table, especially when you've been involved in such a cult show? Their answers would have filled several save slots, but here's a selection …

Who's That?

Lalla Ward now spends much of her time writing and painting children's books, but to many she will forever be the second Romanadvoratrelunder (Romana) to Tom Baker's Doctor. Lalla, like most of the celebrities I've spoken to, seemed genuinely puzzled by the whole fandom thing, especially autograph collecting. 'Why do people do it?' she asked. 'You tell me.' Remembering that I was supposed to be doing the interview, I quickly wrested back the reins and asked her to think back to her first signing event. What memories did she have?

'It was in 1985 in Chicago … and I vividly remember it because I got paid more than I had for my whole first season of *Doctor Who*,' she laughed. 'I was just staggered at how many people turned up. It was a real eye-opener, although to be honest, I had a suspicion that we were just the sideshow. That most people were there to dress up!'

So what does she get out of it these days? 'For me, the shows are a great chance to catch up with old friends and meet people for the first time, because of course I never worked with the other Doctors, although I did go to drama school with Peter Davison. However, I don't understand autograph collecting at all. Let's not beat about the bush – the whole thing is very odd!'

Peter Purves, who played Steven Taylor to William Hartnell's Doctor, enjoys meeting the fans, but he agrees with Lalla. 'It's nice that people are enthusiastic,' he says, 'but I don't understand it, especially when the same people turn up again and again.' In fact Peter admits that he has 'no real sense of nostalgia. I'm more interested in what's happening now.'

Seventh Heaven

For Sylvester McCoy, signing events have more of an immediate appeal. Sylvester has had a varied career, but will probably be best remembered for his stint as the seventh Doctor.

Sylvester has been doing signing events almost since they offered him the job. 'I started on a Tuesday,' he commented, 'and by the Thursday I was at my first convention.' So what's the appeal? 'Would some power the gift to give us; to see ourselves as others see us,' he grinned, quoting the words of the poet Robert Burns. 'And I have – and it's very strange! Really though,' he continued, 'I get to exercise a little-used comedy muscle. When I first started, I was always asked the same questions and I would give the same answers. Then, slowly, I started to improvise and have fun'.

For those who don't know, Sylvester's early career was spent touring with the Ken Campbell Roadshow. He played a circus stuntman called Sylvester McCoy – which is where he got his stage name. So the whole experience is like a return to his comedy roots. 'It's a little like doing stand up, which I really enjoy,' he says.

Any memorable moments? 'Well, certainly the oddest was early on at an event in Minneapolis. I was asked if, now that I was so universally famous, I was afraid of being shot. Well I hadn't been until they'd said that!'

Mary Tamm, who played the first incarnation of Romana, also had clear memories of how intense the fans can be. During one event, she recalled, 'the crowds were so frantic that we had to be surrounded by security 24 hours a day. It was totally exhausting. One lady even followed me into the loos and pushed a book under the cubicle door for me to sign!' Which was the cue for a rush of similar reminiscences.

Mad Moments

Sylvester's oddest autograph request came, he claims, on a cruise ship. With Sylvester, you're never sure if there's a large dose of leg-pulling going on, and there was certainly a playful glint in his eye as he related this apparently 'true' tale of how he prevented a would-be suicide. 'Some woman had decided that having met the Doctor, her life's ambitions were fulfilled and she was going to throw herself off the ship. Now I was inclined to let her jump, but my wife's much nicer than me and persuaded me to go and talk to her. So I signed an autograph and saved her life!'

Peter's oddest fan encounter began innocently enough. 'A young lady asked me for an autograph. I looked up and couldn't see anything to sign, then she just pulled down her pants and asked me to sign her bare bottom.' Did he? 'Yes! Although,' he mused, 'I might have been more reluctant if it had been a man.'

Luckily Lalla has never had any particularly odd encounters. 'I don't know why,' she smiled, 'but people seem to think that I'm terribly posh and treat me in a very deferential way. Which I'm all for! I actively promote the image of inaccessibility. Please,' she says, with almost heartfelt urgency, 'don't give me your knickers to sign!' Now ... you have been told.

The Movellan & the Evil Henchman: Tony Osoba

**'Suddenly, we became aware that the audience were really restless …
Eventually, whatever was bothering them became too much for one
American, who shouted out "Excuse me, sir, your headdress is on fire!"'**

Tony Osoba is in a confessional mood. Despite being a Scot, he doesn't
really like haggis, favours Tottenham Hotspur and Rangers equally, and
was never really scared of the Daleks.

Tony is one of those actors who seem to have spent their entire lives
in the public eye. Although he loves the theatre, he's appeared in over
200 TV shows playing everything from Glaswegian tough nut 'Jock'
McLaren in the prison sitcom *Porridge* to Detective Sergeant Charles
Jarvis in *Dempsey and Makepeace*. He also has two *Doctor Who* credits
to his name, having appeared in both 'Destiny of the Daleks' (1979) and
'Dragonfire' (1987). In fact there seem to be very few types of role that
he hasn't taken. Although six foot one, he's even played a jockey. Perhaps
needless to say, that was on the radio!

Born in Glasgow, to a Scottish mother and a Nigerian father, Tony
found his childhood 'a safe and happy time; although,' he admits, 'we didn't
have a great deal of money. My parents got divorced when I was only six,
so my two sisters and I were brought up by my mother. My father was very
successful at the time and resented not having custody of us. So he made
life quite difficult for her. However, she was a determined woman – very
supportive – and would always back us in anything we wanted to do.'

Back then, what Tony wanted to do more than anything in the world
was design cars. He covered his school exercise books with pictures of
them, and if he ever got a toy it had to be a Dinky car. 'If I got anything
different, I was always disappointed, although I was well brought up, so
didn't show it', he laughs.

When it came to exam time, Tony wrote to all the major car firms to
ask what the best course of study was to be a car designer. They all replied,
but the news wasn't good. 'All of them said, "We can't guarantee that you'd
join the car design department, but if you did, you might only get the task
of designing the rear roof!" and I wanted to do the whole thing!'

It was then that his thoughts turned to acting. 'Although the idea came
upon me over two or three weeks, it wasn't a whim. It was something that

I gradually grew to realise I'd always been interested in. I remember, with quite a degree of trepidation, quietly saying to my mother that I'd like to talk something over with her, and of course she was alarmed! So I said "I want to be an actor" and, all credit to her, after her initial surprise, she was hugely supportive. I had a while before I went to college, so I went to what was the foremost theatre in Glasgow at the time, the Citizen's Theatre, and asked if I could work there. I said I didn't want to be paid, I was just happy to come and do anything, and of course they said "Great!" I learnt lots of different things on different shows – such as going up into the flies and working the thunder sheets – but then the director asked if I'd like to do some tiny acting parts so, even before starting college, I had a bit of a grounding. Then, while in college, I was in a show that made Leonard Rossiter hugely famous, called *The Resistible Rise of Arturo Ui*. It was an enormous success and we took it to the Edinburgh Festival.'

Initiation by Fire

After studying at the Royal Scottish Academy of Music and Drama, Tony moved to London. It proved to be an exciting time to be a young man in the capital. 'The world really did seem to open up,' Tony recalls. 'There was a celebration of youth, led by pop music, which fed into everything. There was a feeling that you could do anything you turned your mind to. Starting out as an actor, jobs weren't plentiful, but oddly it did feel like something would come along. It was a very positive time.'

After spending a year in Amsterdam in a production of the rock musical *Hair*, Tony joined the Royal Shakespeare Company during Trevor Nunn's epic Roman Season – in which Nunn produced all of Shakespeare's Roman plays. It was a thrilling experience, although one event almost put paid to Tony's career before it had properly taken wing. Tony: 'We were doing *Coriolanus*. Nicol Williamson was playing Coriolanus, Patrick Stewart was Aufidius, King of the Volscies, and I and two other actors were playing the older, wiser Council of the Volscies. The way Trevor had arranged it, we appeared in a box above the stage. I had a massive helmet with a long semi-circle of peacock feathers stretching out as wide as your arms. To get into the box, I had to shuffle sideways to allow for this headdress. The third wise Volsci was the wonderful Don Henderson, who was carrying a torch with a real flame. It was the very first night and Patrick was on stage giving a long speech about attacking Rome. Suddenly, we became aware that the audience were really restless. We'd only been going 15 minutes – so we hoped that they weren't bored yet! Eventually, whatever was bothering them became too much for one American, who shouted out "Excuse me, sir, your headdress is on fire!"'

What the audience could see and the actors in the box couldn't, was the apparent sacrificial burning of an actor alive, before their eyes, as Tony's headdress went up in flames! Tony quickly untied the helmet and, at a loss as to what to do next, he passed it to a rather alarmed Don Henderson. Luckily, front of stage was a huge water drum, into which Don threw the burnt offering. Needless to say, by that time, any chance of continuing the scene was shot!

Doing Porridge

It was just two years after Tony's near-immolation that he landed the job that would turn out to be one of his happiest acting experiences – *Porridge*. Tony takes up the tale: 'I was doing a documentary series called *Churchill's People* with a wonderful director called Michael Hayes. By chance, he bumped into Syd Lotterby in the corridors of the BBC. Sid mentioned that there was a role for a young actor in the new sitcom he was directing and Michael suggested me. They had already made about four episodes out of the first six in the series, so I went along to the rehearsal rooms in Acton and was introduced to Ronnie Barker. Ronnie was a huge star, so it was all a bit intimidating.'

Was he nervous? 'I was nervous, but not as nervous as I should have been, because Ronnie and Syd were really kind and supportive. I can't speak highly enough of them. Even though Ronnie was the star of the show, he was very generous and never resented other actors having their moment. I remember David Jason appeared in three episodes. He was maybe 30 at the time and he was playing Blanco, who was Methuselah's age, and had to spend hours in make-up. Ronnie kept a weather eye on it, because he was a perfectionist. Not in a dictatorial way, but he always wanted to do the best. The whole thing was an enormously happy experience for me. I looked forward to going to work every day!' Although Tony's character, Jock McLaren, was only meant to be in one episode, they liked him so much that he became a regular guest in the show.

'Doing porridge' is British slang for serving a prison sentence, and *Porridge* remains one of British television's most popular sitcoms. In 2004 it was voted Number Seven in Britain's Top 50 comedy greats. Much of its popularity was due to the beautifully-realised characters of Fletcher (played by Ronnie Barker), Godber (Richard Beckinsale) and McLaren, who spend their time inside trying to win little victories over the system.

Perhaps not surprisingly, the show was particularly popular in prisons – something that Tony discovered could be quite embarrassing. 'There was one time I was at a party, and this man came and sat next to me and says, "I know you, don't I?" and I say, "No, I don't think we've ever met." He starts looking round and eventually whispers "Pentonville. Pentonville wasn't it? Yeah, Landing 14. That was it!" I didn't want to make him feel like a fool, so I ended up saying that I'd never been to Pentonville, as if maybe I'd been to another prison!'

Daleks and Dragonfire

If *Porridge* was 'one of the jobs' that Tony looks back on 'with the greatest of fondness', then the other is certainly *Doctor Who*. Ken Grieve, who directed 'Destiny of the Daleks', and Chris Clough, who directed 'Dragonfire', were 'just two of the most delightful directors I've ever worked with,' Tony says. 'Is it just a coincidence that they both worked on *Doctor Who*, or does *Doctor Who* just attract wonderful directors? You tell me.'

Tony's first appearance, playing the robotic Movellan named Lan in 'Destiny of the Daleks', was all 'fun and laughter. We Movellans had the most extraordinary costumes. Long silver body-hugging tights, long silver dreadlocks and Cleopatra-type eye make-up. I knew Suzanne Danielle [Agella] and Peter Straker [Commander Sharrel] and we were always laughing. Peter would always have this twinkle in his eye and, as soon as the cameras weren't rolling, he'd be: "What on Earth do you look like?" To which I always replied, "Well, you're no better. Look at yourself!" We giggled a lot.'

Those costumes were pretty unforgiving too. 'We all were pretty slim in those days but you couldn't have an extra slice of something at lunchtime, that's for sure!' Tony chuckles. 'I also remember they were very cold. A lot of the location work was shot down in a quarry in Poole in Dorset – and it was freezing. As with so many things, they're done outside at the coldest time of the year. Don't ask me why! And of course every time we did a take, the sand would kick up and the poor old Wardrobe Department would have to come round and brush you down to try and keep these white costumes pristine. In fact my character, Lan, got shot by a Dalek, and of course I had to fall to the ground. You were always aware of the costume but, in a situation like that, you couldn't fuss about it. You just had to fall down and let someone else deal with the mud and mess! Strangely, I had the same problem of keeping an all-white costume spotless through the working day on "Dragonfire".'

That death sequence gave Tony a rather odd claim to *Doctor Who* fame. 'I've been told,' he says, 'that Lan is the only character ever to be shot by a Dalek and come back to life, at least in the classic series. I think David Tennant's Doctor has been shot and come back, but Doctors don't count, because they have all these magic tricks!'

Tony's next appearance in *Who* came eight years later when he played Sergeant Kracauer, leader of Kane's forces on the space-trading colony Iceworld. 'Dragonfire' gave Tony the joy of working with two very close friends, Tony Selby, who returned to the show to play Sabalom Glitz (first featured in 'The Trial of a Time Lord'), and Shirin Taylor, who was the customer that Ace pours a drink over. The three friends were actually interviewed about their experiences for a 15-minute documentary called *Friends Like Who*, which was made to mark the DVD release of 'Dragonfire' in the box set *Ace Adventures*.

Tony has very fond memories of the recording of 'Dragonfire' and especially applauds the set designers and constructors 'for a very atmospheric set, although the fragility of parts of it meant being aware and on guard at all times.'

So how did the two shows and the two Doctors compare? 'On "Destiny of the Daleks", my feeling was that we knew we were making a programme predominantly aimed at children and teenagers, although quite a few adults still followed it. Eight years later, that seemed to have changed. Nothing was spoken of, but the perception was that we were doing it for a slightly older audience – teenagers and adults. As for Tom's and Sylvester's Doctors, certainly they were very different personas. Tom Baker always studied and thought long and hard about each scene. Some of the older Doctors, like Hartnell's, might have got lost in their thoughts. Tom's Doctor did that too, but he was never bumbling. Tom's character was based on Tom's natural authority. His Doctor was a Doctor with no doubts. The humour was there, but the Doctor himself wasn't a humorous character. Sylvester's Doctor was slightly softer, more humorous. But underlying everything were the intellect and otherworldliness that make the Doctor so unique, and both Tom and Sylvester had those.'

Tom Baker has said that playing the Doctor 'killed his career stone dead', because he'd had so much fun playing the role that even in the theatre he'd look down and see *Doctor Who* scarves in the audience, and want to please the fans rather than play the character. It's a comment that Tony completely understands. 'It's difficult for actors to carry the burden of a successful role,' he comments, 'but even so, it would be enormous fun to be the Doctor.' Would he have liked to have been considered for the role? 'I'd have loved it,' he confirms. In fact, he already has one vital qualification for the job.

'As a kid, I never really found the Daleks terribly frightening,' Tony says. 'The original ones did look like they had a sink plunger for an arm – and they couldn't go up stairs. So I always thought I could handle them if it came to it! Meeting a Dalek face to face for the first time wasn't quite as intimidating as you might imagine either. Seeing them being manhandled off the props truck and then being rather cumbersomely manoeuvred into position, rather lowers the reading on the fright scale. Eventually we were even relaxed enough to sit with our back propped against one while enjoying a hot drink during a coffee break. Nonetheless, there was the knowledge (and an inner satisfaction) that you were in the presence of one of the meanest and most iconic all time "bad guys" of British television – and all due respect for that!'

The Werewolf: Jessica Martin

'John [Nathan-Turner] … declared that anyone who could embody Judy Garland would be able to embody the role of an alien Goth girl who turns into a werewolf.'

The one thing that Jessica Martin knows from experience is that in life, unlike the movies, there's no Willy Wonka factor. No golden ticket. If you want something, you have to go out and make it happen. Which is exactly what she did.

'I suppose that I wanted to act from a very early age,' she says. 'The biggest influence on me as a child was watching old black and white movies on TV on a Sunday afternoon. I idolised people like Greta Garbo, Jean Harlow, Judy Garland and contemporaries like Jenny Agutter and Hayley Mills. They were great role models. I spent a lot of my childhood wondering what it would be like to be in one of those wonderful old films, but it didn't happen for a long time because I followed quite an academic path. I did A Levels and went on to university. So it was a deferred dream, but it did actually come true.'

Jessica makes it sound easy, but making it happen required a hefty dose of talent. 'Well, it's funny that you should use the words "make it happen", because I do feel that you have to go out and meet opportunities head on. I studied English and Drama, so there was a purpose in my academic career. I came out of university with a place at the Webber Douglas Academy of Dramatic Art, but I couldn't take it up, because I had no money. But what I did have were two "selling points". One was that my father's a jazz pianist, so I'd been singing and performing with him from a very young age. I also had a talent for mimicry, which at the time I never took particularly seriously.'

Copy Cats
All that changed after a chance meeting at the Edinburgh Fringe Festival with an aspiring young impressionist called Rory Bremner, who is now a noted comic and satirist. Back then Rory was just another student with another Fringe act. 'I was doing a late-night, after-cabaret act with some chums,' Jessica recalls, 'and was doing impressions of people like Julie Andrews – who is still a classic – but also Toyah Wilcox and Kate Bush, who were very *de rigueur* at the time.' Rory was 'very impressed' and although that initial meeting was fleeting, the two caught up with each

159

other later in London.

'Time went on, I graduated and was going nowhere fast with an act that was dying on the fringe comedy circuit. Then, at one of the venues, I saw Rory absolutely bringing the house down.' Rory was doing a weekly radio news review show called *Week Ending* and they just happened to be looking for a female impressionist. Initially Jessica insisted that she didn't have a wide enough repertoire for the job, but Rory convinced her to give it a try. 'I used to quickly gen up on whichever woman was in the news,' Jessica says, 'and true enough, I found my repertoire expanding very rapidly. So I got fast-tracked to mainstream success through my impressions.' An audition for the satirical puppet show *Spitting Image* followed, along with regular appearances on the London Weekend Television show *Copycats*.

Jessica was 22 and suddenly 'had the television world at my feet … It was unbelievable, when I think back now,' she says. 'One day I was down in the dumps and I couldn't see how I was ever going to have a career, then within a year everything was happening. But for me the incredible thing was that I started getting spin-off things – pantomimes and musicals. I'd always wanted to act, but people were surprised when they found out I could do it. I wasn't just someone off the telly who could do silly voices.'

JNT

It was three years into a burgeoning career as an 'all-rounder' when Jessica's agent called to say that she'd been offered a character in *Doctor Who*. 'I was told that it was a fascinating and challenging character, so I was very curious. I went to the BBC's offices and I met the legendary JNT – John Nathan-Turner. I didn't know he was legendary back then, but now I do!' she laughs.

JNT was *Doctor Who*'s longest-serving producer and a larger-than-life personality. 'He was this leonine character in a Hawaiian shirt, with curly hair and jangling jewellery,' Jessica remembers. 'He looked for all the world like he was going to get up and do a turn, not audition someone. But he was utterly charming. The first thing he said to me was that he and Gary (Gary was John's partner in life as well as his favoured studio floor manager) had seen me on an episode of *Tarby and Friends*. I'd never met Tarby in my life, but suddenly I was his friend and I did this six-minute turn as Judy Garland. John had gone nuts for it and declared that anyone who could embody Judy Garland would be able to embody the role of an alien Goth girl who turns into a werewolf. So that's how I found out I was going to be this character of Mags in "The Greatest Show in the Galaxy".'

Fortunately, Jessica didn't have to actually howl at the Moon or crawl around on all fours! 'John just liked me and that was that. He was the boss man and he gave me this role and I don't think I've played anything so interesting or challenging in straight acting since.'

Getting the role may have been a breeze but costume and make-up were a 'crack of dawn job ... I was probably up at six to go into make-up for seven. I had short, spiky, blonde hair with very dark roots back then, so they created this wig of extensions for that kind of wolfish look that Mags had. Then there was the basic make-up, which was very intricate, again very vulpine. I also had to go through the very painful procedure of having big yellow contact lenses fitted. It was like having ping-pong balls stuck in my eyes. I had plastic false fangs that I had to put in my mouth too, along with a gel substance to create the salivating, blood-like ooze that had to come out.'

In the first couple of episodes, Jessica's character, Mags, has very few lines, so she also had to get to grips with the skill of making her presence felt on screen without saying anything. 'Well, it's true, I don't have a lot of lines in those first few episodes. It was almost like a silent movie for me. However, I had a great lesson in screen-craft from T P McKenna [who played Captain Cook in the story]. He said to me that the essence of acting on screen is to listen. If you're listening, then you can always react, and that's half of what acting's about. So, I have a lot of close-ups where I'm in pain – I'm trapped – I'm this alien with painted eyes, looking woeful and doleful. But believe me, I've been in shows with actors who have said nothing through the whole show but have stolen scenes because they can get up to all sorts of funny business. It's a dangerous weapon in the wrong hands!'

Ups & Downs

'The Greatest Show in the Galaxy' was a story that almost never was. After location work finished, asbestos was discovered at the BBC's studios. This meant that the production crew were suddenly faced with nowhere to record. JNT's ingenious solution was to set up an actual circus tent in a car park at Elstree. 'But then John was like that,' Jessica says. 'He was just marvellous at boomeranging whatever curve was thrown at him.'

The resulting impromptu sound stage created something of a party atmosphere, as Jessica recalls. 'The atmosphere on set was simply tremendous. To this day, I'm still in touch with Sophie Aldred [who played the Doctor's companion Ace]. Sophie and I are the same age almost exactly – our birthdays are a week apart – and we had the same background. We'd both been to university and kind of landed in a pot of jam without really a lot of effort, and we were thrilled to pieces with ourselves really! T P McKenna ... was a hell raiser. He liked to drink and he liked to spin a yarn. I remember that he and Sylvester [McCoy] hit it off immediately and I became the perfect straight man to them both. I would ask a question and they'd go off on an anecdote ... Christopher Guard [Bellboy] was drop dead gorgeous and a bit of a secret rock star, so we spent time writing songs together ... Peggy Mount [the Stallslady] was a great friend ... Danny Peacock [Nord] was a bit of a dangerous, edgy anti-hero in the show and in real life too ... So all in all, it was a bit of a party. In fact we would literally have a little party and a get-together after each day's filming.'

Given that there was such a natural rapport between herself, Sophie and Sylvester, was there ever a hint that Mags might stay on to be a companion? 'No, but you're not the only one to say that. Although my friendship with John Nathan-Turner continued right up until his death, I never asked. Maybe I should have been pushy. But I do think, even now, that there are a lot of untold storylines from that one serial. You could have had a whole spin-off *Torchwood*-type thing, because there was a lot of mirroring going on with the characters of Captain Cook and Mags. We were basically a mirror image of the Doctor and Ace, with T P McKenna as the bad Doctor.' It's an intriguing idea and one that Jessica is obviously taken with. 'Perhaps I should get onto the writer, Stephen Wyatt, and ask him if he could do something. Perhaps as an audio ... that would be great.'

Jessica has already returned to the world of *Doctor Who* playing the voice of the Queen in 'Voyage of the Damned'. 'It was merely half an hour in a voice studio,' she says, 'but I've probably had as much fan mail from doing that as I have for Mags. It was nice for the wheel to turn and, indeed, to get credited, as I didn't expect it.' That half an hour places Jessica in the rarefied world of those actors who have appeared in both classic and new *Who*. So how do her kids feel about it all? Are they impressed by Mum? 'It's very hard to be cool with my son. He's not into the showbiz thing at all. But he is proud of my *Doctor Who* work, and my daughter's always telling her friends that Mum was in the show, although of course her friends all say I wasn't in the "real", new *Doctor Who*!'

Jessica also reveals that she has a new project up her sleeve, which returns her to another world she loves – that of old movies. 'Today, I'm sitting in my art studio working on my graphic novel. It's taken a year so far but I've written the story and now I'm illustrating the book. It's an adventure set in the world of film and, right now, I'm more excited about this than my acting. It's like being your own movie producer. Being able to put things down and show it on the page exactly as you envisage it is great fun. Watch this space, please.'

The Other Brigadier:
Angela Bruce

**'... I fell in love a bit with Robert Jezek,
who was my second in command, Sergeant Zbrigniev.'**

Angela Bruce is a revelation. On screen, the woman who stepped so ably into Nicholas Courtney's army issue boots as UNIT's Brigadier is larger than life: bold, confident and utterly fearless. Off screen, she seems terribly fragile and unsure of herself. 'I was brought up in a mining village where you get a bit shy about success,' she admitted. 'There's this Northern bluffness. We tend to dislike boastfulness. So, for a time, I thought, "No I can't talk about myself!" I'm a very solitary, private person, so for me to do that is a big thing. But as you get older, you realise that it's okay. It's not being boastful. People do genuinely want to know.'

Born in Leeds, Angela was put up for fostering at the age of three and moved to Craghead in County Durham with the family who eventually adopted her. 'I was supposed to go there just for the weekend, but when the woman from the home came to take me back I said, "Bye bye, Mummy and Daddy" and they just broke down and said, "No, she can't go!" So that was it. I never left. My parents already had two sons and a daughter, so to take me on was an incredible thing and I totally adored them.'

It was only once her adopted parents were dead that Angela felt free to search for her birth mother and, when we first met, she was still in the throes of what was clearly a very emotional journey. 'She is alive – and she wanted to keep me – that's all I know at the moment. But I've got these lovely letters that she wrote. I've got a file on me from my birth to 1960 and it's just extraordinary. Not just learning about my birth mother, but about the attitude that people had to black children at the time. There are things in the file like "Angela has adapted to her colour well", which is an interesting statement to say the least! So I've just started the journey and it's thrown me a little bit. When I found out she was alive, which was this past week, I got very emotional. You don't know how you're going to react. You're also aware that time is of the essence. She's not getting any younger. So I'm hoping to meet this woman – whom I'm part of – and the irony of it is that she doesn't even know I'm looking for her.'

A Happy Home
Despite being 'the only black face in this little mining village,' Angela had a

164

'happy childhood.' Her sister was a nurse, and she'd originally intended to follow in her footsteps, but failed the examinations. Instead she ended up working in catering in a hospital, and although she knew it wasn't where she 'wanted to be,' she'd never entertained any ideas of acting. 'We were just an ordinary family. Acting wasn't even on the radar,' she comments.

All that changed in 1970 when the musical *Hair* opened in Newcastle. 'I'd never been to the theatre before, but I saw a clip of it on television and decided to save up my money and go and see it. I thought it was fantastic. People my age just seemed to be having such a wonderful time.'

At the end of the show the cast invited audience members up on stage to sing and dance, and they were so impressed by what they saw that they asked Angela to audition. 'That was on the Thursday night. On the Saturday night, I left with them to go to Aberdeen, and I stayed with the show for three years. Then we went on to London, and Richard O'Brien, who had been writing *The Rocky Horror Show* while he was in *Hair*, asked me to come in and play Magenta the Usherette in his new show. So that was my introduction to showbusiness!'

Angela's break into prime-time television was just as fortuitous. Lesley Dunlop, who played Ruth Fullman in the hospital drama *Angels*, was leaving the show, and the production team wanted someone from the North to replace her. 'I'm a Geordie believe it or not – the accent has now dissolved – and they asked me to come in. I ended up doing three series, and then Leslie Duxbury, who was writing *Angels* and writing my character, became scriptwriter for *Coronation Street*, so I went and broke up Ray Langton's marriage to Deirdre!'

The British take their soaps almost as seriously as their sci-fi and Angela found that being a 'scarlet woman' had its downside. 'I stood on a glass, cut my foot and had to go to the hospital, but the nursing sister who was there flatly refused to treat me. She said, "I'm not going to help you. You stole Ray Langton from Deirdre!", and then she disappeared. I never saw her again!'

Roles in *The Rock Follies*, *Press Gang*, *Takin' Over The Asylum*, *The Bill*, *EastEnders*, *The Ghost Hunter* and *Messiah 2* all followed. 'I've been lucky,' Angela says. 'I've had some really meaty roles, which are still, for women, few and far between.' Undoubtedly her meatiest role, and the one that won her international acclaim, was playing Mary Seacole in a drama that told the true story of Florence Nightingale's lesser-known contemporary. 'It was the best thing I've ever done'.

So how did her 'down-to-earth' family feel about their famous daughter? 'At first my mother didn't really understand,' she recalls. 'I think she felt acting wasn't quite respectable. I was the last child to leave home and it was a bit, "Go, but without my blessing!" But once I got into television, she was very proud. I remember that we went onto *The Mike Neville Show*, which is like a little quiz show. You got so many questions, and the panel had to guess who you were behind the screen, and then they interviewed you. She was in the audience. So I'm sitting there and I can see all the monitors and there's my mum, with her coat and her bag, looking so proud. It was the most amazing thing I ever saw. Later, Mike Neville got my mum drunk on sherry. I'll never forget that! The next morning, after two sherries, she was seriously hung-over, and it was so lovely to do a role reversal and say, "It's your own fault. You should have known when to stop!"'

The Two Brigs

When *Doctor Who* came knocking, Angela was already a famous face on British television but was nevertheless nervous about working on a show she'd been a fan of since childhood. She needn't have worried. It turned out to be a 'fabulous experience'. Nick Courtney, who made a return appearance as the now-retired Brigadier Lethbridge-Stewart, was especially charming. 'He was a great storyteller, a very warm, humorous and generous man who made me feel very welcome as the new Brigadier.'

Angela's character, Brigadier Winifred Bambera, debuted in the seventh Doctor serial 'Battlefield' (1989), and she based her performance on a fearsome drill sergeant who had been an advisor on a production of *Privates on Parade* that she had appeared in at Colchester's Mercury Theatre. 'We needed to be drilled in marching so that we could then add comedy to the scene,' she says. 'The drill sergeant was a huge man with shoulders as wide as the door frame. The squaddies he drilled found him very intimidating. He told us a story about how, one day, he had told them to start marching off, and he'd then got into conversation with a colleague. When he looked around, they'd marched straight into a lake, as they'd been too scared to stop without the command. In rehearsals he didn't talk, he barked his commands, and it made us all jump. So I modelled Brigadier Bambera on him. Ben Aaronovitch, who wrote the episodes, seemed to like what I was doing with the lines, as did Michael Kerrigan, the director.'

Angela 'was delighted to be offered the part' and 'apart from Mary Seacole' it turned out to be 'the most memorable thing I've ever done, because it allowed me to do every daft thing I've ever wanted to do.' That included her own stunts, under the supervision of Alf Joint, who'd worked on the Bond franchise and *Star Wars* and became a legend in the stunt community when he plunged 430 feet into the Reichenbach Falls doubling for Eric Porter in *The Adventures of Sherlock Holmes*.

'It was just wonderful to be walking around hollering at everybody all day, and get paid for it,' Angela laughs – although there were some downsides. 'The only problem was keeping a straight face. With Sylvester, Sophie and Jean Marsh [playing Morgaine], we all laughed at the drop of a hat. So, even in rehearsals, you just cried with laughter. I also got a gum infection, because we used to have sweets on the location – a bag of pick and mix – which we'd get at 5.30 in the morning. I ate so many that I had to go to the dentist. But it was just a joy. Great fun to work on, and I fell in love a bit with Robert Jezek, who was my second-in-command, Sergeant Zbrigniev. He was lovely.'

A New Family

Eight years have passed since I first interviewed Angela. Since then, she's added *Bad Girls*, *Spooks*, *Holby City* and *Casualty* to her already impressive CV. When I caught up with her again for this book she told me that she still travels a lot – 'I don't want ever to get tied down'– but these days she seems more at one with herself and happy to open up and chat.

Career-wise, she's ready to take more chances too. 'I've done a lot of support in good stuff, but I'd actually like to be able to develop a character, and certainly, after doing Mary Seacole, I think I can carry a show now. I'm ready for it. Maybe Sally Wainwright, who wrote the wonderful *Scott & Bailey* about two female detectives, will write something for me.'

And what about her search for her birth mother? The good news is that the story has a happy ending.

'Yes, I did manage to find my birth mother. At first she panicked and resisted contact, but then I tried again a year later and she was so relieved, as she had lost my address and had had a change of heart. She was worried about others finding out about her past but then, one day, she announced to her son that he had a half-sister, and he was as pleased as punch. I have visited her many times since. Now she tells anyone who will listen that she is my mum. I really regret that we were robbed of so much time, but I am also stunned by our similarities, taking into account the brief time I was in her charge. We have the same laugh, the same sense of humour, and she is a very positive woman and loves my partner. So my experience has been a good one, although I am aware that it's not the same for everyone.'

The Cheetah Woman:
Lisa Bowerman

Her face may have been hidden under layers of fake fur, but thanks to an appearance opposite the seventh Doctor in 1989, Lisa Bowerman has gone on to lend her voice to over 50 Big Finish audios, both in the *Doctor Who* range and as Bernice Summerfield in her own spin-off series. But how did it all begin?

How did you come to be offered the role of Karra in 'Survival'?
It turned out that they were casting in a hurry, as someone had turned the part down due to the horse-riding requirements. I knew the director (having worked with him on a series called *Casualty*) and I also happened to ride. The only other requirement was that I had to be prepared to wear contact lenses. They left the bit about the fun fur out!

It seems that the actors playing the cat people worked exceptionally hard, developing fluid body language and emotive expressions, but were hampered by the costumes … Is that a fair assessment?
I think a lot more could have been done – physically – had the costumes been designed a bit more sympathetically. The script implied that the Cheetahs should have a much more feral/human quality about them, but the designers were obsessed with hiding the line of the human neck. Consequently, you couldn't actually turn your head. All the other Cheetahs were played by dancers, but any real movement or style they developed was completely hampered, not only by the costumes, but by the head-pieces. I was lucky, as my head-piece was lightweight, and designed specifically for me. All the others were very heavy, generically-designed ones, and with the temperatures we were working in, it made things very difficult. The riding boots didn't help with ease of movement either! So I suppose the 'creeping' quality of movement that was eventually developed was to compensate for that.

Can you share some lasting memories of your time recording 'Survival'?
There are so many. Being lost on location on the last day of shooting, and walking miles through the undergrowth in the quarry, trying to find the crew. The unbelievable high temperatures we had to endure. I think mainly, though, the socialising in the evening at Lulworth Cove. On the

last night, we had a big party on the beach, a barbecue, music, and the FX boys had lit the Moon red, and put dry ice in the sea. Brilliant!

Looking back, what do you think is the appeal of 'Survival'?
Odd how things change! At the time of it going out, it was pretty much overlooked and derided for the cat costumes. But time and space can work wonders. It was actually an incredibly strong script by Rona Munro, and I think it has stood the test of time. Also, when you think how post-production effects were in their infancy, the post work on the Cheetah planet scenes is excellent – as well as that guitar scoring. There were great performances too from Sylvester and Sophie, and I know that most people think it was Anthony Ainley's finest hour as the Master.

What was it like working with Anthony Ainley?
He kept himself pretty much to himself – though he helped me out a lot. On one occasion up on set in Dorset, when the temperature was rocketing, they'd forgotten to bring water up to the location. I was feeling the effects of the sun somewhat, and Anthony really gave the production team 'what for' – very much looking after my best interests.

Did you know at the time that this would be the 'last' *Doctor Who* serial?
The answer is probably no. I seem to remember at the time that there was a lot of talk of a threat hanging over it. Nobody seemed too sure what was going on, to be honest. You would ask people, and there'd be a lot of shrugging shoulders!

The writer, Rona Munro, has said that there was a lesbian subtext to the relationship between Karra and Ace. Did you know that at the time?
It's been talked about a lot since but, to be honest, it wasn't mentioned *at all* when we were doing it. I suppose sometimes we're so busy dealing with the mechanics of a production that the subtext can get a bit lost. Having said that, the relationship between Ace and Karra is pretty close – and whether you wish to read anything more into that, is entirely up to the viewer.

Can you tell us a little about how you came to be offered the role of Bernice Summerfield?
It's actually rather a long story. I'd met Gary Russell years before, doing

a fan video called *I Was a Doctor Who Monster*. Apparently, when Big Finish first started and they'd decided to produce adaptations of the Bernice stories, my name came up in connection with possible actors for the project. I ended up auditioning for the part in Nick Briggs' front room, with a microphone strapped to an up-lighter … for Nick, Gary and Jason Haigh-Ellery. To be honest, I wasn't too sure about just how legit the job was!

How well do you think that Bernice's character has developed over the last 15 years?

I'm constantly amazed at how the different producers and writers have managed to keep her fresh, interesting and someone the listeners still seem to care about. The fact is, she hasn't stayed the same (which would have been artistic suicide), but she's managed to maintain the qualities that have made her character so well-liked. That's down to the strength of character that Paul Cornell created in the first place. She's totally recognisable, she solves things through her wit and humanity, but importantly she's also fallible, and certainly not superhuman – but a heroine, nonetheless!

For many fans, Big Finish kept the '*Who* flame' alive during the show's hiatus. Did you ever imagine, when you started recording Big Finish audios, that *Doctor Who* would really come back to TV?

I don't think anyone thought it would return to TV. Certainly not in the early days after the series was shelved. You always got the impression that the BBC was rather embarrassed to be associated with the programme in those days. There was no notion about the commercial potential either – they just wanted to sweep it under the carpet! But having been to some of the conventions back then, there was no doubt that the enthusiasm was still there amongst the fans. The flame never died. It just took someone with imagination to get it going again. Enter Big Finish! Luckily the Bernice audios went down very well. The BBC heard them and subsequently gave Big Finish the opportunity to get the licence for *Doctor Who*. Once they'd got the original actors in place, there was no stopping them.

What do you think is the appeal of the *Doctor Who* audios?

What I think they got right back then – and now – is that they have the most brilliant original stories, with some really talented writers, terrific casts and the technical know-how to put them together in a professional way. There's always a hunger for good drama. The fact that it had *Doctor*

Who in the title was an added bonus. It is so wonderful that someone like Russell T Davies (who'd always been a fan) was a listener, and has acknowledged the role that Big Finish played in proving that *Doctor Who* still had an audience out there.

You were also involved in the animated *Doctor Who* story 'Dreamland' with David Tennant's Doctor. Which experience – television, audio or animated *Doctor Who* – has been your favourite to date?
I can't really say which has been my favourite, as they all have fun elements to them. Of course, the TV storyline I did was very hard work physically – but when would you ever get to have an experience like that again? The audios are always a joy to make, as was the animation. although that was a very brief affair, as I was only in the studio for a day. The one thing I do know is that *Doctor Who* and Big Finish have introduced me to some wonderful people and without them I would never have made some of my very best friends. How can I not love *Doctor Who* just for that?

Chapter Four: The '90s

**'The universe hangs by such a delicate thread of points, it's useless
to meddle with it. Unless, like me, you're a Time Lord.'
(The Doctor, *Doctor Who*)**

It's been called the naughty '90s – a decade of good times and excess. This
was the era of royal divorces and Presidential indiscretions. Of Lara Croft
and Wonderbras. Of the Second Summer of Love and – for those just
worn out by the very idea – Viagra.

If the '80s were the vanilla ice cream of the 20th Century, then the
'90s were undoubtedly Ben & Jerry's Phish Food. This was a decade of
sensation-seeking; of damn fine cherry pies, killer tomatoes and Pepsi
Max. A time when we finally shook off the legacy of boom and bust
economics and dared to believe that (however it all turned out) things
could only get better. There was a party going on, and whether you were a
Ninja Turtle, Reservoir Dog or Batman, everyone was invited. Everyone,
it seemed, except the Doctor.

When the seventh Doctor and Ace strolled off arm in arm at the end
of 'Survival', the *Doctor Who* production office already knew that this was
to be the last *Doctor Who* serial for some time. Possibly the last *Doctor
Who* serial – ever. It was to give the show some sense of closure that
the then script editor, Andrew Cartmel, wrote this speech for Sylvester
McCoy, which was overdubbed on the closing moments of the show:

'There are worlds out there where the sky is burning, and the sea's
asleep, and the rivers dream … People made of smoke, and cities made
of song. Somewhere there's danger, somewhere there's injustice, and
somewhere else the tea's getting cold. Come on, Ace — we've got work
to do!'

It made a touching finale to that episode but also expressed the hope
that somehow, somewhere the show would go on.

Although *Doctor Who* had always been popular – and a real money-
spinner – Auntie Beeb had never really approved. In 1963, the show's first
director, Waris Hussein, felt that the Corporation didn't really know what
to do with *Doctor Who*. Twenty-six years on, and despite its success, the
feeling was the same. *Doctor Who* was just a bit too strange and a bit too
clever for the stiff-backed Corporation. However, if the BBC believed that
closing down production would finally rid them of the headache that was
Doctor Who, then they'd seriously underestimated the fans. The show –

and its champions – simply refused to roll over and die.

Ironically, it was during this 'hiatus' that the Whoniverse experienced a massive explosion of industry and creativity. Fans formed their own clubs, published their own fanzines, wrote stories, produced films and recorded audio dramas. Many of these fans would later go on to become professionally involved in the new, rebooted show in the 21st Century.

Concerted attempts were made during the '90s to produce a full-scale, professional *Doctor Who* film too – but they all died in pre-production. All but one. It took the efforts of another *Who* fan, British producer Philip Segal, to negotiate a deal with Universal Television (licensed to the Fox Network) for a TV movie … ably assisted by scriptwriter Matthew Jacobs whose father, Anthony, had appeared in the 1966 serial 'The Gunfighters' … Needless to say, Matthew was a fan too.

The TV movie, called simply *Doctor Who*, brought back Sylvester McCoy to officially hand over the role to the eighth Doctor, Paul McGann. Paul's exuberant, life-loving Doctor was very much a man of the '90s. Fans might have been divided over some elements of the storyline and what it revealed about the Doctor's back-history, but the movie did well in the UK. In the US, viewing figures weren't high enough to justify commissioning a series, but that didn't really matter. Once again the magic had happened. There was a new Doctor, and the groundwork had been laid for a comeback of epic proportions.

The Appreciation Society:
Antony Wainer

'... I suppose we – and others – held the torch and repeated the mantra that it would come back. Hoping, but without really knowing the truth.'

In these days of constant connectivity, it's never been easier to link up with like-minded people. But before the internet, before Skype, Facebook and Meetup groups, there was the *Doctor Who* Appreciation Society (DWAS). Back in the mid-1970s, it was fan clubs that gave fans like the 16-year old Peter Capaldi an outlet for their passion and creativity. When, at the start of the 1990s, fans were faced with the possibility of a year – maybe more – without any new *Who* on television, it was to organisations like the DWAS that they turned.

The DWAS was founded in 1976 – born out of the Westfield College *Doctor Who* Appreciation Society. The show has always attracted a loyal following, but the DWAS gave UK fans a real focus. Among those who have contributed to the Society's publications and organisation are Stephen Payne, founder of the magazine publishing company Visual Imagination; science fiction and *Who* author John Peel; BBC script editor and producer at Big Finish, Gary Russell; and David J Howe, co-founder of Telos Publishing and co-author of *Howe's Transcendental Toybox*.

Antony Wainer has been the Society's Press and Publicity Officer for the last 12 years. The post is voluntary, as the DWAS is a not-for-profit organisation, run by fans, for fans. 'In 1976, the DWAS was operating from somebody's house and that's still the same today,' Antony says. However, being a fan in 2013 is a very different experience from what is was in 1976. Back then, the DWAS kept fans in touch with each other – and all the latest *Who* news – by snail mail. 'We were quite happy and content getting news from the BBC – when they were prepared to give it to us – and passing it on to the fans in our newsletter but, in the late 1990s, the internet took over and now things happen very, very quickly. News can get to me in seconds of some announcement being made, and the old-style DWAS would not have been able cope if we were still sticking stamps on envelopes.'

The DWAS may have leapt wholeheartedly into the digital world but their remit remains very much what it always was – getting the fans together. 'Conventions and gatherings have always been very important as far as the DWAS is concerned. We did, until quite recently, run an annual event called the PanoptiCon, where large numbers of *Doctor Who* fans could meet to celebrate the programme. Initially the DWAS was the only real provider of that sort of fan event, and we always had good access to the stars of the show. Jon Pertwee came to our very first convention. Nicholas Courtney was the Society's Honorary President until his death, and Colin Baker is the Society's new Honorary President. Today, of course, anybody can independently set up a *Doctor Who* event, if they have the money and contacts to do so. But the one-day events that we still do are very well attended, and recognised as part of what the DWAS does best.'

Proof, if it was needed, that *Doctor Who* fandom has always been about more than just collecting or obsessing can be found in the fact that Society's membership has remained 'pretty much the same regardless of whether the show was on- or off-air.' What is surprising, though, is that despite the DWAS's loyal and steady membership, it seems that many fans of the new show are less interested in classic *Who*. 'The fact that *Doctor Who* has come back is very exciting,' Antony says 'The new series has been modernised of course – it's got a faster pace, better effects – but the beating heart is the same. It does feel like the same programme. If you liked it in the past, you'll probably like it now. However, what we've noticed is that many people who like the new series, haven't gone back to watch the old ones. I find that quite surprising because, if you like the new show, there are hundreds of stories that you've never even seen that you just might like too.'

Mind the Gap

When *Doctor Who* was cancelled in 1989, the BBC always insisted that it would be back. No-one realised that, with the exception of the Children in Need charity episode 'Dimensions in Time' and the Paul McGann TV movie, it would take 16 years for the show finally to return.

Although those are often referred to as the Wilderness Years they were far from barren. There has always been a thirst for new *Who* stories, and the gap was quickly filled not just by the officially-licensed Virgin New Adventures books, Telos Novellas and Big Finish audios but by fan fiction, fan films, fanzines and conventions. 'A gap was there and that gap was quickly filled, but always, behind whatever was happening, was the hope that *Doctor Who* would return to TV,' Antony says. 'None of us realised that it would take so long, but I suppose we – and others – held the torch and repeated the mantra that it would come back. Hoping, but without really knowing the truth.'

These days, the DWAS still carries that torch; although Antony admits that perhaps the Society tends to favour the classic series. 'I guess that the DWAS tends to see itself as custodians of the old series, because we're all a bit older, but we are very, very respectful of the new series and we cover all the new series news online and in our newsletter.'

Antony himself cites the fourth Doctor serial 'The Deadly Assassin' as his favourite, despite the fact that some involved with the DWAS pilloried it when it was first aired in 1976 – 'although the five year-old-me wasn't aware of that,' he laughs. 'I was just enjoying the story. We got to see the Doctor's home world and these wonderful sequences in the Matrix. I just loved all the imagery.'

So what would Antony's ideal fiftieth anniversary story be? 'My hopes – which I think may be dashed – are that the anniversary story would have lots of Doctors in it. But I'm a traditionalist. Celebrating 50 years, but only having two Doctors from the last six years, seems a small way to mark this great anniversary. I suppose in wanting a multi-Doctor story I want the BBC to recognise the show's legacy,' he says. Which is surely something that all fans – old and new – would applaud.

The Target Man: Nigel Robinson

Long before videos, DVDs and TV on demand, the only way for fans to revisit favourite stories was via the written word. Even when the technology became available, the Target range of *Doctor Who* novelisations remained extremely popular. Nigel Robinson was Target's editor and a *Who* author during the '80s and '90s, and was there to see out the old and chime in the new …

Can you tell us a little bit about how you came to be involved in the Whoniverse?
Totally by accident! I'd been a fan of the show since I first saw the fifth episode of 'The Web Planet'. I am sure I must have seen earlier stories as well, but that was the one that captured my imagination. Later, I bought all the Target books as they came out, and I still have the very first issue of *Doctor Who Weekly*! I was never a member of the *Doctor Who* Appreciation Society, though, and had no contact with the fledgling fan groups around at the time. After university, and with time on my hands, I wrote a *Tolkien Quiz Book* with a friend, which was published by Star Books. Star were a part of W H Allen, who also owned Target Books. I then pitched them the idea for a *Doctor Who Quiz Book*, which they took up. I became a freelance copy editor, working on the *Doctor Who* novelisations for about a year or so, before I was brought on board as a member of staff to handle the complete Target list. When I left W H Allen to go freelance again, I started work on novelising some of the *Who* scripts like 'The Edge of Destruction' and 'The Time Meddler', and then wrote a couple of the New Adventures. Recently Big Finish and the BBC's AudioGo have approached me to script some original stories and adapt some of the 'lost' Hartnell stories. Apparently I have a reputation of being the 'Hartnell writer' – I'm flattered and have no problem with that!

You were editor of the Target range between 1984-1987. Where there any golden rules that authors were expected to abide by?
There wasn't a rulebook as such, but there were unwritten rules, given the nature of the age group we were largely aimed at. When I was briefing writers, especially the original Hartnell writers who were unfamiliar with *Who*'s popularity in the '80s, I would always suggest that they wrote for an intelligent and sophisticated 13- or 14-year-old. But a 13- or 14-year-old who was considerably more intelligent and sophisticated than they probably

were at that age! There were a couple of writers who wanted to be a little too 'grown up'. One in particular became very irate when I cut an inappropriate reference to recreational drug-taking from one of his books. It was a great reference, and very witty, but inappropriate for a large part of the readership.

I did insist that each novelisation should be of its own era. So, for instance, I never allowed anyone to describe the first Doctor as a Time Lord, because the Time Lords hadn't been invented when Hartnell was the Doctor. I think during my time I allowed only two exceptions to that rule. In 'The Mind Robber', I edited Peter Ling's prose to include a reference to the (Delgado) Master, so there wouldn't be any confusion with the Master of the Land of Fiction, and in 'The Massacre', the Time Lords were indeed mentioned for a very good reason – although that reason escapes me at the moment! Of course I later did sort of break my own rule in 'The Edge of Destruction', when I described the TARDIS danger signal as the sound of a 'tolling bell'. I didn't exactly refer to it as the Cloister Bell, so I suppose I was bending my own rules rather than breaking them!

In the pre-video era, Target books were the only way for fans to revisit the series. Do you think that in the age of live streaming and TV on demand, 'the book of the show' still has a place?
Sadly, no, although I would love to be proved wrong! I think that an expanded novelisation of, say, 'Father's Day' by Paul Cornell, or 'Cold War' by Mark Gattis, would be fantastic. There is so much wonderful material you have to leave out of a 45-minute story – but that would probably only appeal to hardcore fans and wouldn't be financially viable. Back in the day, the Target books were the only way of revisiting a classic story, but modern-day Targets would be redundant. The way forward lies in original novels or audios based on the established characters, and there is some great stuff coming out at the moment.

It's been said that the Target novelisations were written at such a breakneck speed that they were sometimes done before the script for actual the TV serial was even finished. Is that true? It didn't happen when I was editor. I think, though, that Terrance Dicks' adaptation of 'The Five Doctors' was delivered before the final edit of the TV show. I was shown an early manuscript and I recall that there were quite a few differences between Terrance's original treatment and what appeared on screen. Certainly in what I read Sergeant Benton made an appearance, whereas of course he didn't in the transmitted version.

You wrote four Target novelisations, focusing on first and second Doctor adventures. What's the appeal, for you, of those early Doctors?
They are the two Doctors I grew up with. I still think Hartnell is the best Doctor ever, and it's fascinating how he developed from the dangerous anti-hero to the beloved if irascible grandfather figure. And, with a couple of exceptions, he enjoyed the company of some of the best companions as well as experiencing the widest variety of adventures any Doctor had. The stories are challenging and never once talk down to their audience.

Which was your favourite Target novelisation and why?
It would be invidious for me to pick out just one. *Fury from the Deep* was excellent, and the success of that spurred Victor Pemberton to embark on another career as a writer of bestselling sagas. Donald Cotton's *The Myth Makers* was totally different from anything else and a delight to edit. Ian Marter always delivered top-rate stuff and – when he was good and not writing to unrealistic deadlines – there really was no-one to beat Terrance Dicks. As far as I'm concerned, in terms of getting kids into reading, Terrance and his eminently readable prose is up there with the likes of J K Rowling and Roald Dahl. But, if I really did have to pick just one, then it would be the very first one, *In an Exciting Adventure with the Daleks*, written by David Whitaker. I recently reread it and was astonished by his prose and sense of characterisation. His *The Crusaders* novelisation is wonderful too – crisp, elegant prose, wonderful, well-rounded characters. I can quote huge chunks of that book from memory! And, again, he never wrote down to his readership.

You've also written Virgin New Adventures novels. How easy was it to write stories that 'fit' into an already existing (and complex) Whoniverse ... and were there any restrictions placed on writers about what the Doctor could/couldn't do?
As I recall, we were given more or less *carte blanche* to do what we wanted with the Doctor, the TARDIS and Ace as these were all BBC properties and licensed to Virgin and the New Adventures. There were the odd copyright restrictions such as being unable to use established monsters such as the Daleks or the Cybermen (which, of course, later changed). I think – certainly in the beginning – we all tended to overdo the continuity references, largely because we could and we were all fans – and what fan wouldn't want to include as many references to the show's past as they could? Plus, to be honest, the Whoniverse wasn't that complicated back

in the early '90s when the New Adventures first came out. If anything, it's the New Adventures and then the Missing Adventures, and all the other subsequent spin-off media, that made it complicated!

As a writer, which *Doctor Who* story from the classic or new series appeals to you most and why?
From classic *Who* I really admire stories like 'Horror of Fang Rock' and 'The Robots of Death', which is odd as Tom's Doctor isn't my favourite. But they're both great base-under-siege stories, with a terrific TARDIS team, and are very well written, with a small group of rounded characters you can actually believe in. There's some lovely humour in 'Robots', particularly, and the Voc Robots themselves are a classic *Doctor Who* design. Of the recent *Who* stories, 'Vincent and the Doctor' is up there with the very best, I think.

If you were asked to write a 50th Anniversary story, what would you write?
I'd probably do something without any past Doctors, just because including all the existing (and ageing!) Doctors would make the plot far too crowded for the telly … although it would probably work very well in a book. Certainly I'd do nods to the past such as the clips in 'The Name of the Doctor', which were wonderful. The Hartnell/ Clara scene sent a shiver down my spine! What about focusing on some of the past companions and how the Doctor has affected their lives? I loved the name-checking of Ian and Barbara, Ben and Polly, Ace, Tegan and Harry in *The Sarah Jane Adventures*!

You've also written a horror series of books for children as well as sci-fi series for adults. What's more satisfying/challenging – writing for children or adults?
Neither. They are both satisfying and challenging in their own ways. Of course you have to adapt your writing style and subject matter for your readership but, in the end, it's all about telling a story, isn't it?

The Illustrator:
Andrew Skilleter

'[John Nathan-Turner] … liked me but I must have been in awe of him. He was the bloody producer of *Doctor Who*, for God's sake, and I was but a humble artist!'

The room that I laughingly call my office is less of a workspace and more of an Aladdin's Cave. Floor-to-ceiling shelves groan under the weight of paper, plastic and pewter. Dusty reference books languish behind action figures and role play game miniatures. Every time I adjust the blinds, a 'Pyramids of Mars' mummy topples over and impales itself on a rather alarmed looking Tom Baker action figure. (No, despite what my niece thinks, it's really not a doll.) Balanced on top of the digital radio are assorted miniature Daleks, being held at bay by a teeny Matt Smith brandishing a sonic screwdriver. And there, staring down on me with a look of cosmic disdain, is a framed print of Anthony Ainley's Master, signed by the great man himself. It's an Andrew Skilleter print from the late 1980s and it's still one of my favourite pieces of *Doctor Who* art.

You might not be familiar with Andrew's name, but if you've ever read a Target or Virgin New Adventures novel, or picked up a *Doctor Who* video, then the chances are you'll know his work. He has 49 books and 24 video covers to his credit … so far. He also produced the iconic *Radio Times* cover for 'The Five Doctors'. But, arguably, it was when the show was in its hiatus that Andrew's prints and lushly-illustrated books found their most appreciative audience. Starved of on-screen *Who*, fans relied on video and printed paper for their fix. The work of Andrew Skilleter, in publications such as 1995's *Backlight: The Art of Andrew Skilleter*, gave us a *Doctor Who* freed from the straitjacket of budgets and technical problems. In Andrew's imagination, the Whoniverse looked exactly like every fan always imagined it – fabulous.

Making Memories

Andrew's first professional *Doctor Who* commission came in 1979 for the *K9 and Other Mechanical Creatures* volume – an illustrated *Doctor Who* special published under the Target imprint. 'I was asked,' Andrew says, 'to provide a very busy cover illustration as well as devise and create a number of puzzles in black and white. That came not long after I had visited Mike Brett, the art director at W H Allen, who gave me my very first book cover work, and later commissioned me to do the first in a long list of *Doctor Who* Target book covers.'

The process of producing cover art has evolved over the decades, as digital technology has gradually replaced pen and ink, brush and wash. 'The process is very different now, but looking way back at the way I produced a *Doctor Who* cover for Target, I would generally start with a pre-release information sheet, outlining the title and the story in brief. It was up to me to find reference images. Reference is everything with *Doctor Who*, and the lack of it in the early days was a constant problem. No videos, no internet and no good colour copiers!

'Once I had put together a rough – a preliminary sketch or drawing – outlining the composition, I'd post it to the art director, who would call me and perhaps discuss it or simply give me the go-ahead. I would produce parts of the drawing on tracing paper, transfer it to a rigid, smooth art board and then draw it up ready for painting. I would then generally paint the background followed by the subjects in gouache, which is a water-based pigment. Finally it would be packed and posted to the art director. The cover then had to be approved by *Who*'s producer too. As I adopted the airbrush and later started to work with acrylics, the process became increasingly sophisticated until today, the referencing and composition is all done digitally, even for traditionally-drawn or painted work.' Despite such a painstaking procedure, it's a tribute to Andrew's skills at conjuring up the world of *Doctor Who* that he was never asked to do a repaint.

Although Andrew has always been an extremely flexible draftsman, it was probably those early covers that established him as 'the man who draws *Doctor Who*.' 'In the days before video and computers, the Target books were long-awaited, and many fans retain fond and intense memories of them. My Who Dares poster prints launched at the 20th Anniversary Longleat Celebration in 1983 also made their mark and, again, these are fondly remembered by the fans today.'

Who Dares

Those poster prints – including the one of the Master that I have on my wall – were created as part of Andrew's own foray into publishing with his Who Dares business. It was this period of frenetic creativity that produced some of his most conceptually dazzling work. Alongside his own poster prints, calendars and bookmarks, Andrew also worked on David Banks' classic *Cybermen* volume. In it, Andrew included speculative portrayals of post-'Silver Nemesis' Cybermen, which have since been an influence on other *Who* publications. *Blacklight: The Art of Andrew Skilleter*, a large-format, colour hardback was published by Virgin in 1995, collecting together his finest paintings, with explanatory text by Andrew himself.

Having contributed so much to the *Doctor Who* story, is he a fan of the show himself? 'I've never been a fan in the true, dedicated sense, as I was with *Dan Dare* from a fairly young age, but as I was into sci-fi and space fantasy, I was a regular watcher from the beginning. However, I became completely involved in the show once I started to work for it, particularly from a visual perspective. I became captivated by the aliens, and the Cybermen in particular. If I had to choose only one single piece of art as a favourite from all my *Doctor Who* work, then the one that comes to mind is my cover for the *Cybermen* book. It brings together the classic *Doctor Who* Cybermen with my own personal vision and technique, and I spent a long time on it.'

At the height of his involvement with *Doctor Who*, Andrew visited a number of location and studio recording sessions, including those for 'Warriors of the Deep', 'Resurrection of the Daleks', 'Silver Nemesis' and 'The Greatest Show in the Galaxy'. There he was able to watch the shows take shape while getting up close and personal with the subjects he'd spent so long drawing. 'I recall visiting the location of "Silver Nemesis" with my wife at the old disused Greenwich Gas Works in London and being dropped in the wrong place and having to discover a way in!' he says. 'The main reason was to see my friend David Banks, who was playing the Cyber Leader. It was a bleak location and a heavily-contaminated area, which later became the site of the Millennium Experience.'

Andrew also got to know *Who*'s producer John Nathan-Turner who, he recalls, was always 'very hands on – in the nicest possible way – and everything I did was discussed and seen by him. I think he liked me but I must have been in awe of him. He was the bloody producer of *Doctor Who*, for God's sake, and I was but a humble artist! But he loved the visual world and my art; I suspect he liked to have creative people around him. But, to my disadvantage, I was never one to become part of a clique. I would always try and get up to London personally, but I was not as up front as I am today, which was a shame as, I think, I could have forged an even closer professional relationship with him.'

Andrew says that the Doctor that captured his imagination most was the fourth – Tom Baker. But which one is the hardest to capture? 'Probably Peter Davison, as the likeness is all about tonal values and making sure you don't over-paint the detail of the face … Having said that, though,

I'm largely pleased with all of the Davisons as the fifth Doctor that I've painted.'

Andrew continues to produce *Doctor Who* art as private commissions as well as sell his own prints and books (at www.andrewskilleter.com). Recently he also undertook a special project to mark the passing of Elisabeth Sladen. 'It was,' he says, 'a spontaneous one-off … but it turned out to be a very demanding piece of work, as there is a thin line between celebration and sentimentality. This was a personal tragedy for her family and friends and not just the passing of a fictional character.'

Even in the '80s and '90s, *Doctor Who* had such limited budgets that the sets and special effects were often pretty lacklustre. Art could often bring the characters to life in a way that hadn't been possible on screen. Now, new *Who* has the budget to show it all. Has this made illustrating the world of *Doctor Who* more challenging? How easy is it to translate this new, super-polished world of CGI effects into 'portable' art? 'I was fortunate to have established myself in a pre-digital age. I and my contemporaries took a pride in the mastery of traditional techniques to deliver the "wow" factor. Now almost anyone can do it using Photoshop. It makes time-consuming traditional painting irrelevant, certainly commercially. That's why I'm embracing digital more and more. Not to replicate what I've done, but to explore new creative horizons. I've always been interested in the "next thing", the next challenge.'

The Producers:
Gary Russell and Nick Briggs

When the final episode of the seventh Doctor serial 'Survival' aired on 6 December 1989, few fans really believed that the show would never be back. But when in August the following year, the *Doctor Who* production office finally switched off its lights and closed its doors, it seemed that the Whoniverse really had come to an end. In the years that followed the show's 'hiatus', there can be little doubt that it was the unremitting fever of the fans that kept the *Who* flame alive. Gary Russell, Nicholas Briggs and Jason Haigh-Ellery were three of those fans who determined not to let the show they loved die … which is where Big Finish enters the *Doctor Who* story …

GARY RUSSELL

What were your very first *Doctor Who* memories and what was it about the show that so caught your imagination?
Most definitely the last episode of 'The Tenth Planet'. I have very vivid memories of that, although I didn't have a clue what it was about, of course. But I must've watched the show regularly afterwards and I know that from the repeat of 'The Evil of the Daleks' in 1968, I was hooked. I don't know why, though. It never scared me. I loved the music and title sequence, but what made me fall in love with this show more than any other, I haven't a clue. But I'm glad I did.

Tell us about yourself and where you fit into the Big Finish story.
I set up a fan group back in 1984 with Bill Baggs doing thoroughly illegal, copyright-shattering *Doctor Who* audio dramas called Audio Visuals (AV). I met Nick Briggs through that and a few years later he, myself and John Ainsworth wrapped AV up. But audio was in my blood. I'd been taping *Doctor Who* on cassette tape since the '70s, so I understood what did and didn't work on pure audio. Nick was the same. I think we both instinctively understood the medium. After the 1996 *Doctor Who* movie, I chatted to my old chum Jason Haigh-Ellery and said maybe we should do AV-like things again but legitimately. He and I approached the BBC for a licence and were turned down flat. So we went off and sorted out getting a licence to do Bernice Summerfield on audio, dragging Nick along for the ride (and expertise). A year later, the BBC came to us and asked us if Big

Finish would be interested in doing *Doctor Who*. They thought it amazing that no-one had suggested this before. Best of all, it was the same three people who had turned us down 12 months earlier! They were convinced they'd had this brilliant idea and had never met us before. But I wasn't complaining, I just grabbed that licence and ran! I spent the next eight years running the *Doctor Who* side of Big Finish until fleeing to Cardiff in 2006 to work on *Torchwood* and *Doctor Who* on the telly.

Did any of you have a background in audio/drama/production or was it a matter of learning 'on the job'?
I learned as I went along, especially from Nick, who just had a natural flair for both audio and storytelling.

Was there ever a time when you thought 'This is a really big mistake …'?
No, but there was a point where I thought I was doing too much!

What would you say was your biggest Big Finish 'wow' moment?
During the recording of 'The Sirens of Time', Nick was directing Sylvester, Colin and Peter in the studio. Jason and I were making tea and I just looked Jason in the eye and said, 'We've done it. We're making *Doctor Who!*'

It was a massive acknowledgement of the success of your work when Big Finish storylines began to be adapted for TV. Did you ever feel the need for such 'official' recognition?
Nope, not at all. It was flattering, yes – but I was more excited that Rob Shearman was being used on the show because Russell T Davies loved his Big Finish plays, rather than the actual thing of a script being reworked.

Which Big Finish audio do you feel most captures the spirit of the original TV series?
Of the ones I produced – too many to list. I guess the most obvious would be 'The Spectre of Lanyon Moor' or 'Sword of Orion', and yet even they have something that makes them rise above the TV show and makes them special; the sort of stories that only work on audio. That's what it's all about – ensuring you are using the medium rather than slavishly trying to make a TV episode in sound.

What has been Big Finish's most successful title and what do you think is its appeal?

Sales-wise? Probably 'The Sirens of Time', because it was the first. Critically – 'The Chimes of Midnight'. But they're from my run. I'm sure Nick's custodianship has produced infinitely more successful ones. But although I love both of those, I have favourites of my own, often because of the making of them rather than critical/financial success.

What one *Doctor Who* character would you like to feature in a story, but haven't yet?
I wanted to use the Zygons. Had I not left Big Finish when I did, the seventh Doctor would have gained a Zygon-in-disguise as a companion from the American Wild West.

Big Finish played a huge part in keeping the flame alive during the show's hiatus. Did you ever feel that yourselves?
Not at the time, no. I just wanted to make 12 *Doctor Who* stories a year that 75 percent of our audience would like. And the 25 percent who didn't would hopefully enjoy the next month's …

NICK BRIGGS

What were your very first *Doctor Who* memories and what it was about the show that so caught your imagination?
It's so difficult to remember when *Doctor Who* first entered my life. I was born in 1961. I don't remember seeing the first episode, obviously. I may have been sitting in front of it. Who knows? But my earliest memories of anything are of *Doctor Who*. I remember William Hartnell. I remember 'The Celestial Toymaker' and 'The Tenth Planet'. I remember being upset when I saw the *Junior Points of View* programme on BBC TV with [presenter] Robert Robinson saying that the Doctor was dying. They showed a clip of – and this is how I incorrectly remember it – William Hartnell writhing in agony on the floor and changing into Patrick Troughton. Ah, the imagination of a child! Now I have a young son, I know how much the imagination can embellish things. So *Doctor Who* is, as I've often said, sort of hard-wired into me.

I'm not sure what it was about the show that caught my imagination. But it certainly did catch it, in a big way. I loved it. It made me tingle with delight. It seemed to offer everything I wanted in stories and adventures. And, of course, I really loved the Daleks. I always wanted them to win.

Steven Moffat has pointed out to me, rather vehemently, in front of a hall full of pupils from his old primary school, that this, in fact, means I have completely misunderstood the whole premise of the show. He was quite scary when he said that!

Tell us about yourself and where you fit into the Big Finish story.
Gary was my choice to take over running Audio Visuals, the amateur *Doctor Who* plays we did, after Bill Baggs. So we'd worked together doing *Doctor Who* for fun. We often spoke about how, one day, we'd like to do it for real. Audio *Doctor Who*, with a licence from the BBC! Just imagine. And then, he and Jason made that happen, through grown-up meetings with important people. Gary came and told me the good news. He said I'd be doing all the directing and lots of sound design and music, because he knew that was my thing. I asked about writing, and he said only *Doctor Who* novelists could do the writing. I begged and begged and, bless him, because he's a kind man, he changed his mind and let me write the first one … and more or less any scripts I wanted to thereafter. Gary was very generous to me. He also let me do the Dalek voices – and look where that led me! So I was there at the beginning, and worked on most of the first few releases. And I continued to have a steady stream of work from Big Finish, regarding it as my mainstay. I also did a lot of promotion for the initial launch, getting us on the Steve Wright radio show on BBC Radio 2 and various other shows and in the *Big Issue* magazine (Scotland edition only, strangely enough). They put Daleks on the cover, even though we didn't get the Daleks for some time.

How did the idea of making own audio dramas set in the Whoniverse evolve and how tricky was it turning the idea into a reality?
We'd been doing it for years for fun. So it didn't feel tricky at all. Gary and I knew exactly how it worked, then he and I set about finding other people who could do it. We got Alistair Lock on board to do music and sound design, then we asked for submissions and got all sorts of other talented people on board. I sort of handled the sound design side, because Gary kept saying he couldn't really tell if anything was in stereo or not. He can. He just says that for effect … I hope. And then Gary recruited all sorts of writers. I used to moan like mad about a lot of the scripts. I was a right royal pain in the arse to Gary. I think he had the patience of a saint, patted me on the head and set me to work on my own projects to keep me out of mischief.

Did you have a background in audio/drama/production or was it a matter of learning 'on the job'?

We'd learnt by doing the Audio Visuals stuff. I'd also done some professional work for Bill Baggs. I'd done quite a bit of sound design and music for him. But Gary and I were very clear about how to do audio drama. We finessed that as we went along. I eventually found us the Moat Studios and then worked very closely with the brilliant Toby Robinson, who is still our mainstay studio guy, to sort out the best way to evolve how we worked in studio.

Was there ever a time when you thought 'This is a really big mistake ...'?

Never. Blimey, no. It was our favourite thing. And it was really successful from the start. Gary was very sharp at picking up on this and said to Jason, 'We have to go monthly.' And by jingo, he was right.

What would you say was your biggest Big Finish 'wow' moment?

Just getting into the studio and doing the first one. That was seriously 'Wow'! It's strange to remember that, back in those days, I was so tense and excited that I could never eat lunch. No wonder I was so skinny.

It was a massive acknowledgement of the success of your work when Big Finish storylines began to be adapted for TV. Did you ever feel the need for such 'official' recognition?

From the moment we started, my take on it was that the BBC recognised what we were doing as the official continuation of *Doctor Who*. That's what BBC Worldwide, in the form of Steve Cole, said at the time, and that was Gary Gillatt's editorial take in *Doctor Who Magazine*. So, I suppose it didn't surprise me when the TV series sought to mine some of our ideas. I would have been shocked if they hadn't, I suppose. I know that might sound arrogant, but in order to create stuff I like, I kind of have to get caught up with it. Second-guessing what people want or worrying about those who don't like what you do, is the death of creativity. If I read even a slightly bad review of something I've done, I find it impossible to work ... usually just for a couple of hours, but sometimes for weeks. So I've learned to screen any of that stuff out. So, official recognition or not, I was as happy as can be, playing in my own, BBC-licensed sandpit.

Which Big Finish audio do you feel most captures the spirit of the original TV series?

That is an impossible question to answer. We all have very different ideas of what *Doctor Who* was. I mean, I thought William Hartnell was writhing on the floor in 'The Tenth Planet', didn't I? Seriously, I can't answer that question. They all have bits in them that capture the spirit of the original TV series as experienced by whichever writer or director or sound designer or composer is working on it ...

What has been Big Finish's most successful title and what do you think is its appeal?
'The Sirens of Time' is the most successful, narrowly followed by 'Sword of Orion'. Ironically, these are two of the stories with the most mixed reviews. But it just goes to show that reviews are the views of one person. Often it is a person with an agenda or a set of views that are atypical of the larger audience. Reviewers have a different approach to material. Their job is to listen to, read or watch stuff ... so they develop a sort of abnormal perspective. I can say that, because I used to review TV and films ... and that's absolutely true. You start to think your viewpoint is in some way definitive, or that what you say counts ... which it sort of does. But I think it's unhealthy. 'The Sirens of Time' is the most popular, because it's the first, and the first of anything almost always sells the best. 'Sword of Orion' was the first eighth Doctor story to feature a classic 'big' monster – the Cybermen. These are the kinds of things that affect people when they buy things. Both of these stories continue to sell, over and over again. If you're asking about creatively successful, I like things that stand out and are different. Joe Lidster's 'The Rapture' was a real, controversial departure and should be applauded for that. I love Alan Barnes's 'The Girl Who Never Was'. A brilliant exit for Charley Pollard. And I love strange stuff like Eddie Robson's 'The Condemned' – urban, bleak, but with a sparkle of *Doctor Who* magic. I love so many of them, and so I should. It's my life.

What one *Doctor Who* character would you like to feature in a story but haven't yet?
I think we've pretty much covered my wish-list, apart from the impossible dream of somehow being able to work with the first three Doctors. I know. It's impossible. I know we can't bring them back to life. But that's my unattainable dream. It seemed pretty unattainable that we'd get Tom Baker back into the role. But, my goodness, I slogged away at that, and with the generous help of many, we managed it. Phew. And Tom is as much a joy to work with as all the others. Working as executive producer,

I've really got to know the Doctors far more than I thought I ever would. They're bloomin' great.

Big Finish played a huge part in keeping the flame alive during the show's hiatus. Did you ever feel that yourselves?

We didn't think it was a hiatus. We thought *Doctor Who* would never come back. But yes, we kept it alive in people's minds, didn't we? Not in the minds of the bigwigs at the BBC. They didn't have a clue that we even existed. They thought *Doctor Who* was rubbish and dead, until Russell T Davies brilliantly persuaded them otherwise. Thank goodness for Russell. As you know, he saved our bacon!

Where do you go from here ... and will *Doctor Who* always be part of the Big Finish story?

I'll carry on until I don't want to carry on anymore. And I don't see me stopping any time soon. I do love my job as executive producer. It gives me real creative freedom. But that freedom is only possible because of the great team I work with. Jason is a good friend and a lovely boss. David Richardson is stupendously hard-working and one of the finest human beings I know. Paul Spragg is so brilliant at what he does, and his commitment to Big Finish and his attention to detail are really quite breathtaking and inspiring. He also makes terrible jokes and I love terrible jokes. Kris Griffin, our marketing guru, or 'gnu' as we call him, is the most amazing man. An inspiration. There are loads of other people who I just think are superb too. We're very lucky to have them all, but I'm guessing you'd rather this interview didn't just turn into a list of brilliant people. But, as with any job, it's the team that counts. We're humans and things only work well for humans when you get along with other humans. Big Finish, the home of great humans, creating adventures for a great Time Lord.

The Filmmaker:
Keith Barnfather

**'It was always the scope of *Doctor Who* that entranced me …
any time, any place, anywhere.'**

At the grand age of 84, you'd expect actress Damaris Hayman would
be happily enjoying retirement in her quiet Cheltenham home – but
no. When approached by Reeltime Pictures' Keith Barnfather about
returning to play Olive Hawthorne from the perennially-popular Jon
Pertwee story 'The Daemons', she jumped at the chance. 'I shall retire, I
think, in my coffin! Miss Hawthorne was my all-time favourite role and I
was enchanted by the thought of being her again for a little while.'

The White Witch of Devil's End is due to be released at the end of
Doctor Who's 50th Anniversary year, and seems sure to be a hit with the
many fans of 'The Daemons', from which it takes its inspiration. But then
Reeltime have been making the sort of films that *Doctor Who* fans hanker
after for almost 30 years.

Many of us may dream about being involved in the world of *Doctor
Who* in some small way, but people like Nick Briggs, Gary Russell and
Keith Barnfather have made that dream a reality.

The BBC have always guarded their intellectual properties very
carefully, so Reeltime built their reputation around direct-to-video *Doctor
Who* spin-offs that focused on characters and monsters licensed directly
from the writers who created them.

'It was always the scope of *Doctor Who* that entranced me,' says Keith, '…
any time, any place, anywhere. Right from the start, when I formed Reeltime
in 1984, I had a desire to do drama. The company's "bread and butter"
was corporate and business television, but then we started doing the *Myth
Makers* series, profiling actors who had appeared in *Doctor Who*. Through
them, I got to meet most of the cast of *Doctor Who*. Finally, after three years,
when I felt ready to take it on, I searched around for a story and character
from *Doctor Who* that we could both record and clear the rights to.'

That first *Doctor Who* spin-off was called *Wartime* and featured John
Levene playing Sergeant Benton in a UNIT-themed story. 'It was to John's
very great credit that he was prepared to trust us to do it right. I'm very
proud of *Wartime*. The locations were fantastic and it was a marvellous
first effort,' says Keith.

Other spin-offs followed. Reeltime's factual *Doctor Who* output has always exceeded its drama, and one of the company's biggest hits was its documentary about the *Twenty Years of a Time Lord* celebration at Longleat in 1983, because everyone who was there wanted to see if they were in the video! But it was perhaps *Downtime*, in 1995, that made people really sit up and take notice. *Downtime* was a sequel to the second Doctor stories 'The Abominable Snowman' and 'The Web of Fear' and was notable for its all-star cast. Nicholas Courtney, (Brigadier Lethbridge-Stewart), Deborah Watling (Victoria Waterfield), Jack Watling (Professor Travers) and Elisabeth Sladen (Sarah Jane Smith) all reprised the roles that had made them legends in the Whoniverse. *Downtime* also introduced the character Kate Lethbridge-Stewart, who would go on to appear in another Reeltime drama, *Daemos Rising*, before featuring in the television show itself.

Expanding Universes

It was a massive acknowledgement of the impact of Reeltime's work when some of their stories began to be adapted as Virgin New Adventures novels. 'It's always nice when you are either praised or recognised for any work you do,' says Keith. 'Virgin were very happy to tie up novels with our dramas as it was a good promotional tool for them too. We both benefited. The same was true of Silva Screen, who produced CDs of the music Mark Ayres had done for us.'

Thanks to new technology, both professionals and amateurs are increasingly able to afford to make their own videos and publish their own books. So how does Keith feel about the possibility of more people joining the business? 'These developments,' he comments, 'have helped us at Reeltime. When we started, the cost of hiring kit was horrendous, truly horrendous. Now we own our own broadcast HD kit and edit suite. So it would be churlish of me to bemoan the availability to anyone else. I'm pleased young filmmakers have the tools that I didn't. Good luck to them.'

Is there any one character from *Doctor Who* that Keith would like to include in a Reeltime drama but hasn't? 'Well, we've just been making *The White Witch of Devil's End* with Damaris Hayman reprising her role as Miss Hawthorn, so I suppose that answers your question! I was really amazed and delighted that Damaris was prepared to take it on. We had recently recorded an interview with her for our *Myth Makers* series so I already knew that she still had a hunger to act. But I really didn't expect her to be so keen.'

The drama is really an anthology – a set of connecting stories about

Olive's life, told in her own words. When considering who best to approach to write these stories, Keith contacted old friend David J Howe at Telos Publishing, whom he knew from their involvement in the *Doctor Who* Appreciation Society. Together they chose several authors who they felt would be sympathetic to the material, and brought in Big Finish writer Matt Fitton for a final script-polish.

For many years now, companies like Reeltime, Big Finish and Telos – all founded by *Who* enthusiasts – have done more than simply mine the existing *Doctor Who* universe. They've added to it, and continue to do so. And the world of *Doctor Who* is big and bold enough to embrace it all.

The Fanzine:
Stephen James Walker

Fanzines formed the backbone of *Doctor Who* fan activity in the '70s, '80s and '90s. From humble beginnings, fans found ways to get their writing and artwork down onto paper and into the hands of fellow fans. As photocopier technology developed, so fanzines became increasingly sophisticated and professional in their look, and many hundreds of titles were produced. There was the irreverent *Second Dimension*, with its surreal Anna Higgins cartoon strip about *Rupert the Time Lord* written – like the Rupert Bear originals – in rhyming couplets. There was the dry but definitive factual publication *In Vision*. There was the ever-opinionated *Doctor Who Bulletin*, which, by 1994 had evolved into the professional newsstand magazine *Dreamwatch*. And there was *The Frame* – a 24-issue *Doctor Who* fanzine that ran from February 1987 to the spring of 1993, and set the benchmark for all fan publications to come. One of the editors of *The Frame* was Stephen James Walker.

How did you first become involved in *Doctor Who* fandom?
I was only a young boy when *Doctor Who* began back in 1963, but fortunately for me my father used to tune in every week, so I saw it right from the start, and I was instantly captivated by it. The first two Doctors, played by William Hartnell and Patrick Troughton, were my childhood heroes! For some reason, the show just enthralled me more than anything else. That continued with the advent of the third Doctor, played by Jon Pertwee, at the start of the 1970s. However, being a fan up to that point had been a very solitary experience. Most of my classmates at school also watched and enjoyed the show, but none of them was as devoted to it as I was! Then somehow I learned that there was a *Doctor Who* fan club being run by a chap named Keith Miller in Edinburgh, and I immediately wrote off to become a member. That was my first involvement with organised fandom. I can still remember the delight I used to feel whenever one of the club's irregular newsletters popped through my family's letterbox! Then, a couple of years later, a fanzine called *TARDIS* started up, and that quickly led on to the creation of the *Doctor Who* Appreciation Society (DWAS). Again I joined straight away – I think I was about the twelfth member! That was in 1976. Then, the following year, the DWAS held the first ever *Doctor Who* convention, organised by Keith Barnfather at a

church hall in Battersea, and that was where I first met other fans of the show in person, including David Howe. From that point on, for the next 30 years or so, I became more and more heavily involved with fandom. I made lots of like-minded friends along the way and was lucky enough to meet almost every leading cast member and significant behind-the-scenes contributor ever to have worked on *Doctor Who* – two rare and much-regretted exceptions being William Hartnell and the first actor to play the Master, Roger Delgado, who both sadly died in the mid-1970s.

What lay behind your decision to launch *The Frame* in 1987?
I first started writing fanzine articles about *Doctor Who* around 1978. I was particularly interested in chronicling the show's history, and became very friendly with the first head of the DWAS Reference Department, Jeremy Bentham. When Jeremy later resigned from the DWAS and started up his own fan group called Cyber Mark Services (CMS), I became involved with their endeavours. Chief amongst those was a monthly loose-leaf reference work called *Doctor Who – An Adventure in Space and Time*, which had been devised by two fans named Tim Robins and Gary Hopkins. Initially I proposed and took charge of a sister publication to that, called *The Data-File Project*, which ultimately presented extended plot synopses of all the stories from *Doctor Who*'s first two seasons. You have to remember that this was back in the days before commercial video releases or extensive TV repeats of *Doctor Who*, and fans were really crying out for that type of basic information about the show's early history. Then, in the mid-1980s, when Gary Hopkins gave up editing the main *Space and Time* publication, he invited me to take over from him, and I did that for the next three years. By that point, I'd also started contributing occasional articles to the official *Doctor Who* magazine, then published by Marvel. Anyhow, it was toward the end of my stint working on *Space and Time* that David Howe approached me at one of the regular monthly fan gatherings we both attended at a London pub, and asked if I would be interested in working with him on a brand new fanzine. If I recall correctly, David had just stepped down as head of the DWAS Reference Department then – having been Jeremy's successor when he left. So it was initially David's idea for the two of us to produce a fanzine together, but I readily agreed, and we then worked on it jointly from the start.

So how did things progress from that initial idea to actually launching the fanzine?
We had our first planning meeting at David's house in Surrey, and he

invited another friend of his, Mark Stammers, to come along. As well as being a fellow *Doctor Who* fan, Mark was a graphic designer by training and profession, and David thought it would be useful to have him on board. So it was agreed at that meeting that the three of us – David, Mark and I – would be joint editors of the new fanzine. We also put our heads together to come up with a title for it. We didn't want to use something really obvious like the name of a *Doctor Who* monster – there had already been lots of other fanzines with clichéd titles like that. If I recall correctly, David initially suggested *The Net*, as that was the title of an unrelated drama production that our very first interviewee, director Christopher Barry, had worked on prior to his involvement with *Doctor Who*. I wasn't too keen on that, though, so I put forward the alternative of *The Frame*. My thinking was that this related obliquely to a lot of the things that we wanted to do in the fanzine. We wanted to include a lot of previously-unpublished photographs and artwork, making it a very visual publication – and of course photographs and pieces of artwork are often presented in a *frame*. We also wanted the text to be high-quality and authoritative, with analytical pieces in which the writers would *frame* persuasive arguments. And we were covering a TV show consisting of *frame*s of film and videotape! So we all agreed on that title, and then set about putting together our first issue.

In terms of design and quality, *The Frame* straddled the line between being a 'zine and a full-scale professional magazine. Can you give us an idea of the sort of workload involved in putting together such a publication?

The workload was huge, but it helped enormously that there were three of us collaborating on the 'zine. There was a certain amount of subdivision of labour. David took the lead on the organisational side of things; arranging interviews, liaising with printers, dealing with individual and shop orders and so on. Mark naturally took the lead on the design aspects, and fortunately was able to make use of some of the high-spec equipment and facilities of the firm where he worked at that time. I probably took on the biggest share of the writing and text editing work. But all three of us were heavily involved in every aspect of the 'zine, working closely together on it. We all at that point had full-time 'day jobs' as well, so this was all accomplished in what would otherwise have been our spare time – principally during evenings and weekends. I would often find myself staying up till three in the morning working on one aspect or another of *The Frame*!

How well did the publication meet your expectations?
I think we were all delighted with what we managed to achieve on *The Frame*. Of course there were occasionally things that didn't work out quite as we had intended. There were a couple of times when our printers didn't do quite as good a job as we would have liked, and a couple of others when a planned article fell through and we had to put together a hasty replacement, which wasn't ideal. But I'm a bit of a perfectionist, so I probably spotted flaws that no reader of the 'zine would ever have noticed or been aware of! Overall, *The Frame* certainly lived up to my expectations, and I am still enormously proud of it to this day.

Did you have a background in journalism/magazine production or was it a matter of learning 'on the job'?
I can't remember a time when I wasn't keen on writing. Whenever, as a child, I was asked the standard question 'What do you want to be when you grow up?', I would always reply, 'An author!' Strangely, though, I didn't study English at university; instead, I took a BSc (Hons) Degree in Applied Physics! But I never intended to work as a scientist afterwards. I just chose that subject because I was interested in learning more about it. My first paid job was in an administrative post at the BBC, working at Broadcasting House. After that I joined the Civil Service in 1983, and remained there for the next 22 years! I worked as a policy adviser, mainly on individual employment rights issues, gradually climbing the ladder of seniority. That job actually involved a great deal of writing – drafting correspondence, policy papers, briefing notes and speeches for successive government Ministers, including on some occasions even the Prime Minister. And all the time I was doing that, I was also working on my various *Doctor Who* projects in every spare moment I could find!

A little-known fact is that I also tried at one point to break into TV scriptwriting, in partnership with another friend and long-time *Doctor Who* fan named Dave Auger. The furthest we ever got was being commissioned by TVS to develop a children's drama in the fondly-remembered *Dramarama* strand. It was called 'Playback' and concerned, in essence, a haunted VHS tape! It was going to be directed by Michael Kerrigan, who by coincidence had not long prior to that handled the *Doctor Who* story 'Battlefield'. However, this was just before the ITV network underwent one of its periodic shake-ups, which unfortunately resulted in TVS losing its franchise, so the programme was never made. Dave and I stopped writing together soon after that, because we were simply too busy with other things. This was a familiar situation for me! A few years earlier, I had had to turn down the chance of writing one of the Target range of *Doctor Who* novelisations, *The Edge of Destruction*, because of my workload on the *Space and Time* fanzine; and later on I would sadly just miss out on contributing one of Virgin's New Adventures range of original *Doctor Who* novels, which would have been entitled *Mistaken Identity*, because I found I couldn't fit that in at the same time as working on the non-fiction books for which David, Mark and I had already been commissioned. Too much to do, and not enough time to do it in! Nowadays, I am known primarily as a non-fiction writer and editor, but that wasn't always my intention – it was largely down to circumstances – and I would like to get back to writing some more fiction one day.

The '80s and '90s are often seen as the golden age of fanzines. What do you think 'zines offered fans that 'official' magazines didn't?
Funnily enough, one of our motivations for starting *The Frame* was that the official *Doctor Who Magazine* published by Marvel wasn't really catering to our tastes. Its coverage was too superficial for us, and the design aspects of the show – which we considered integral to its success – were more or less ignored. It also tended to reuse the same stock photographs over and over again, whereas we knew that there were a lot of previously-unpublished ones that could be unearthed from private collections with a bit of research and effort. So in *The Frame* we set about putting together a fanzine that was more in line with what we ourselves wanted to see being done. Later, when *The Frame* became a big success, the staff at *Doctor Who Magazine* realised that a lot of other fans had similar interests to us, and they started running the same type of material as well, essentially emulating what we were doing. But we didn't mind that. As the saying goes, imitation is the sincerest form of flattery!

More generally, though, there were a lot of things fanzines could do that the official *Doctor Who Magazine* couldn't. They could be more contentious and critical in their content. They could be more satirically humorous. They could include a lot of fan fiction and artwork. They could delve into aspects of the show that would have been too obscure or abstruse for *Doctor Who Magazine*'s more mainstream readership.

The great thing was that by the 1990s technology had advanced to the point where photocopying and even proper printing had become much more readily accessible to the general public – with the advent of high street print shops and so on. This meant that any fan who wanted to start up a fanzine had a realistic prospect of being able to achieve it. And with the burgeoning of organised fandom in that decade, and the proliferation of independent *Doctor Who* conventions, there was a large and readily accessible market as well. Of course lots of fanzines faltered after just one or two issues, either because their originators had underestimated the amount of work involved or because they simply weren't good or distinctive enough to attract a readership; but the best of them could thrive.

Who was your most interesting interviewee and why?
That's a very difficult question to answer, as all of our interviewees had interesting things to say. However, I was very pleased indeed that I managed to track down and interview Anneke Wills, who played the Doctor's companion Polly in the mid-1960s. No-one in *Doctor Who* circles had known her whereabouts for years before I contacted her. In fact she had spent time in various places around the world, and at that point was living in an artists' community on an island in Canada. I'm proud to say that it was as an indirect result of me contacting her that Anneke was later able to reconnect with her roots in England, which eventually led to her coming back to live in this country full time.

Others I particularly enjoyed interviewing for *The Frame*, either on my own or with others, included producer Innes Lloyd and designers John Wood, Raymond P Cusick and Barry Newbery. David and I actually visited Barry several times in order to complete our interview with him, because he worked on so many different *Doctor Who* stories and had so many fascinating things to say about them, and we got on so well that we kept in contact afterwards. In fact, Barry and I still exchange Christmas cards every year even now!

Who would you have liked to have interviewed, that you didn't have the chance to?
For me, 'the one that got away' was Terence Dudley, who both wrote and directed for *Doctor Who*. Terence had a long and distinguished career that also encompassed producing – including on the popular BBC telefantasy shows *Doomwatch* and *Survivors*, both of which I loved. I'm sure I would have found it fascinating to have an in-depth discussion with him. I did in fact meet him briefly several times, and on the last of those occasions, at a convention in Birmingham in the summer of 1988, I asked him if I could arrange to interview him for *The Frame* at a later date. He readily agreed, but as neither of us had a pen and paper handy, he suggested I

get his address from the convention's organiser, Paul Vanezis. Naturally I spoke to Paul about this, but he was understandably very busy at the time. He said he would get in touch with me later to pass on Terence's contact information. Unfortunately he never did – no doubt it slipped his mind – and before I could get around to chasing it up, I sadly heard that Terence had died, on Christmas Day 1988.

Why did you decide to cease publication of *The Frame*?
Peter Darvill-Evans, then the editor of the officially-licensed *Doctor Who* books at Virgin Publishing, was a great admirer of what David, Mark and I had been doing on *The Frame*, and on the strength of that he commissioned us to write our first professionally-published non-fiction *Doctor Who* guides. Our first proposal was to write a book all about the Daleks, but that fell through due to a last-minute objection by the agents of Terry Nation, the Daleks' creator. So then we came up with the idea of doing the large-format, heavily-illustrated *Doctor Who* 'decades' books – *The Sixties*, *The Seventies* and *The Eighties*. While we were still working on those, we were also commissioned to write a series of seven standard-size *Handbook* paperbacks, one for each of the seven TV Doctors up to that point. So basically it got to the stage where the time we were spending on all of these books, as well as our other commitments – including work and family commitments unrelated to our *Doctor Who* projects – made it impracticable for us to continue doing *The Frame* as well. There just weren't enough hours in the day for us to fit everything in. Something had to give, and unfortunately that something was *The Frame*.

If you could do things over what would you do differently?
Nothing! I have no regrets.

Do you think that, today, social media, blogs and websites now meet the same fan needs or do print fanzines still have a place?
I do think that to some extent those various types of online communications provide the same sort of outlet for fan interaction and comment as fanzines did back in the 1980s and 1990s. Having said that, though, I also think there's still a place for print fanzines. The online fan activity may have a greater immediacy to it, but it all feels rather ephemeral and chaotic to me. A print fanzine – or indeed a fan-produced book – somehow has a greater sense of permanence and 'weight' to it. There are some excellent ones around, too, such as *Nothing at the End*

of the Lane, published by Richard Bignell, who has done a wonderful job of unearthing previously-unknown information and photographs relating mainly to 'classic era' *Doctor Who* of the 20th Century. That's a publication right up my street! Then there's *Vworp, Vworp*, a really beautifully-produced and highly-visual fanzine devoted to *Doctor Who* in comic strip form and the history of *Doctor Who Magazine*. Again, the type of fanzine I really appreciate! Another one I buy regularly is Kenny Smith's *The Finished Product*, covering the Big Finish *Doctor Who* audio plays, which is exactly the same kind of A5, photocopied fanzine that proliferated in the 1980s, giving it a great nostalgic quality for me. So yes, there's definitely still a place for print fanzines.

What advice would you give to a *Who* fan, thinking about starting their own *Doctor Who* print or e-publication?
I think it's important to consider carefully what you're trying to achieve – be it with a fanzine or a blog or whatever – and how you're going to make it distinctive and different from what other people are doing. What unique perspective or unusual angle can you bring to the subject matter that will make your project stand out from everyone else's? But most of all, do something that pleases you, and that you really enjoy doing. If you aren't going to be having fun with it, then there's really no point!

The Kid: Yee Jee Tso

**'A few times I went out with fans from conventions, but I don't think
to be honest that I can share the actual events with you … LOL.'**

Yee Jee Tso loves sci-fi. But then that's probably pretty easy to guess from
his CV. As well as playing misled street kid Chang Lee in the 1996 *Doctor
Who* TV movie, Yee Jee has also appeared in *Sliders, Stargate Atlantis, The
Outer Limits, Dark Angel* and *Battlestar Galactica*, and played computer
wizard Jared Chan in the big-budget movie *Impact*.

'I'm a sci-fi fan, for sure,' he says enthusiastically. 'I loved *Star Wars* –
the original trilogy – *Dune, The Hitchhiker's Guide to the Galaxy, Star Trek*
as well as many others. But by far my favourite sci-fi show to have been
involved in is *Doctor Who* – in all seriousness.'

Growing up in the '80s, Yee Jee was, he says, 'the epitome of the latch-
key kid … I watched an exorbitant amount of TV when I came in from
school, and yes *Doctor Who* was one of many shows that I enjoyed.'

That young latch-key kid was born in Hong Kong but grew up in Canada,
where his parents emigrated when he was just six months old. Living in
a predominantly Jewish neighbourhood, he quickly learned to appreciate
challah and matzah ball soup! It was there too that he first got the acting bug.

'A lot of friends from my neighbourhood were involved in music and
drama,' he comments. 'In my first year at high school, one of my best friends and
I got parts in one of the school's very elaborate musical theatre productions. It
was a rare feat for a first year student to get in, never mind two in the same year.'

Yee Jee seemed to have a natural flare for the subject, and under
the mentorship of the drama teacher, Mike Denos, he was encouraged
to throw himself into the acting world. That support did come with a
warning from Denos, however: 'If you can think of anything else you can
do in life and be happy, do that. Otherwise, go ahead and pursue an acting
career.' That advice is something that Yee Jee has never forgotten.

A Big Break

The two friends continued to perform in school productions until a local
talent agent spotted them in a show. 'He invited my friend to join his
agency. I met with him and expressed an interest in joining the agency too
and he said, "I'll send you on a few auditions but you're not really on my
roster. You'll have to take some acting lessons." I did as he suggested and
he did send me for some auditions. One of the first was for a predominant

casting director in Vancouver. I was nervous as all-heck, stuttering and stammering my words and acting very, very nervous and eager-to-please. In all respects it was a complete disaster. Luckily, they wanted those qualities for the character, so I got the part!'

That first gig cemented in Yee Jee's mind the desire to be an actor. 'Filming was on location at an abandoned railway tunnel. The cast were dressed in 1890s period attire and ... I was sitting on an apple box [a type of specialised box used in film production]. Directly in front of me was the camera crane in all its technological glory and coolness, set against this historic backdrop. It was such a surreal juxtaposition – the old and the new – that it blew me away. I thought, "How cool are movies!" From that moment on, I was hooked.'

Despite that early success, Mike Denos's words of warning stayed with the fledgling actor. 'I try,' he laughs, 'to maintain a level head and grounded perspective on the whole acting thing, because acting may be a lot of things, but it's rarely consistently or reliably rewarding.' As a result, Yee Jee has his fingers in lots of other professional pies, from web development to photography, but it's acting that really floats his boat.

After that first 'wow' on-set moment, Yee Jee continued to take acting lessons and got himself 'a more supportive agent' to help progress his career. And progress it did. His first big break came in 1991 when he landed a recurring role in Nickelodeon's only teenage soap, *Hillside*. That was quickly followed by two seasons in the Canadian teen drama *Madison*, where he played two different characters. 'That really allowed me to "stretch my legs" with something long-term-ish ...' he says.

Yee Jee now has over 60 professional TV, film and stage credits to his name, but he still considers the *Doctor Who* TV movie to be a major landmark.

Movie Memories
Yee Jee played Chang Lee, a street kid who finds himself manipulated by Eric Roberts' wonderfully menacing Master. At the time, he was just 21. A lot of time has flowed through the continuum since then, but still he retains a special place in his heart for the movie and its fans. 'They've been very supportive. I mean: really, really supportive. A few times I went out with fans from conventions, but I don't think to be honest that I can share the actual events with you ... LOL. I could probably fill a book with crazy stories from my past!'

Can he share some memories of his time filming the movie? 'This is the first time I've shared this memory. At one point during the filming, one of the location crew members – I don't remember his name now –

approached me about an "opportunity". I agreed to meet with his associate, who was a musician. Anyways, long story short, I was very young and naïve at the time – one might say "a real dumb-ass" – and this fellow took me for five grand. Back then $5k was like $20k today. It was supposed to be a "loan", with signed contracts, the whole nine yards, but in the end the contract wasn't worth the paper it was written on. Lesson learned!

'However, I have many, many fond memories of that time as well. That one was just meant as a peek behind the curtains, so to speak. One time that particularly sticks in my mind was when we were in the middle of shooting the scene just before the fireworks. We've all come back from the dead and the Doctor is about to board the TARDIS and say his goodbyes. So it's meant to be an emotional moment. The location was this manmade water feature … There were a lot of people and equipment around. It was very busy and intense, and of course someone had to fall in the water. And that would be me! But I didn't just misstep – I completely fell over backwards and got soaked head to toe! Wardrobe had doubles of some of my costume, but not all. So I was quite wet when we shot that scene. I don't think I'll ever forget that day!'

Yee Jee also loved getting to know his British co-stars. 'Either I have a distant British ancestor or I get it from my dad, who went to college in England, but I've always shared that British sense of humour – kind of cheeky and silly and self-effacing. So it was a joy working with Paul [McGann] and Sylvester [McCoy].'

Since filming the movie, Yee Jee has returned to the world of *Doctor Who* with Big Finish. His first role, playing Dr Goddard in the webcast 'Real Time', paired him with sixth Doctor Colin Baker. 'Excelis Decays', in 2002, reunited him with Sylvester McCoy. 'Tales from the Vault' teamed him up with Daphne Ashbrook (who played Grace Holloway in the TV movie) in an Amicus-style portmanteau story that romped through four different *Doctor Who* eras. 'It's been lovely to work on those,' Yee Jee says. 'It's such an honour and so much fun to be able to create new characters and work with people from different eras of the show. I'm really so very grateful for every opportunity to do that.'

So what's next? 'A lot of actors have a "dream role" that they want to play,' Yee Jee says, 'but I don't. I'd love to sink my teeth into something brilliantly written and directed amazingly well. I've been fortunate enough to have been involved in productions that qualify, but mostly in smaller roles – besides Chang Lee. A meaty lead role in a truly awesome film – that's my dream role, regardless of what type of character.' And returning to the world of *Doctor Who*? 'Definitely!'

The Doctor's Doctor:
Daphne Ashbrook

Harry Sullivan was the first. Martha Jones was the feistiest. But there's no doubt that Dr Grace Holloway was the Doctor's doctor – the one who captured his hearts ... even if she did inadvertently stop them first. Daphne Ashbrook played the lady who did what no other companion had done until the TV movie ... kiss the Doctor ...

What would you say was your 'big break' career-wise?
Well, my first on-screen job was a part in the ABC series *Hardcastle and McCormick*. So I guess that was my 'foot in the door' moment. But when I landed a lead in the series *Our Family Honor*, that was a pretty big deal. It was a great part – kind of a *Romeo and Juliet* scenario, and an unbelievable cast. I played a New York cop, Ray Liotta was my partner, Kenny McMillan was my grandfather, and Eli Wallach played the head of the crime family – just to name a few. We shot the exteriors in New York City, every other month, for a month. I was in heaven. Tom Mason played my uncle and he is such a wonderful actor. The pilot was also directed by one of my all-time favourite directors, Bob Butler, and I learned so much from him. The whole thing was just a gift.

How did you come to be offered the part of Grace Holloway and what was your audition like?
It must have been fairly uneventful, as I don't remember all that much about it ... except watching all the British actors rehearsing their lines in the lobby – they were auditioning for the Master role. *But*, Philip Segal has said that I was late for the audition and came running in and was a bit frenzied. They liked that, and thought my behaviour suited the role. I have no memory of this. But whatever works, right?

Were you aware of *Doctor Who* before you accepted the part?
I knew *nothing*. Not until I was in Vancouver and rehearsing with Paul McGann and the director Geoffrey Sax. They started to ask what I knew about the show, and slowly they started to educate me. Between late nights shooting and waiting around on set with Paul and Sylvester McCoy, I started to get a bit of an understanding. But I really didn't *know* about it until many years later, when I started to meet the fans of the show. The depth of love for this show has been truly amazing to see. I'm just starting to get it. At the time,

it was just a great part, in a great script, and working with great people, in a great city. Which has always been enough ...Who knew I was going to have the privilege of being a part of the greater *Doctor Who* family!

In the movie, Grace declines the Doctor's offer to travel with him. If it were real life, would you have said yes – and where would you have asked the Doctor to take you?
I would have said yes and I would have asked him to take me to his home on Gallifrey. I want to meet his family!

Due to copyright issues, Grace Holloway has never appeared in any Big Finish audios. If you could revisit the character, which Doctor – other than the eighth – would you like to travel with and why?
God, it's hard to choose, but it would have to be Sylvester – Number Seven. He's such a dear friend and I *know* I would have a blast with him. But Tom Baker seems like a wild ride. He has this mirthful approach to the Doctor and there's always a good dash of danger thrown, so travelling with him would be intriguing – very hard to turn down. But I do love them all. And Number Eight will always be *my* beautiful Doctor!

You're the only woman to have appeared in both *Doctor Who* and *Star Trek* on TV. What other sci-fi franchise would you like to appear in and why?
The recent *Star Trek* movies would be amazing. *Star Wars*, of course; *X-Men* I love; *Men in Black* would be awesome ... Okay, okay, I *love* sci-fi ... so sue me.

So, who's the better kisser, Julian Bashir or the eighth Doctor?
Really! I never kiss and tell!

You recently encouraged fans to join you for RegenerEight – a mass online rewatch of the *Doctor Who* movie accompanied by live chat. Can you tell us a little about that, and did you really crash Google hangouts?
RegenerEight was, I think, an idea from my Web Dalek, which is the *nom de guerre* of my web/PR person. I don't think I knew that it was even technologically possible, but we did it. There were at least 7,000 people who watched the movie and listened to the commentary with myself, Gary Russell, Yee Jee Tso and [host of the regular Podshock *Doctor Who* podcast] Ken Deep. Around 10,000 people were chatting or blogging while the event took place. Eighty-one countries were represented. And let me just say, we

had no idea … The only way we could track who was going to actually participate was by RSVPs on Facebook and Google. So we went into it thinking that there might be as many as 300 people involved! And yes we did crash Google hangouts … Luckily, we had back-up and directed people to YouTube and my website (www.daphneashbrook.com) to make sure everyone could attend the party. But those numbers are just conservative tallies – and not counting all of the people who had *Doctor Who* parties and were counted only once. The whole thing was absolutely amazing!

The commentary from Gary, Yee Jee and Ken was perfect. We all had our different perspectives to offer, and it just worked like a charm. Gary was in Wales, Yee Jee was in Vancouver, Ken was in New York and I was in Los Angeles. Honestly, I was a bit terrified. I just couldn't have lived with myself if the whole thing had gone bust. So the scariest moment was at the start, before we did the countdown to press 'Play' in unison, and one or the other of us kept getting knocked off the live stream. I think my voice was a little shaky at the start, but once we got rolling, it was a blast! There have since been many requests to get a copy of the live stream, so we will soon be making it available.

You've worked on four *Doctor Who* audios for Big Finish. Which classic series Doctor/companion has been the most fun to meet and why?
I've loved meeting everyone I've worked with at Big Finish. They are all so wonderful. But I think my favorite was when I met Katy Manning while we were recording 'Tales From the Vault'. She is such a kick, and I felt immediately like we were old friends. She's such a delight!

Your autobiography is called *Dead Woman Laughing*. What's the story behind the title?
Subtitle – *An Actor's 'Take' From Both Sides of the Camera* … It's about my life a bit, and being in this crazy business, having been in it my whole life. I grew up in theatres watching my mother and father rehearse or perform in plays. I then started in the theatre at six myself. But the title came about as follows: I'm lying 'dead' on the cloister room floor during the shoot of the *Doctor Who* movie, and I start to laugh. It was toward the end of the shoot, and I was getting punch-drunk. But I just couldn't stop laughing. It's a problem being believable as a corpse, while laughing.

Anyway, I said something like, 'Dead woman laughing.' And Paul turned to me and said, 'That's the title of your book.' I never forgot that. Something like 15 years later, I was asked to write a book, and there it was. I always found that the many characters I've played where I die, and the many where I've been killed, make entertaining stories. As I worked on the book, I realised that I have had some close calls with 'meeting my maker' as well. So I thought the title would definitely work.

You've just released an album, *Grace Notes*. If you could choose any one song to sum up your life so far what would it be?
Depends on what day you catch me on. 'Useless Desires' for the days when I feel frustrated. 'Horses', when I miss my daughter. 'Diamond in the Rough', when I'm struck by the beauty of others – which is often. 'This Must be the Place', when I need to lighten up. And 'One Big Love', when I'm feeling the love. Oh, and 'Furry Sings the Blues', when I worry about the loss of our culture, individualism and small businesses that succumb to large corporate interests. Every song means something to me. Sorry, I cheated.

Which one character/show/film are you most often recognised for?
I think, at the moment, *The OC* character I played, Dawn. I played a recurring character on that, and was a bit infamous, being such a perfectly awful mother to Ryan. I'm a mean, alcoholic, cigarette-smoking, bad-boyfriend-choosing jail bird. Oh, and I abandon my own son. What a fantastic role! Also, a show I did last year called *Hollywood Heights*, where I played a kind of white-trash but well-meaning mother. They really wrote some great stuff for me – lots of funny lines. People come up to me about that role in the oddest places. But it's always fun!

How has *Doctor Who* changed your life?
It has kept me from becoming a bit of an isolationist. I am very shy, believe it or not. And I tend to hide out a bit. But the *Doctor Who* fans are always *so* kind, and generous, and funny and smart – don't get me started! I feel like I am a part of a family, who will forgive my flaws, and offer the occasional hug. It means so much. It also gives me the chance to meet *all* the wonderful people who have contributed to *Doctor Who* over these many years. I have made some of my closest friends through *Doctor Who*. Thanks Doc.

Finally, do you have any message for Peter Capaldi as he steps into the Doctor's shoes?
Peter, buckle your seatbelt … it's going to be an amazing ride! Welcome to the *Doctor Who* family!

Chapter Five: The '00s

**'I've seen fake gods and bad gods and demigods and would-be gods;
out of all that, out of that whole pantheon, if I believe in one thing …
just one thing … I believe in her.'**
(The Doctor, 'The Satan Pit')

Whether you call them the noughties, the aughties or the 20-ohs, the new decade brought with it new – and old – problems. In Asia, a Boxing Day tsunami claimed the lives of over 230,000 people. In Kashmir, an earthquake added another 80,000 to those lost. Hurricane Katrina and the Black Saturday bushfires brought devastation to both the US and Australia. New diseases such SARS (Severe Acute Respiratory Syndrome), swine flu and bird flu reminded us all of the power of a very old word: pandemic.

While Mother Nature bared her teeth, we humans were notching up a pretty impressive death toll of our own. Coups, conflicts, greed and the growing War on Terror proved once again that when it comes to killing, we are the masters of the game.

However, the '00s weren't all tragedy and terror, death and disaster. The growth of the world wide web, digital technology and personal computing brought people of all orientations, colours and faiths together in a way that hadn't been possible a decade earlier. Even if all we did with that shiny new tech was share pictures of cute kittens, at least we were connecting with our fellow men. Thanks to Facebook, Twitter and instant messaging we could all now ignore the people we were with, to chat to someone else 200 miles away.

It was this theme of 'just connect' that gave the re-booted *Doctor Who* its distinctive feel. When Christopher Eccleston brought the first new Doctor in almost a decade to our screens, his creation was a brusque, bold and no-nonsense character. Gone were the quirky clothes and the even quirkier personality ticks. This was a stripped-down Doctor. A war-damaged, guilt-wracked loner who, like Hartnell's Doctor, needed the warmth of human contact to reconnect with his better self. And reconnect he does. By sacrificing himself to save his companion Rose, Nine laid the groundwork for a more 'human' and compassionate Ten.

David Tennant's tenth Doctor burst onto our small screens – in a blaze of regenerative energy – on 18 June 2005. During the actor's five-year tenure, he would become one of the most popular Doctors ever. Part of that popularity was due to David's natural charm and commitment to the role – he's a lifelong fan. But the Rose-Doctor will-they-won't-they storylines also proved incredibly popular. Some fans believed that focusing on the soap opera of the Doctor's 'love life' was missing the point of the show. Others applauded the decision to explore aspects of the Doctor's personality that had previously been off-limits. Whatever your feelings, with David Tennant at the helm, *Doctor Who* enjoyed a level of popularity that hadn't been seen since Tom Baker's era.

By the time that Matt Smith donned his All Saint's layer boots and tweed jacket in January 2010, *Doctor Who* was once more riding high in the ratings. 13.8 million viewers tuned to watch the 2007 Christmas Special 'Voyage of the Damned'. However, every regeneration brings change, and Matt Smith's Eleven has seen something of a return of old school *Who*. His fish finger and custard-loving Doctor is more alien and more disconnected than Ten … although, he does gain a wife/surrogate daughter in the form of River Song. What we can expect when the youngest actor to play the Doctor – Matt Smith – hands over to the oldest since William Hartnell, only time will tell. It always does.

The Animator: Steve Meyer

It's November 2003. Richard E Grant has just become the ninth Doctor and Steve Meyer is part of the team responsible for bringing the all-new *Doctor Who* back to the small screen for the first time since the TV movie in 1996. Three years later, Steve has the opportunity to work with Patrick Troughton – 19 years after the much-loved actor died. Yes, really …

Tell us a little about yourself.
I've worked in animation for 20-odd years, designing and art directing everything from *Terry Pratchett's Discworld* to *Rupert The Bear*'s new adventures and a million things in between. I was Cosgrove-Hall's designer, art director and producer between the mid-1990s and 2003, working on the BAFTA-winning *Foxbusters* and nominated *Albie*. I animated Leonardo da Vinci's drawings for the Victoria and Albert Museum and developed animated projects for John Lloyd's *QI* company. I'm now creative executive at Impossible Pictures, working across genres, but focusing mainly on factual shows. Among other things, I've just made a show about dragons for National Geographic and I'm currently making a series about the First World War for the History Channel in the US.

How did you get involved in the Flash-animated *Doctor Who* 'Scream of the Shalka'?
I was approached by BBC Interactive's Martin Trickey and James Goss, for whom I'd made *Ghosts of Albion*. That was an online Flash-animated serial based on a Victorian-set horror story written by Chris Golden and Amber Benson and voiced by a great cast including Rory Kinnear, Anthony Daniels and the legendary Leslie Phillips. James and Martin were intending to breathe new life into the then fairly dormant *Doctor Who* world with a streaming .swf file online series. Part of the brief was that it had to be able to be viewed by anyone with a 52k dial up internet connection. Aargh! That caused serious design and directorial issues. But I was excited to be able to take the things we'd learnt on *Ghosts* a bit further, with a slightly bigger budget.

How much freedom were you given about how the 'Scream of the Shalka' world – and Doctor – should look, and which specific elements were you responsible for?
The small team and I at Cosgrove-Hall Films were pretty much responsible

for everything, from the design and animatics (moving storyboards cut to a timeline and a voice track) to the final delivery of the Flash files to the Beeb.

There were only around half a dozen of us working on the hour-long animation, including Jon Doyle and Claire Grey, who also worked on our later *Who* animation projects. I have to say, though, it felt longer than an hour when we were trying to deliver it in less than four months! Along with lots of other roles on the production, I designed every character and most locations and props. So it was very intense, very exhausting and a lot of fun! I personally got to re-imagine the exterior, and particularly the interior of the TARDIS, a new Doctor, the Master and some monsters. That's a pretty amazing thing for anyone who has ever been a fan of the show. The fast, low-key, low-budget nature of the production probably gave me more freedom to do more than any *Who* designer before or since, so I count myself very privileged.

What influenced your designs for the Doctor and the Master?
It was decided that the ninth Doctor, as he was then, should look like the actor who voiced him in the animation. I watched *Withnail and I* a lot – not a chore – and took it from there. Richard's was a pretty dark and troubled Doctor in Paul Cornell's script and I think that is reflected in the gothic look to the design. It also reflects the fact that, given half a chance, I'll make anything I design look gothic or steampunky ... even *Rupert the Bear*! The other character designs have, I hope, a flavour of the great actors who voiced them, though they were never intended to be exact likenesses. Not least because a number of the actors played more than one role in the show. The great Sir Derek Jacobi, who voiced the Master beautifully, is not the basis for the look of the robot character. He much more closely resembles earlier incarnations of the Master.

Initially the BBC intended 'Scream of the Shalka' to be the first in a new series of *Doctor Who* adventures. How did you feel about being involved in what was then the show's relaunch?
To be honest I was so up against it to deliver the show on time, I don't think I was very aware of what was going on more broadly in the world of *Who*. I saw some other scripts towards the end of production but, by then, the announcement had been made that Russell T Davies and executive producer Julie Gardner were going to make *Doctor Who* the brilliant big-budget show it deserved to be ... and the rest is history. I never

doubted and always hoped that our limited animation project would be superseded at some point by a proper full-on live-action TV series. Given how brilliant that series and its incarnations of the Doctor have been, I'm not complaining!

How did you feel about being involved in resurrecting one of the great 'lost' *Who* serials?
It was a great project. Mad and wonderful on so many levels. Small budget, again, but not as technically constrained as 'Shalka'. The challenges of trying to make it sit comfortably alongside the surviving episodes of the show were daunting. Hearing the audio recording of Nicholas Courtney seeing his animated likeness for the first time was worth all the late nights in the studio!

If the lost episodes of 'The Invasion' were ever found, how would you feel about watching them?
We all hope for a *Raiders of the Lost Ark* moment and for the original missing episodes to turn up in some far-flung corner of the BBC universe, and I for one would love to see the lost episodes. To see how close, or not, we got to the original team's vision and directorial decisions. It wasn't always easy to decipher from the surviving sound.

'The Infinite Quest' was another animated *Doctor Who* project that you worked on. This time, the animations were aired in 12 weekly parts in a segment of the children's spin-off show *Totally Doctor Who*, before being released in compilation form on DVD. Can you share one memory of working with David Tennant on that?
When we were voice-recording 'Shalka', a young actor and big *Doctor Who* fan, who was working on a radio show in the studio next door, turned up in his lunch hour to play, uncredited and for free, a doomed caretaker murdered by worm-infested zombies! As far as I know, that was the first appearance of a Mr David Tennant in an episode of *Doctor Who* … oh and 'The Infinite Quest' was great to work on as well!

If you could work on anything in the Whoniverse, what would it be and why?
Well, designing a monster for the live-action TV show would of course be something any designer would love to do. But I'm very happy to have worked on *Who* in the small way I have.

The Gaffer: Mark Hutchings

'I've done over 100 episodes. I've seen every Doctor – Christopher Eccleston, David Tennant and Matt Smith – come and go. I've seen producers come and go, directors come and go and I've been there right through it all. I'm the last man standing!'

Mark Hutchings is talking about his incredible career. As gaffer, he's worked on every episode of new *Who* since the very first, 'Rose', and will be back recording the new season with the new Doctor, Peter Capaldi, in January 2014. He's also been involved in *Torchwood*: 'Children of Earth' and *The Sarah Jane Adventures*. It's quite a record, but for those of us not in the business, what exactly is a gaffer?

'Basically,' Mark laughs, 'a gaffer is head of the lighting department and solely responsible for anything electrical on the set. I work in cahoots with the DOP – the director of photography. So he tells me how he wants the set lit and then I take over. I draw up the plans and rig the lights to make sure that everything's ready and looks the way that the DOP wants it.'

The term gaffer originally referred to someone who moved overhead equipment to control lighting levels using a gaff – a hook on the end of a long handle. An alternative name – often heard in award ceremonies – is chief lighting technician.

Light, or sometimes the lack of it, is a vital filmmaker's tool, and it's especially important in sci-fi for conjuring up that sense of the otherworldly. Imagine the film *Alien* without all those dark shadows and creepily-lit corridors. 'In drama, lighting is very important to create mood,' agrees Mark, 'but exactly what's needed changes from scene to scene. You may want shafts of light coming through a cloud. Well you can't just wait around for one to show up – you have to create it. So the gaffer and his team will do that; but first you also have to put smoke into the set. Obviously we have a Special Effects Department to produce the smoke, and it's not until you put smoke into the set that you'll see the shafts of light and know if you've got it right.'

With a show as involved as *Who*, there's really no such thing as a typical day's filming, but Mark gets involved at a very early stage. 'I'll be given the script, then the DOP and I are told by the director what feel he wants for the episode. You then do what's called a tone meeting where the DOP tells you what colours he wants on various lamps, whether he wants it light or dark or moody – basically the look he wants on screen. So you work out which coloured gels you're going to use and what sort of lights you're going to use to get the episode to look how the DOP wants it.'

Mark's being modest of course. Tim Palmer, director of photography on 'Let's Kill Hitler' and 'The Wedding of River Song', described him in his blog as 'the inimitable Welsh BAFTA-winning gaffer Mark Hutchings, who really runs the show. We would be all at sea without Mark.'

Happy Families

It all sounds like one big, happy family. Is it? 'Well, you spend more time in work than you do at home, to be honest, so you do become a big family. You end up becoming friends – you have a bit of fun. Obviously you have a laugh when you can, although once the camera's rolling it all gets very serious. It's work hard and play hard, as they say.'

For Mark, working on *Who* has been very much a dream job. 'I was a fan,' he says. 'I'd watched *Doctor Who* as a kid so, for me, getting to work on the show as a gaffer was fantastic. Going back seven, eight years, when I first applied for the job, so many people were after it. I couldn't believe it when I got the phone-call from BBC Wales to say I'd got the job.'

Since then Mark has been busy making his own contribution to the world of *Doctor Who*, and has even got to know the Doctors themselves. 'We always have a bit of banter with the actors. With Matt Smith, because he's a Blackburn Rovers supporter, we have a bit of a laugh about football. He's English and we're Welsh – the show's recorded in Cardiff – so when England play Wales at rugby we quite often have a playful £10 bet. And of course when the Olympic torch came through Cardiff, Matt carried it down to the Bay. The leg that he did was very early in the morning, so a lot of people didn't see it, but we all had a hold of the torch.'

What about David Tennant and Christopher Eccleston? 'David wasn't really interested in football or rugby but you still chat about family or what he's been up to. Christopher was always really nice. He was into his training. He used to come home from work and you'd quite often see him on Cardiff Bay going for a run. He used to keep himself very fit. Then there was Lis Sladen. God bless her – she's passed away now – but she was a very, very lovely lady and we did have a lot of fun on *The Sarah Jane Adventures*. In fact I've been so lucky working on all the *Doctor Who*s, *Torchwood* and *Sarah Jane*.'

As time rolls on and we look forward to seeing what the next season of *Who* has in store, Mark is equally excited. 'I hope to work on it as long as I can,' he says. 'It's work in Cardiff and that means I can keep all the Welsh boys employed. The show's not only been great for me but for Wales too. Hopefully it'll continue for many years to come. In fact, the way I'm going, I've been at it so long, I might end up being one of the Doctors!'

The Model Maker: Mike Tucker

**' ... from the classic series, seeing the reaction to the motion control
sequence where the TARDIS is plucked out of space
by the Time Lords in "The Trial of a Time Lord"
would probably be a high point.'**

If you spent your childhood painstakingly painting up 1/5-scale Sevans models of Daleks, Ice Warriors and Cybermen, then you'll appreciate what I mean when I say that Mike Tucker probably has one of the coolest jobs in the Whoniverse. Actually, make that two of the coolest jobs. When he's not making award-winning miniature effects for *Doctor Who* he's got a pretty formidable back catalogue of *Who* books and comic strips to his name.

What might be surprising is that Mike's *Doctor Who* career hasn't been limited to just the new series. Surprising because there are only a handful of people who have worked on both classic and new *Who*. Mike's involvement with the show actually dates from Season 23 – Colin Baker's last – and includes all of Sylvester McCoy's tenure plus the charity Children in Need special 'Dimensions in Time'.

Even before new *Who* had been aired, Mike was involved, working on a special series of 'TARDIS cams' – short films for BBC Interactive showing the TARDIS landing in a variety of different alien environments. The job was perhaps one of his trickiest in terms of time and budget. 'We had,' Mike says, 'a very short deadline, and a tiny budget in which to deliver four very different planetary landscapes over a period of four days.'[5]

Since then, Mike and the team at his company, The Model Unit, have worked on some of the new series' most demanding stories. For 'Aliens of London', their showcase sequence was of the Slitheen spacecraft circling over London before crashing into the River Thames – taking out Big Ben's clock tower on the way down. Achieving the necessary level of realistic carnage meant building a section of the clock tower from plaster along with a timber wing of the Slitheen spacecraft, all to scale. They also got to trash Downing Street, building a scale model of the Prime Minister's famous Number 10 door for the digital effects team to work with.

For the Blitz sequences in 'The Empty Child' and 'The Doctor Dances', Mike and his team were once again called in to provide a series of miniatures. This time, a three-and-a-half-foot foam and latex barrage

---

5 There were actually six TARDIS cams in total (all of which have been released as bonus items on *Doctor Who* DVDs), but some of them used the same alien environments.

balloon was required, which could be puppeteered against a black backdrop to give the effect of the balloon's realistic movements in the air.

For 'The Christmas Invasion' (2005) the script called for the arrival of a Sycorax ship to be accompanied by every window in London being shattered. Mike and his team were given the task of shattering the windows in one of the tower blocks on Rose Tyler's estate. Working at 1/6th scale, they constructed a six-storey tower block, complete with interior rooms, balconies, satellite dishes and Christmas decorations. A total of 111 individual window panes were shattered on each take!

Mike has even added 'new' optional-alternative effects to the DVD release of the 1964 story 'The Dalek Invasion of Earth'. Ensuring that the replacement effects had a suitably retro feel meant that contemporary photographs of London landmarks such as Trafalgar Square and Battersea Power Station had to be combined with blue-screen model photography to create digital matte painting backgrounds. Smoke elements and digitally-generated saucers were then composited into the final shots.

So how on Earth did Mike get to do such an awesome job? 'Originally I wanted to build models for the Science and Natural History Museums – I loved the forced-perspective dioramas that used to be common in both of those museums. Then I caught an edition of the BBC magazine programme *Pebble Mill at One* that featured an item on the BBC Visual Effects Department, and that was it, I was hooked on a new career path.'

Plain Sailing

Believe it or not, making it happen proved to be 'relatively straightforward,' Mike says. 'The day after that edition of *Pebble Mill* had aired, my mum wrote to the BBC asking for information about careers in the Visual Effects (VFX) Department, and they wrote back with an information pack. Following that, I arranged to visit the workshops and spent a day watching what was being done and talking to the designers. At the end of the day, the then Head of Department, Michealjohn Harris, gave advice on what college courses to take that would be useful and said that he'd put my name on file for future reference. I then followed the advice he gave and, following the successful completion of my Theatre Diploma, I joined the VFX Department as a holiday relief assistant. I was also given a lot of encouragement by the retired Head of BBC Wales Drama, David J Thomas, who arranged visits to the BBC Wales studios whenever the VFX team were working there.'

One of Mike's early jobs was working on a cult sci-fi show that aired on what was then the BBC's only other channel – BBC2. That channel had always been reserved for niche programming, although it was perhaps more a reflection of the BBC's attitude toward sci-fi rather than the show's viewing figures that qualified *Red Dwarf* for a place in its schedules.

'I'm proud of pretty much everything we did for *Red Dwarf* – for Series Three to Six at any rate,' Mike comments. 'The show's VFX Director, Peter Wragg, was generous in passing on his knowledge of the techniques that he had used during his time working with Gerry Anderson at Century 21, and we ran with it. Strange as it seems, very few of the BBC VFX crew were interested in model work. They preferred going on location, so we pretty much had a free hand to go off and do what we wanted in terms of making the show a calling card for the Department.'

When Mike finally got the opportunity to work on *Doctor Who*, which was in 1986, he was suddenly faced with the enormous challenge of being involved in a show of which he was a self-confessed fan. 'I don't think that you can be my age and interested in effects without being a fan of some aspect of the show!' says Mike. 'However I was smart enough to realise that any fan-ish enthusiasm needed to be tempered with professionalism. So I kept my delight at working on the show in check. Nonetheless, to be given the job of building the TARDIS miniature for "The Trial of a Time Lord" was a surreal moment. It was only as my time on the show went on that the producer, John Nathan-Turner, realised quite what a fan I was. But by that time he had also realised that it didn't get in the way of me doing a good job. In fact he recognised that it actually added another level to the work that I did. I think that the same is true of the new series, where fans permeate the production team all the way to the top.'

All Change

From a technical and budgetary point of view, classic and new *Who* are obviously very different shows. However, what Mike reveals is that it's not just about having the money to go around but, creatively, things are much more delineated. Where, in the past, the BBC's own VFX Department would be expected to handle most of the work in-house, *Doctor Who* now requires extensive outside expertise. 'The sort of multi-tasking crews that the BBC used to utilise have been replaced with specialised crews. On the effects front, that means there are four or five effects companies working on any given episode when there used to be one. For example, on "Time and the Rani", Colin Mapson's effects crew was comprised of six people and we did everything – the monster masks, animatronics, props, miniatures, pyrotechnics and atmospheric effects. On the much more recent "Cold War", there were four effects companies – the Mill doing CGI, Millennium FX doing the creatures, Real FX doing pyrotechnics and atmospherics and my team doing the submarine miniatures. Plus there was a separate Props Department. That obviously costs more, but it means that each company can concentrate on its own individual area so that the quality improves.'

Put simply, television is no longer made in the way the BBC did it in the '60s, '70s and '80s. Back then, shows would use a multi-camera set up that required a number of cameras – usually four, in *Doctor Who's* case – working simultaneously on the studio floor. Two would be used for close-ups, two for wider action shots. In that way, the whole programme could be recorded in a series of continuous takes, with instant editing carried out by the vision mixer cutting between cameras on the fly, reducing costs considerably. 'Now,' Mike says, 'multi-camera dramas have been replaced with single camera shoots, so each episode is more like making a mini feature film.'

Considering that Mike's involvement with *Doctor Who* spans 25 years, what would be his most memorable moments so far? 'Wheeling the new Dalek onto set at the Millennium Stadium in Cardiff was quite a good moment from the new show,' he recalls. 'The work we did on "Cold War" was very pleasing too, but the single best effect we've done on the new show has been the Nestene lair being destroyed at the end of "Rose". It cut seamlessly into the live action. But from the classic series, seeing the reaction to the motion control sequence where the TARDIS is plucked out of space by the Time Lords in "The Trial of a Time Lord" would probably be a high point.'

Successful Sidelines

Aside from his model work, Mike has also been involved in quite a few *Doctor Who* 'side projects' too … although it's hard to imagine how he finds the time to do anything else, without an actual TARDIS stashed away somewhere.

He was for instance involved in refurbishing the props and models for the *Doctor Who Experience* attraction. It sounds like fantastic fun, and presumably he was quite excited to be working on some of the old props and models? 'Absolutely,' Mike says. 'The Ice Warrior was an especially nice one to work on just because of the age of the piece, but in terms of seeing an old prop returned to its former glory, the Giant Robot underwent a complete transformation. Someone had taken the very odd decision to spray over the original metalwork. It took a long time to clean off all of that paint, but when we had finished, and the prop was polished back up to a high shine, it just looked fantastic. I didn't think it would look quite as good as it did.'

His other sideline is as a successful writer. His first book was the non-fiction volume *Ace!*, co-written with Sophie Aldred. He's also written for BBC Books' Past Doctor Adventures range and the Big Finish audio dramas, and contributed comic strip stories to the *Doctor Who Battles in Time* and *Doctor Who Adventures* magazines. Perhaps most popular with the fans were his Past Doctor Adventures, co-written with Robert Perry, which featured the seventh Doctor and Ace and picked up from where classic *Who* stopped, forming a kind of 'Season 27'. What was the appeal of writing for that particular Doctor and companion team? 'It just made sense,' Mike says. 'I'd worked a lot with Sophie and Sylvester. I'd also spent a lot of time with the script editor Andrew Cartmel and writers Ben Aaronvitch, Ian Briggs and Marc Platt talking about the characters, and I considered the seventh Doctor to be "my" Doctor. Certainly I think that paid off in terms of how Robert Perry and I captured the characters on the page. There was also some freedom in terms of where you could take the stories, whereas previous incarnations were anchored a little in their respective eras.'

Does he have a favourite out of his books? 'It's always tricky to pick out one book or story because they all have different meanings to me. In terms of a crowd-pleasing blockbuster then *Storm Harvest* (1999) probably comes out on top, although *Illegal Alien* (1997) is still a favourite – but that could be mainly down to the fact that it was my first published novel.'

The Fight Coordinator: Kevin McCurdy

'Dave was like a big kid! Especially when he saw the swords we'd be using, he was like, "This is greeeaat!" … swinging it around over his head.'

Kev McCurdy is having the time of his life. When we meet, at London's Shakespeare's Globe, he's taking time out from rehearsals for *Macbeth*, on which he's the fight director.

The Globe is a modern day reconstruction of the theatre that was built and owned by Shakespeare's acting troupe – the Lord Chamberlain's Men – in 1599. It's made to period specifications with oak-beamed, whitewashed walls and a thatched roof … incidentally the only thatched roof allowed within London's City limits since the Great Fire in 1666. Although outside the theatre the Southbank is a bustling tourist trap, inside it's easy to lose yourself in the romance of the period. I can see why Kev loves working here.

'I've been at the Globe on and off for four years, he says, 'and to be honest there's not a lot of difference between live theatre, TV and film. My brief is still the same. On TV you can hide a lot of things with the right camera angle, but I don't like hiding. If you're going to land a punch – land it. It's more fun. We do pull punches and kicks but we actually land them, and once the actors get used that, they let rip – and they're happy to kick the crap out of each other!'

I've seen most of this season's plays at the Globe and the stage fights have been very, very physical, but it sounds like the best is yet to come. 'We're doing the Scottish Play now and we've got a hit to the head, which you actually see, a slap to the face, which you see and hear, a strangulation, Banquo being murdered. All that is full contact. Then there's the fight at the end. I've always wanted to do an axe fight. The Native American Indians and their style of fighting have always struck me as interesting. When I was approached to do the play, the director, Eve [Best], was really accommodating. So we're using tomahawks, which I don't think has ever been done before.'

Play Time
Kev has a wild and crazy life. 'I get paid to teach people how to swordfight,'

he says, 'how to use martial arts and how to chuck themselves against walls and not get hurt. The sort of stuff that we used to do as kids ... and it's great!' However, becoming one of only 27 people in the UK who are qualified by Equity to play at being big kids hasn't been easy.

Kev started out as an actor, but got 'swept up' in the movement training he did at drama college in Wales. 'We did movement – mime, dance and stage fighting – and I just fell in love with the combat training. It was a real stress-buster as well. Three years in drama college is tough. It's very competitive. So combat training was a good way of getting the stress out in a controlled environment.'

While working as a jobbing actor, Kev continued training 'doing every single workshop going' until he became an Equity-registered fight director in 1996. Then his life changed overnight. 'My life just went whoosh, basically,' he says, 'and I haven't stopped since then. I've been really fortunate, but then I have been working like a mad loon! I'm not the type of person to say "No", and for a long time, I just grabbed every single job, making mistakes – as you do – but learning, learning, all the time. Now I've been a professional for 17 years – still learning, still making mistakes – but I'm starting to refine things and be more selective. I've done movies now, major TV stuff, West End plays, and it's all great. Everything is a challenge because every single day is different.'

Back in 2006, when Kev and I first met, he had just given a demonstration of the swordfight he choreographed for the *Doctor Who* story 'The Christmas Invasion'. The fight was one of the highlights of David Tennant's first complete story as the newly-regenerated Doctor and Kev had clearly loved every second working on the show. 'I'm involved in quite a few shows in Cardiff like *Pobol y Cwm* [a Welsh-language soap opera], so I was already in the area. But then I had a phone call from the BBC production office asking if I could come and see them, and I thought "Yesss!" Their main concern was if I could use a broadsword, which I thought was interesting at the time, because I didn't know what the story entailed and *Doctor Who* doesn't have that many swordfights ... but it was great. From Day One, Dave was like a big kid! Especially when he saw the swords we'd be using, he was like, "This is greeeaat!" ... swinging it around over his head. We had four days to rehearse it, seven hours a day, and I really pushed them, because that's what I'm like with people. I said, "Look, my job is to make you look good, and if you don't look good then it's my fault," and they went for it.'

It helped that both David Tennant and Sean Guilder, who played the

Sycrorax Leader, were already fairly handy with a sword. 'Dave's done some swordfighting on stage and Sean was in the series *Sharpe*, so we were able to spark off one another, which was great. It was hard work, though,' he admits. 'At the end of the day, you're knackered and your muscles are crying out "What are you doing to me!"' Did he have any complaints that he was driving the actors too hard? 'Oh yeah,' he laughs, with a wicked gleam in his eye. 'On Day Two! But they were so good-natured about it all. I fought with both of them as well, so they could watch my reactions, because that's how I work. I don't just say, "We're going to do this," and then kick back for three hours. I want to get up and do it too. We get paid to play, and it's no fun if you don't join in!'

More, More, More!

Rehearsals are one thing, but on the day of filming, Sean had to wear a very heavy and restrictive costume. Fortunately, that presented few difficulties. 'If anything, Sean's movements were actually enhanced by the costume,' Kev recalls. 'Sean's a very physical guy and he'd created this very staccato movement for his character. So when he got the costume on, there was only a little adjustment needed to make the fight moves "work". But we knew it would be great when we saw him in the costume for the first time. That was a real "wow" moment. We thought, "Okay, this is really going to rock!"'

Given the passage of time, I ask Kev if there's anything he would have changed about the fight if he could – and his answer is a bit of a revelation. 'No, I wouldn't have changed anything, but it would have been nice to have seen the full fight, as it was edited right down. In fact, there's only me, Dave Tennant and the BBC who have got copies of the full fight, which was eight minutes long. Every time we showed it to the director he'd say, "I want more!" So we would go back and put another 30 moves in, and then he'd say, "More!" So when we actually saw the finished episode, we were saying, "Oh, is that it?" It did show off the work we'd done nicely enough but, at the same time, it would have been good to have included the full thing.'

Since working on 'The Christmas Invasion', Kev has been 'full on' with jobs on a number of very high-profile Hollywood films, including *John Carter* and *Season of the Witch*. How did they compare with working on smaller British productions? '*John Carter* was mental! That's all I can say – mental!' Kev grins. 'I enjoyed it. It was testing, mentally as well as physically. There's so much going on with a big production and, when you're in the middle of that, it's hard to switch off. At some point you have to walk away – look after yourself and your people. I was leading the core stunt team and my brain was on for the whole time. From the time I got up in the morning to the time I got back to the flat at night. Then I had to decamp – get everything that I'd filmed that day onto my laptop – before I could relax. By that time it was normally about half past ten. Then I'd have to wind down, have food, go to sleep, and then I was awake at a quarter to five to be on set for seven … and start all over again.'

Season of the Witch proved to be a much more positive experience. 'Nicholas Cage,' Kev says, 'is one of the nicest guys I've ever met. I'd been brought in to train him for eight days – two times a day – and he was picking things up so fast that, by day three, we were running on nearly 60 moves. He's like a machine, but so gentle and so honest. He came in every morning and wanted to work – wanted to be good. He was always asking, "You will tell me if I'm rubbish, won't you?" And I did [laughs], and he was absolutely fine with that. He liked the fact that the pool of people around him were honest. And then I got told that I was going to be the choreographer for the movie – that blew my mind. We were over in Budapest for three months and then went to Austria for three weeks filming on a mountain. I tell you, the job I've got is amazing!'

Raising the Bar

Many fight specialists have their 'trademark' moves. Ray Park is well known for a two-sword twirl that, even if he's hidden under a mask, makes his character instantly recognisable. Is there such a thing as a 'Kev move'? 'No,' he says. 'My style is very truthful, because all the stuff I've done, I've done for real. I've represented Wales for taekwondo. I've done a lot of martial arts. I've trained in sabre, foil, broadsword, rapier, Roman gladius, katanas … I have a friend in the USA who's in the Special Forces who teaches me one on one. The people I've talked to, the experiences I've had, the people I've mixed with … I've got lots of stories … but we won't go any further!'

The secret to 'keeping it real' is, Kev believes, not designing a fight as a stand-alone set-piece. 'I found out very quickly that looking at it from the fight director's point of view was a waste of time, because actors want to know why they have to do something.' What's their motivation? 'Exactly! So I start with that question. I look at the build-up to the fight, and sometimes the director might say that he wants a massive fight at a particular point. We then work together so that it makes sense in terms of the story. The fight might end up being scaled down, but I can then make it more vicious, because there's a backstory behind it to build on. If a fight sticks out for the wrong reasons – if you're watching the acting, then the set-piece, then the acting – then it doesn't work. It should just flow. A fight is a physical representation of a verbal statement.'

For a guy who's already achieved so much, Kev still has a few things on his 'wants list'. He collects swords and would love to have 'all of *The Lord of the Rings* armoury … plus a workshop to make my own.' He's a huge admirer of the old-school fight masters. 'Douglas Fairbanks Senior and Junior were both wonderful artists. Basil Rathbone – a brilliant fencer. Bob Anderson, who did *The Lord of the Rings* – superb … *The Princess Bride* has some spectacular swordfights – they're Bob's … *The Mask of Zorro* with Tyrone Power and Basil Rathbone is, for me, possibly the best on-screen swordfight ever, closely followed by *Scaramouche* with Stewart Granger … Then there are martial artists like Jackie Chan. I'd probably fall down in a quivering heap if I ever met him. Or Yuen Woo-ping, who worked on *The Matrix*. He's like ridiculous-years-old and still moves like a god! If by the time I leave this Earth I've produced anywhere near that quality of work, I'll be very happy.'

But Kev's 'dream' is to get a nomination for the World Stunt Awards. 'Just to be there. To be nominated on a world stage for the Best Fight. I don't care if I don't win. Just being nominated would make me happy.'

If anyone can make that happen, Kev can. This is a man who regularly puts in 16-hour days and 110 percent. He 'hates', he says, being in a comfort zone. He likes to 'push it – raise the bar' – although you'd never guess it from his chilled out persona. 'Spending your days beating the crap out of people, and being beaten, is very cathartic,' he smiles. 'When I'm back home in Cardiff, walking about, I'm just so relaxed. Really it's not hard work. It's lots of fun. I'm having a ball!' And what about that DVD of the full-length 'The Christmas Invasion' swordfight? Sadly, no, I couldn't persuade Kev to run me off a copy … just for myself and a few friends, naturally …

The Companion's Companion:
Noel Clarke

'I came from a one-parent family. It was a tough life, but I never thought about killing myself. Even at 13, sex wasn't on my mind. Killing myself definitely wasn't!'

Barking: 2006. Noel Clarke is one of a handful of actors who have made the journey to Invasion – a small UK *Doctor Who* event attracting around 300 paying guests.

Fast forward to 2012 at the MCM London Expo – a convention devoted to all things cult, cool and fantastical. Down below, in the vast halls of the Excel Centre, things are hotting up. This year, the show's expected to attract over 60,000 visitors, and it's not too hard to imagine that most of them have come out to play today. Fortunately, up in the green room, things are far less frenetic. It's here that the show's guests come to chill out before they head back into the maelstrom for signing sessions and photo-shoots. It's here too that Noel Clarke and director Johannes Roberts have come to promote their latest project, the movie *Storage 24*, which Noel wrote, produced and stars in. He's also just nabbed a spot in J J Abrams' hotly-anticipated *Star Trek: Into Darkness*. Which will make Noel a member of quite an exclusive club: actors who've been in both *Trek* and *Who*.

In just six years, Noel Clarke has turned himself into one of showbusiness's hottest properties. No wonder he's smiling.

Such success isn't lost on an actor who, a decade ago, couldn't even get an agent. 'I'd always wanted to act,' he says. 'Ever since I was about five years old … but for a long time it just didn't happen … I grew up with my mum, and to tell a West Indian parent, who came to this country and had to struggle and work hard, that you want to act … well!'

Feeling the pressure to 'get a real job' Noel headed off to university, working at a local gym to help pay the bills. It was there that he met director Rikki Beadle-Blair, and that meeting changed his life forever.

Proving a Point
Rikki asked Noel to audition for the lead in his upcoming project, *Metrosexuality* – a groundbreaking six-part drama about the lives and loves of a group of London 20-somethings. Roles in the cop drama *The*

227

Bill, procedural crime series *Waking The Dead* and hospital soap *Casualty* all followed. Noel finally hit pay-dirt in 2002 playing cheeky chappie Wyman Norris in the hugely popular British comedy *Aufwiedersehen Pet*.

Aufwiedersehen may have been the show that made him a household name, but for Noel the high point came in 2003 when he won the Olivier Theatre Award for Most Promising Performer in Christopher Shinn's play *Where Do We Live?*. It wasn't just about winning the approval of fellow thesps. It was about proving to the people who hire and fire that he could deliver.

'I love TV and I love theatre, but they're a different kind of thing. With theatre, you're on every night, but with TV, I can do ten bad takes and one good one, and a director can edit it and make me look like I'm actually doing a decent job! But what you do in the theatre is really testing the craft, and for someone who wasn't classically trained – theatre-school trained – it was tough. People wouldn't see me. Casting directors wouldn't see me. They wouldn't take me seriously. But after doing a few plays and then getting the Olivier, all of a sudden people were like: "Oh, all right. Maybe he can do it after all."'

Not only can he 'do it' but he quickly proved that acting wasn't his only talent.

Back in Barking, Noel had just finished a stint in *Doctor Who* as Mickey Smith, Rose Tyler's on-off boyfriend, and was looking forward to the release of his first film, *Kidulthood*. The movie, a thoughtful trawl through urban culture, surprised many with its uncompromisingly dark storyline and hard-hitting themes. The critics loved it. The tabloids damned it for glamorising violence and drug taking. Suddenly Noel, who wrote and starred in the film, found himself a frontline spokesman for Britain's disaffected youth.

But how 'real' were the events portrayed in *Kidulthood*? Noel was keen to point out that everything in the movie was based on things that had actually happened in his own area of West London – a year's worth of newspaper clippings formed the backbone of the story.

'Sex, drugs, violence. It's all out there. You can't pretend it isn't. My mother's a nurse and she says three girls a week come into her ward – all for the same reason. Because their mothers have found out that they are having sex with their boyfriends and told them to stop. And they try to top themselves. In my film, in the first ten minutes, a girl hangs herself. So, it may seem bleak but it's really relevant to what's happening to kids today.'

Does he understand that sort of desperation? 'Not really. I came from a one-parent family. It was a tough life, but I never thought about killing myself. Even at 13, sex wasn't on my mind. Killing myself definitely wasn't! It just shows how society's changed. Kids are thinking about this nonsense. Hopefully, this will strike a chord with some people.'

It certainly did. A sequel, *Adulthood*, followed in 2008 with Noel again doing the writing honours. The film also marked his directorial debut. It became one of the highest-grossing British films of 2008, making a reported £1.2 million in its opening weekend.

Back in 2006, Noel's game plan was simple: 'Onwards and upwards, you know? Hopefully I can just keep on acting ... but if Hollywood called, I don't know. I wouldn't pass it up. I guess I'd go where the work was, but obviously I'd want to do good work. The thing is; it's very difficult to go there cold. You have to build up some sort of reputation, and that's what I'm trying to do at the moment. People are starting to know who I am, and I think that's the time when you can go across and say, "I've done this and this and I've done that and now I'm ready."'

Is it still a problem finding good roles for black actors? 'It's not so much of a problem any more. People like Will Smith and Jamie Foxx have opened it up and there are a lot more black actors coming out and playing leads. They're creating more opportunities and hopefully those opportunities will also help British actors who want to go over there.'

Having it All

Six years on and Noel's done it all – acting, writing, directing, producing, and Hollywood too. So what have been the highlights, the lowlights and the surprises?

Noel is disarmingly modest about his achievements. 'It all sort of happened by accident ... and I've just kind of gone with it really ... I probably wouldn't have wanted to have got into producing this early, but things sort of happen. Highlights have been just being able to put work out. For me, there haven't really been any lowlights. But people looking in from the outside would probably say that *4.3.2.1* was the lowlight, because it wasn't received as well as *Kidulthood* and *Adulthood*.'

Pseudo crime caper *4.3.2.1* is a film that, Noel readily admits, 'really divides an audience,' but for him it was the breakout movie. He was no longer 'that hoodie guy or the guy that does those hoodie films.' It's also the film that has had the best sales so far, winning big audiences internationally. The studio is naturally keen to do another one.

But before that, Noel's thoughts are on *Storage 24*, which had been a 'work in progress' since before *Adulthood*. The film's inspiration came from something very Earthly – a 24-hour storage facility that Noel's wife used to visit for work. Surprisingly, too, the film initially had a quite a different feel. 'Those places, the corridors are really creepy. Sometimes they're quiet and sometimes there was this annoying music, but they had no windows and you'd get to the end of a corridor and realise you're into the next corridor. So the idea grew from me wondering what would happen if we got stuck in there and there was someone trying to kill us. How would we get away? Originally there was going to be a serial killer … but after a while I thought, "Why am I doing a serial killer when an alien would be much better …?" I like that stuff and it would open it up internationally, because people would "buy" the monster. So I wrote that. I've got a couple of writing partners – I say partners but really they're protégés that I'm bringing up to write and direct – and they had a little go at it once I'd written it. And then I hired Johannes with that draft. He liked it and away we went.'

Noel makes it all sound very easy, but as most filmmakers know, getting a film made in any country is tough – never mind in Britain where sci-fi is still often dismissed as 'kids' stuff'. Here, Johannes chips in: 'Yes, it's very tough … but you find a way. It's not like the British Film Council were knocking down my door to get this sci-fi movie done. But you have to have the drive, and that's what Noel has.'

In fact when Noel talks about 'sales' and 'opening up the market' you realise that behind that casual exterior is a one-man dynamo with a very shrewd business mind. But does he actually like sci-fi? 'I'm a big fan,' Noel confirms, although he says he'd be hard pressed to name a favourite genre film. 'I like too many to say there's a favourite. But maybe *Blade Runner* …' So *Storage 24* is really a sci-fi homecoming for the man whose career hit the stratosphere with *Doctor Who*.

The Boyfriend

Noel's role as Mickey Smith was notable in that the stories in which he debuted were the first in which *Doctor Who* companions had been seen to have a private life away from the TARDIS. Much of the success of the rebooted show hinged on the Rose-Doctor-Mickey triangle. Even today that storyline divides fans, but Noel himself was happy with the way the series – and his character – developed. Noel felt that Mickey – being a bit of a 'selfish buffoon' – wasn't widely liked by fans during those early stories; it was only when the character joined the TARDIS crew that he began to develop 'a bit of backbone'.

Noel grew up watching Peter Davison's Doctor, and when we first met, one of the 'real thrills' for him in playing Mickey Smith was getting the chance to meet his boyhood idol. 'He was my hero,' Noel said. 'I'm gutted that he's not at this event today, but I met Adric at Collectormania ... and I was so chuffed ... because he hung around with Peter Davison and his Doctor was just the coolest.' What about Eccleston and Tennant? 'I went on record saying that Eccleston was the best Doctor ... the best for the modern age, a darker Doctor, and I won't take that comment back, but I tell you David Tennant is great! Tony the Tiger greeeat!'

Although Eccleston's ninth Doctor was, he says, 'more intense' than Tennant's 'emotional' tenth, he feels that without the contribution of both actors, the show would not have been as successful. 'Chris helped re-establish the show ... but David lightened the tone and brought in a wider audience.'

Sadly *Storage 24* doesn't feature any cameos from the good Doctor, but it's taken Noel back to a genre he clearly loves – and with the door left open for a sequel. 'Well, on this movie we changed the ending halfway through the shoot. I went to Johannes with an idea and he went, "Man, that would be cool." And even though I've written it and he's directed it, it wasn't until we saw the final version and it ends the way it ends that I said, "Dude, we've got to do another one." And I think people will want it too. It ends in a way that makes you excited. But at the moment the sequel's just an outline. I'm not going to write it until we see how this one does.'

Does his busy schedule leave him time for a return to *Doctor Who*? 'I'm always open to offers,' he says with a smile.

So how does Noel's mum feel about her son's choice of career now? 'She's all right with it but,' he adds, 'I'm sure that somewhere in the back of her mind she still thinks I should "get a real job!"'

The Costume Designer:
Ray Holman

Wizards vs Aliens, Silk, Law and Order: UK, Sea of Souls, The Sarah Jane Adventures, Sherlock, Torchwood and *Doctor Who.* Costume designer Ray Holman has worked on them all. Since graduating in 1984, Ray has become something of a behind-the-scenes star in world of *Doctor Who.* His first involvement with the show came with 2006's 'Blink'. That was followed in 2007 with work on 'Turn Left'. Then in 2009/10 he was hired to work on Series Five, creating costumes for Matt Smith's new Doctor and companion Amy Pond. He has also won a Welsh BAFTA for Best Costume Design for *Torchwood* in 2008 and was nominated in 2009 and 2010. But just what does it take to reach such heady heights …?

Can you tell us a little about yourself and how you ended up in the enviable position of designing costumes for *Doctor Who*, *Torchwood* and *Sherlock*?
I studied Theatre Design at the Royal Welsh College of Music and Drama in Cardiff and specialised in designing, cutting and making costumes in my final year. I also had to design sets and props. I was spotted by the Head of Costume at BBC Wales and they trained me as a wardrobe assistant and then as an assistant costume designer until I became a full costume designer. So, I worked my way up from the set floor through to designer level at the BBC and ITV. I have designed for comedy, light entertainment and loads of different types of drama, mainly for television.

The Doctor's costumes are as iconic as the character himself. As a designer, is it thrilling or terrifying to be asked to create a new look for a new Doctor?
It's both terrifying and exciting, but it's basically quite a responsibility, because there are so many people waiting to see what you come up with.

Day 1: You're designing a new costume for a new Doctor. Where do you start?
Well, we didn't have any kind of brief, so Matt and I were free to explore many options. We spent days at a costume hire company trying on different kinds of looks, including coats from different periods of history, and going through the iconic fashionable looks from the 20th Century. I'm

not sure if it helped or confused us more, but we had to start somewhere. We also had to consider the costumes worn by the previous Doctors. One interesting and often forgotten point is that the Doctor picked up his clothes from a hospital changing room in 'The Eleventh Hour', so it all had to make sense in relation to that moment in the script when he dresses and faces the enemy on the roof of the hospital.

How much of the eleventh Doctor's final 'look' came from you, how much from Matt, how much from scriptwriters, etc?
Matt played a big part in the end decision. Ultimately, I don't have to wear the costume – he does – and as the fitting process went on, he started to research great minds like Einstein, which is where the idea for tweed came from. I helped form the look as a whole. The executives came to approve the final look once we thought we were close. It wasn't until that meeting, with everyone in the room, that the bow tie was decided upon.

Presumably some items of costume were off the menu simply because they were too similar to what other Doctors had worn? Or was it always a case of anything goes as long as the finished design works?
We started out trying to avoid the major iconic things worn by previous Doctors but, ultimately, I think the individual end style will always come from the actor who wears the clothes, whether you are reusing an idea or not.

Can you describe Amy's look?
Amy's look in one word is 'adventurous'. She's a woman who knows what she wants.

Was there any attempt to make Amy's costumes resonate with the Doctor's? To create a visual 'bond'?
I dressed Matt and Karen as the individuals they are. They were cast by people who thought carefully about how they would work together on screen, so it helps when you get such capable casting.

Which *Doctor Who* costume, apart from the Doctor's and Amy's, were you most pleased with and why?
Most of Series Five was incredibly populated with characters and extras, but one of my all-time favourites was Rosanna's costume from 'The Vampires of Venice'. Her purple velvet dress was built from scratch in order to mesh with the CGI creature she becomes. The big, gold lace

collar we made reflected the spikes the creature had, and I also made huge, red silk petticoats for underneath the frock, although we didn't see much of those. Also, I loved doing the costumes for 'Vincent and the Doctor'; and Tony Curran, who played Vincent, loved his coat. I especially liked the French-style and fabrics. Another favourite were the Silurian Warriors. We made them from scratch in the Department, and for that I will always be very proud of my team.

You also reworked Captain Jack's costume for *Torchwood*. Can you tell us a little about that?
Captain Jack was a Second World War Royal Air Force officer in *Doctor Who* and looked fabulous, but his costume was strictly historical. For *Torchwood* it needed to have a lot more adventure to it. So I made a theatrical version of the coat, so that when he runs and stands on the top of tall buildings, it moves and blows with the wind. Ultimately I had to make the period parts of his costume work in a much broader sense, so that he didn't feel like he was stuck in a single period. He was also the head of a secret organisation so needed to be enigmatic and sexy.

If you could redesign one of the earlier Doctors' costumes, which Doctor would you choose and how would you change the costume?
Oh, I would never presume to do that! They were all brilliant reflections of the time.

Bow toes – cool or not?
In the end, cool. They are a smart and brilliant part of a gentleman's wardrobe, whether in a period sense or now in a modern fashionable sense. I'm very pleased that elements of Matt's costume in the form of Harris tweed, bow ties and elbow patches have worked their way into mainstream fashion. It's a huge compliment.

What's harder, working on an historical series where costumes have to be perfectly accurate or sci-fi and fantasy where it's all from your own imagination?
I think it's difficult to choose which one is harder or easier, because each and every project I work on presents a different set of design problems. Period accuracy is hard work, but fantasy has its own challenges. One of the harder things to do is good 'old contemporary'. The characters have to be 'just right' and tell the story written, which is often overlooked. All the

costumes in *Broadchurch* are thoroughly thought-through, but they are not noticed as much because, if they are right, they are a visual part of the storytelling process and not a hindrance.

For all those cosplayers who would love to copy Matt's look, what is the quintessential eleventh Doctor costume?
Tweed, boots, shorter trousers, bow tie, elbow patches. Never forget the patches – that's what Amy Pond called him, 'Patches'.

Finally, what are you doing at the moment – can we expect to see more of your work in future episodes of *Doctor Who*?
I'm currently working on *Silk* again, and I want to keep myself available for Series Two of *Broadchurch*, which I love. I've just been nominated for another Welsh BAFTA for *Wizards vs Aliens* (Series One) and we will be working on Series Three later in the year. But as for *Doctor Who*, I probably will not do another one, as life is pretty busy right now. But you never know. In this business, things change all the time!

The BFI: Dick Fiddy
& Justin Johnson

The British Film Institute (BFI) was founded in 1933 to promote the art of film and television, as well as act as an archive for the nation. So it seems more than appropriate that, in *Doctor Who*'s 50th Anniversary year, they should have led the celebrations. Dick Fiddy and Justin Johnson were two of the team behind the concept of the BFI Southbank cinema in London screening one *Doctor Who* serial a month – one for each Doctor – leading up to the anniversary itself in November. But deciding exactly which serials to include created quite a bit of debate …

Tell us a little about yourselves and your relationship to the wider Whoniverse …
Dick: I'm Dick Fiddy and I'm the TV Consultant for the BFI. As far as *Doctor Who* is concerned, I was just of the right age when the series started. I probably saw most of the classic *Doctor Who* when it went out – even the episodes that are now lost. I was a real nut for the show, as were most of my friends, and before the organised functionality of the internet pulled the fans together, my friends and I used to meet in the playground to talk about it and – I guess – stick out our hands and pretend to be Daleks! But I think it was *Doctor Who* that really got me interested in television in all sorts of way. It was one of those shows that lodged in the back of my mind, and eventually that misspent youth – watching too much television – became a job!

Justin: I'm Justin Johnson and one of my roles here at the BFI is scheduling film and TV screenings for younger audiences, and obviously that includes *Doctor Who*. I'm just a bit younger than Dick – my Doctor was Tom Baker. I can just about remember 'Planet of the Spiders', where Jon Pertwee regenerates into Tom Baker, and I can absolutely remember – even though it's such a cliché now – hiding behind the sofa. I don't know why, but 'The Seeds of Doom' sticks in my mind, and I was terrified of the Krynoid. I also remember going through every box of Weetabix for those cardboard *Doctor Who* cut-out figures they had. So, I'm certainly a fan, although not in the scarf-wearing, Dalek chasing, convention-going way. But I'm somebody who watches the shows, reads about the shows and has a real nostalgia for them.

Where did the idea for the BFI to mark the Anniversary *of Doctor Who* with a year-long celebration come from?

Dick: Well, we've screened episodes from the classic series in the past and we've worked extensively with the BBC's production office arranging previews, so we knew that this was an anniversary worth celebrating. In what way we should celebrate was initially up for grabs. It was actually Justin's idea to have an ongoing celebration that stretched over the whole year.

Justin: Originally there was the thought that we'd do something around November, themed on time travel. But in 2012 we'd shown every Disney animation – one a week for a whole year – to celebrate the release of their fiftieth animation. That had worked really well. So my feeling was that, with there being eleven Doctors up to Matt Smith, we could run a year-round celebration, screening a different story from a different Doctor each month up to the anniversary in November. The thought was that we'd run each screening like a mini convention and try to get the best possible guests on board to talk about the episodes. So not only would it be giving something back to the fans, but it would also give those people who only started watching in 2005 the opportunity to soak up some of the history of the show.

How difficult has it been to turn that idea into a reality?

Dick: I think one of the main problems we've had is that we're in danger of becoming victims of our own success! Our biggest auditorium is a 450-seater and when you put on events like this, there's a massive demand. We could sell the tickets ten times over. Inevitably some people are going to be disappointed. Also, it's been pointed out to us that it's a London-centric event. But the one way we can – and have – been able to reach out is by putting the guest talks online.

Justin: I think we've been lucky in the sense that all of the approaches to guests we've made so far have been met with a really positive response. Most of the people we've approached are used to getting a fee when they go to a convention. But we don't make any money from these events – we're a not-for-profit organisation – and all of them have been happy to come along and give up their time for free. It's astonishing actually what the reaction has been from the press and the fans and the people who have been involved in the show who have been in touch with us. We've had a phenomenal response and it's all been amazingly positive. We're finding out that the people who support the show and the people who have been involved in the show are really genuine.

How easy has it been to choose just one serial from each Doctor's tenure, and which one has caused the most debate?
Dick: [Laughs] Debate … yes … there was quite a bit of debate. We all have our favourites and, of course, sometimes they coincided, sometimes they didn't! For the earlier Doctors, certain stories seemed to spring to mind, but when you start to look at the logistics, you want to put different things into the mix, otherwise you suddenly find yourself with 11 Dalek stories! So you start to think about which stories represent the show's strengths and which best represent a particular Doctor – or his companions – because you're trying to cover as wide a base as possible.

Justin: That was the most enjoyable part – where we wrote down our favourites and then compared the results. We got someone else involved as well who's sort of an *uber*-fan, and it was very enjoyable looking at the lists and working out what to go for. One of the reasons we didn't publish a complete list up front – apart from the fact that it's quite nice to reveal it bit by bit – is that it's an ever-changing list! We didn't think we would be playing 'The Mind of Evil' in March initially. However, because the restored colour version was coming out on DVD later in the year, we went to the BBC and asked if there was any way we could show it. Amazingly they agreed, even though, at the time, it wasn't finished. So we got to screen it just a couple of weeks after work had finished on it – that was too good an opportunity to miss.

Were there things that you would have liked to include in the celebration, but couldn't?
Justin: We would have liked to have shown some of the fan projects that are out there. There are so many but, for copyright reasons, we could never show them and charge money for them. That period between *Doctor Who* finishing and when the show came back in 2005 saw some really interesting fan films made, and it would have been nice to revisit them.

How do you think that the classic and new *Who* compare?
Dick: One of the interesting things about the show and the BFI's history with it is, if you look back 20 years ago, we didn't screen that many episodes. That was because things like *Doctor Who* were considered 'culty'

and not very inclusive. They appealed to a very small group of people at that time – almost overridingly male. The new series has become much more democratised. It has a wide fan base now. Lots of girls as well as guys love it and it has a huge following in the gay community too.

Justin: Now the episodes are more like mini movies in that they're very self-contained. They can stand on their own and you can dip in and out of the show. You don't have to slavishly follow it. But the four- or six-part serials of the '60s and '70s allowed much more time for a story to unfold. That meant that the characters were more important – perhaps you even cared about them a bit more. Although those stories were slow, there was something about them that got under your skin. And having to wait a whole week was nerve-wracking!

What qualities make a film or a TV series iconic, and in what ways does *Doctor Who* qualify?
Dick: There's no magic bullet. Some shows like *Fawlty Towers*, which ran for only 12 episodes, have very short runs but still become iconic. Other shows need longevity. I think if *Doctor Who* had finished in 1967-68 it would be tremendously and warmly remembered, but it wouldn't have the same place in the pantheon of British television. I think longevity is the key. And – of course – the most amazing piece of luck when someone hit on the idea of regeneration. It wasn't like a new actor playing Sherlock Holmes or James Bond. It was a continuation of the same story, albeit that the Doctor had a new face. No-one at the time could have foretold what an impact that would have on the show's history.

You could certainly argue that the first regeneration, when Patrick Troughton took over, was the most important single moment in the show's history. Hartnell was very popular and had made the part his own. He brought a sense of menace and otherworldliness to the Doctor, and Troughton very cleverly maintained that but didn't in any way try to mimic Hartnell. He made the Doctor completely his own. It's often overlooked now, but that transition was very, very important to the survival of the show, and thank goodness he got it right.

What would you say is the one aspect of *Doctor Who* that makes the show unique?
Dick: For me – the adventure. The idea of being able to go anywhere at any place in any time, just opens so many doorways. And I like the way

that David Tennant's and Matt Smith's Doctors realise that too, when they're trying to persuade a new companion to climb onboard.

Justin: From my point of view – its Britishness. It's a uniquely British show. The formula of being able to travel anywhere in time and space could be picked up by anyone, but the humour of the scripts, the Britishness of the performances, and the stories are what make it unique. A lot of American shows take themselves very seriously. *Doctor Who* has this self-deprecating British humour, and the Doctor's the exact opposite of the typical 'Hollywood' action hero.

Dick: Yeah, if you think of American sci-fi like *Star Trek* or *Battlestar Galactica*, it's always about the military might of the nation going out there. They're always officials wearing uniforms. But *Doctor Who* is all about individuality and eccentricity. He's the loner – the underdog – and that's quintessentially British. That, I think, is why we all love *Doctor Who* so much.

The BFI's 'Top Stories'
'100,000 BC'
'The Tomb of the Cybermen'
'The Mind of Evil'
'The Robots of Death'
'The Caves of Androzani'
'The Two Doctors'
'Remembrance of the Daleks'
'Doctor Who' TV movie
'Bad Wolf' / 'The Parting of the Ways'
'The Stolen Earth' / 'Journey's End'
'The Eleventh Hour' and 'The Name of the Doctor'